FOR HIS EYES ONLY

They say ignorance is bliss, but anyone who's experienced the stresses and strains that attend even the best-planned wedding will tell grooms-to-be it's better to know what's going on. What's more, your bride (and your mother-in-law) will be forever impressed with your savoir-faire. Here's how:

- Why a lifetime of enforced monogamy is weird but worth it
- The history of rings and the symbolism involved
- What not to say when you're asking her to spend the rest of her life with you
- Great expectations—hers and yours—and how to wed them to reality
- Love and money—and other essential ingredients for creat-ing the perfect wedding day

"A sweet and very funny book—what a kinder, gentler, hap-pily married *National Lampoon* staff might do in a *Bride's* magazine parody. . . . *Marry Like a Man* will give Miss Manners dyspepsia, but all you regular guys will laugh aloud and pass it around."

—ELINOR LIPMAN, author of *The Way Men Act*

"*Marry Like a Man* is chockablock with the kind of hard-won insight and mordant wit that we've come to expe̶ from one of America's foremost authorities on bad re̶ ̶ "
—DAVI̶

PETER N. NELSON is the a̶ ̶ ̶ ̶ ̶ ̶ ̶. His work has also appeared in ̶ ̶ ̶ ̶ ̶ ̶ ̶ ̶, *Elle,* *Esquire,* and *Redbook.* He lives with ̶ ̶ ̶ ̶ ̶ ̶ Northampton, Massachusetts.

PETER N. NELSON

MARRY LIKE A MAN

The Essential Guide for Grooms

A PLUME BOOK

PLUME

Published by the Penguin Group
Penguin Books USA Inc., 375 Hudson Street, New York, New York 10014, U.S.A.
Penguin Books Ltd, 27 Wrights Lane, London W8 5TZ, England
Penguin Books Australia Ltd, Ringwood, Victoria, Australia
Penguin Books Canada Ltd, 10 Alcorn Avenue, Toronto, Ontario, Canada M4V 3B2
Penguin Books (N.Z.) Ltd, 182–190 Wairau Road, Auckland 10, New Zealand

Penguin Books Ltd, Registered Offices:
Harmondsworth, Middlesex, England

First published by Plume, an imprint of New American Library,
a division of Penguin Books USA Inc.

First Printing, February, 1992
1 3 5 7 9 10 8 6 4 2

Ⓟ REGISTERED TRADEMARK—MARCA REGISTRADA

LIBRARY OF CONGRESS CATALOGING IN PUBLICATION DATA:
Nelson, Peter, 1953–
Marry like a man : the essential guide for grooms / Peter N. Nelson.
p.   cm.
ISBN 0-452-26759-5
1. Weddings—United States—Planning. 2. Bethrothal—United
States. I. Title.
HQ745.N45   1992
395'.22—dc20   91-24488
CIP

Printed in the United States of America
Set in Garamond No. 3

Designed by Steven N. Stathakis

BOOKS ARE AVAILABLE AT QUANTITY DISCOUNTS WHEN USED TO PROMOTE PRODUCTS OR SER-
VICES. FOR INFORMATION PLEASE WRITE TO PREMIUM MARKETING DIVISION, PENGUIN BOOKS
USA INC., 375 HUDSON STREET, NEW YORK, NEW YORK 10014.

ACKNOWLEDGMENTS

I would like to acknowledge all the people who helped me gather information for this book, without whose consultation and cooperation I would have been lost. They include Barbara Hanson, Jim Fryar, Tom McClung, Jordie Herold, Carol Duke, Pat Swensen, Kinter MacKenzie, Joseph Nocera, Bill Goldsworthy, the Hockey Hall of Fame, J. Watcyn Lewis, Jay Kreisberg, José Garcia, Sullivan Photography, Paul Shoul, Alana, Mikki, the Albion Bookstore, Gene Roddenberry, Joel Fishman, Alice Martell, David Hirshey, and Warren Rasmussen for fixing my computer. I would like to thank Vatsyayana, Stanley Elkin, Ann Bernays, F. Scott Fitzgerald, Thomas Mann, the *Guinness Book of World Records*, and *Bride's Magazine* for letting me quote from them. Most of the average costs for weddings, receptions, photographers, etc. were furnished by *Bride's Magazine*; figures taken from their readers' poll. I would also like to convey my deepest gratitude to Tony and Doris Porcella, and to Bud and Loey Nelson, for all assistance rendered, and finally, to my beloved wife Diane, without whom neither this book nor my future would be possible. This book is dedicated to her.

TABLE OF CONTENTS

EPIGRAPHS

A positive engagement to marry a certain person at a certain time, at all haps and hazards, I have always considered the most ridiculous thing on earth.

—JANE WELSH (MRS. THOMAS) CARLYLE

I'm old fashioned. I believe that people should marry for life, like pigeons and Catholics.

—WOODY ALLEN

A man looks pretty small at a wedding.

—THORNTON WILDER

Men marry because they are tired; women because they are curious. Both are disappointed.

—OSCAR WILDE

Whether one is carried away by an ordinary young, bashful housewife, or a beautiful, congenial lady friend, or a Valkyrie and guardian angel, is only of interest insofar as the personality is interesting.

—ISAK DINESEN

If I ever marry, it will be on sudden impulse, as a man shoots himself.

—H. L. MENCKEN

The best part of married life is the fights. The rest is only so so.

—THORNTON WILDER

Keep your eyes wide open before marriage, half shut afterwards.
—BENJAMIN FRANKLIN

Marriage is popular because it combines the maximum of temptation with the maximum of opportunity.
—GEORGE BERNARD SHAW

One should never know too precisely whom one has married.
—FRIEDRICH NIETZSCHE

Times are changed with him who marries; there are no more bypath meadows where you may innocently linger, but the road lies long and straight and dusty to the grave.
—ROBERT LOUIS STEVENSON

Seldom, or perhaps never, does a marriage develop into an individual relationship smoothly and without crises; there is no coming to consciousness without pain.
—CARL GUSTAV JUNG

Marriage is the only war in which you sleep with the enemy.
—ANONYMOUS

To be loved, be loveable.
—OVID

Marriage is the triumph of hope over experience.
—SAMUEL JOHNSON

Nothing anybody tells you about marriage helps.
—MAX SIEGEL

Marriage: a community consisting of a master, a mistress, and two slaves, making in all, two.
—AMBROSE BIERCE

Marriage, if one will face the truth, is an evil, but a necessary evil.

—MENANDER

Love consists in this, that two solitudes protect and touch and greet each other.

—RAINER MARIE RILKE

When people are marrying, they are taking a stand, informing society that they are not alone anymore, that they have made a commitment. But the deepest part of marriage, like conversion, is private.

—KATHRYN PERUTZ

Marriage is part of a sort of 50's revival package that's back in vogue along with neckties and naked ambition.

—CALVIN TRILLIN

Marriage is a great institution, but I'm not ready for an institution.

—MAE WEST

It destroys one's nerves to be amicable every day to the same person.

—BENJAMIN DISRAELI

If I were to do it over again I would marry in early infancy instead of wasting time cutting teeth and breaking crockery.

—MARK TWAIN

INTRODUCTION

WHAT THIS BOOK IS AND ISN'T

There is a shelf full of books on weddings in most bookstores. The books on this shelf are written by people such as Amy Vanderbilt, Emily Post, Judith Martin, or Martha Stewart, who generally do a good job relating the rules of etiquette regarding planning and pulling off a wedding ceremony. The authors of such books often get invited to appear on talk shows or to speak at bridal conventions, become experts at weddings, and probably make a pretty good living at it. I'm all in favor of making a pretty good living, but I have no desire to become a professional wedding expert. I don't want to be on talk shows. You could suddenly come down with Tourette's syndrome, or accidentally say something like, "All the people in Florida should be killed," and then where would you be? I don't want to speak at bridal conventions. Why, then, would I write a book about weddings?

Two reasons.

First, there are no books for men. Men are half—well, *almost* half, of all weddings. We ought to have something to say about them, or at least something to read. Yet the bridal library shuts us out. There isn't even a word you could use to describe a library for grooms. Groomal? Groomic? Groomish? *Marry Like a Man* is as close as I could come. It's a book which, if marriage is a journey, might serve as a kind of road atlas, tell you how to prepare and what to expect.

All the other books are written by and for and directed toward women. It makes perfect sense. They're the ones who have traditionally planned and organized and carried off wedding ceremonies, making them the logical market for a book on such things. Women will probably (it is hoped) buy this book and give it to their fiancés. Where weddings are concerned, women tell men what to do, where to do it, when to do it, and how to do it. Get a tux, be at this church, on this day, on this hour, and take a bath first. Men have been cast as passive participants in their own wedding ceremonies. To a degree, we've probably accepted this role, willing to stand on the sidelines, hands in our pockets, saying, "Don't mind me" or, "Whatever you want, dear," being both lazy and considerate at the same time, until the bride usually gets annoyed and says, "I need your goddamn *help* here, oh betrothed of mine." Not only does she want to tell you what to do, but she wants you to *help her* tell you what to do. It can leave even the most sensitive Post-Feminist-New-Age-Guy feeling a little lost. You need a book, some kind of resource. Yet there are only etiquette books, describing how to avoid awkward social situations, handle seating arrangements, proper wordings for wedding invitations, and so on. Nothing to chew on.

Furthermore, if you read the wedding books on the shelf, you notice something else is missing from them. None of them begins to tell the reader how he or she is going to *feel*. One of the most important events of your life, and you have to go into it blind. Books in the bridal library might suggest that you and your fiancée are going to fight. Okay, but why? What kinds of fights? They will hint that you're going to be tense on your wedding day. Okay, but why? What will my concerns be, and what can I do about them?

This book takes you through the nuptial process, step by step. It addresses questions of etiquette and form, only because a wedding is a ceremony laden with tradition, and traditions are there for a reason. I do not, personally, care a great deal about etiquette or form, and would rather make my own rules as I go along. But then, part of getting married, and staying married, is learning to make rules with someone else—your bride, her family, and your family, in which case etiquette and form can be very helpful. This is also a country with a long rich tradition of making exceptions to rules, so this book attempts to address alternatives to traditional wedding approaches as well.

A wedding can't really be controlled, but it can be understood, and executed intelligently. And if it can't be fully controlled, power over it can be taken out of the hands of those who would seek to control it—that is, the Wedding Mafia, a consortium of florists and bakers, caterers and photographers who will set upon you like wolves, if you aren't careful, and tear your bank account to shreds. This book seeks, if nothing else, to be a consumer's guide and warn against the Wedding Mafia, who make their living by assuming a wedding is a once-in-a-lifetime event and that people will pay three and four times what something's really worth for a once-in-a-lifetime event, knowing they're getting ripped off but thinking, "Well, I'm only going to get ripped off once in my lifetime." This book is for couples who intend to stay in control (ha!) and share in both the planning and the costs of the wedding, a hands-on manual for initiates, necessary because the corollary to a once-in-a-lifetime experience is that nobody who does it has ever done it before, so they don't know what to expect, or how to avoid being taken advantage of.

I have tried to structure this book chronologically, beginning with the point where a man is contemplating getting married, taking him through how to propose, how to buy a ring, how to manage a wedding, how to survive a stag party, how to get through the actual day, and finishing at the honeymoon.

I have tried to estimate what things cost. Prices, of course, vary greatly from place to place and year to year, so the costs included in this book are only useful as indexes. It's also true that what people can afford will vary greatly.

I've tried to be fair but have not always successfully avoided gender stereotyping; for example, when I refer to a minister, I will most likely use the pronoun "he," and use "she" when referring to caterers, only because the majority of ministers I talked to were men, and the majority of caterers were women. I am fully aware there are women clergy and male caterers, and that sexism in language is a nasty fact, but not as nasty as littering one's text with the "he/she" or "his/her" kinds of portmanteau pronouns you find sticking out in some texts like, as the detective writer once said, "tarantulas on a wedding cake." I favor facility over absolute politico-linguistic correctness, and assume most readers are sophisticated enough to understand.

Finally, I've tried to be fair to the subject matter, though irreverence comes easy to me. Humor, the marrying man will learn, is sometimes the only reason to keep going. Abraham Lincoln, during the Civil War, when asked how he could continue to make jokes while the nation was experiencing such sorrow, replied, to the effect, "I laugh because if I don't I fear I shall die." Getting married is something like the American Civil War, not on the same scale, probably, but still an ordeal in which it is essential to keep one's sense of humor. Some of the fights you can get into over throughly inconsequential wedding details, like whether there should be mints next to the guest book at the reception, are incontrovertibly stupid and juvenile. Yet you will fight in deadly earnest, believing any ground you give before the wedding will be ground forever lost. You'd better learn to laugh at them afterward, or you're going to be in big trouble. Even with your senses of humor intact, one of you is going to say at least once, "That's it, the wedding is off!" All the more reason to keep your senses of humor about you. Too often, weddings get encumbered in solemnity and form, to the point where everyone forgets what they're supposed to be about. People getting married need all the laughs they can get, not to deny the seriousness of what they're doing, but to remember, through all the tense preparation, that they are preparing for a celebration.

It soon becomes evident, reading about the world's wedding practices, that, though they vary widely in detail, they are in substance the same everywhere—a ritual coupling that creates a new social unit. If there's been a single significant change in marriage in the last 500 years, it might be simply the idea of marrying for love, instead of marrying because your parents told you to, because there were pacts to be made between tribes or clans, or marrying because it was the only way a man could make children. Maybe love is a mystery because we're still inventing it, still reading the manual, or, more likely, still rewriting it.

If this book has a primary metaphor it would be that of a journey, a voyage of discovery, Lewis and Clark, whitewater rafting into the wilderness. This book is not a map you look at in lieu of appreciating the scenery as it passes. It's only a guide to help an inexperienced tourist become an informed traveler. You will still get lost but, eventually, you will find yourself. You will find yourself married. This book covers only the first steps of that voyage, but then, as the Chinese proverb says, "A journey of a thousand miles begins by reading a single book about how to take the first steps."

Or something like that.

1

TAKING THE LEAP: QUESTIONS A GROOM MIGHT ASK HIMSELF

"So you're taking the leap," people will say to you.

"Into what?" you wonder.

You have decided to marry. You are now contemplating the magnitude of your decision. You want to think long and hard about it. Go look in a mirror. If you have any reflection at all, it means you're human (if you don't, it means you're a vampire, in which case you have more pressing problems). And if you're human, you have doubts, you have questions.

WHAT AM I AFRAID OF?

Change. Acrophobes aren't afraid of falling accidentally from great heights—they're afraid when they're up high that they'll suddenly change into someone who wants to jump. Change moves forward through time from the known present to the unknown future; and given a choice between the familiar and the unknown, most people will stick to the familiar. Even a paramecium knows to stick with what's working. But although we may not be fond of change, we are at least capable of it, which is why we evolved into large complex organisms able to put men on the moon while paramecium are still hairy little balls of Jell-O living in puddles.

WHY DO I LOVE THIS PERSON, AND NOT ANOTHER?

It's not always pointless to ask an unanswerable question, but in this case it is. Maybe she strokes your forehead just like your mother used to do when you were sick as a kid. She laughs like your baby sister. She said the exact same thing Ann-Margret said to you in a dream you had when you were eleven. You can take this one apart forever, to ceaseless diversion and no avail. An unexamined life is not worth living, and an unlived life is not worth examining, but an overexamined life is no way to live. Melville said it in *Moby Dick.* You can cut a whale in a million pieces and render it down to the last drop of oil without ever understanding what makes it a whale or why it swims. Chase the whale too long and you'll piss it off. Piss it off too long and it will sink your boat. The moral of *Moby Dick:* let it swim.

WHY IS THERE LOVE?

If there weren't, there'd be nothing to watch on television. "Dragnet" reruns and the weather. We are attached at birth and long for reattachment from then on. In other words, your guess is as good as mine.

WHY IS THERE MARRIAGE?

There is marriage because there is fear, envy, hunger, lust, and loneliness. It all started long before recorded history, when man first climbed down from the trees.

While he was still in the trees, everything was fairly simple. Humans had two basic needs—the need to stay alive, which meant eating, and the need to make more of ourselves through procreation. A tree only had so much food in it, and so much room for primitive children. There was balance. There had to be, or you'd fall out of the tree. Eventually, somebody did fall out of a tree, and started walking upright. Primitive man was nothing if not trendy, and pretty soon, everybody was walking upright. Bipedalism enabled primitive man to walk farther to gather more food. The larger the food supply, the more ape-kid mouths they could feed. Primitive man began to procreate more and more, until one day primitive woman said, "Hey—wait a primitive goddamn minute." Primitive woman was not meant to be pregnant and walk upright at the same time. Modern women aren't too thrilled about it either. Biologists believe human babies are born sooner than they were meant to be born, helpless until the age of four, while other mammal offspring are able to feed themselves a few short hours after parturition. Primitive woman was handicapped by the dependent child. She could even have more than one dependent child at a time. She needed help, a man around the cave to provide her with food. For this reason, some sociobiologists theorize, she invented monogamy.

Primitive man was concerned mainly with spreading his seed as far as it would spread, the most virile and dominant males siring the most offspring while preventing primitive wieners and wusses from doing likewise, to the benefit of the species. It didn't always mean sticking around to help raise the kid—until primitive woman invented monogamy. She enforced monogamy, the theory goes, by concealing her readiness to breed. However she did it, she managed to keep primitive man around to provision her while she and her child were both helpless, something like nesting birds. Today only 3 percent of all mammals are monogamous, whereas 90 percent of all birds mate for life. At any rate, somewhere along the line, primitive man decided both to sire offspring and then hang around to help insure their survival, give natural selection a boost. Having some kind of wedding ritual might have been his way of protecting his brood, publicly designating and identifying who his mate was.

Coming down from the trees allowed us to live in groups larger than one treeful. We evolved as a social animal. As societies formed, codes for mating and breeding must have formed as well, to prevent incest from weakening the gene pool, and to encourage new pairings, bring in new blood to enhance the health of the clan. Think of the movie *Mars Needs Women*. Marriage by capture was probably one of the earliest forms of marriage, where a tribe or clan set out to capture women from another nearby tribe or clan. Early societies were sometimes formed by group marriages, or polygyny. A man had more than one wife when war or disease reduced the number of eligible males or where capture of women greatly increased the number of eligible females. Societies with more males than females practiced polyandry, a woman having more than one husband. Marriage was the glue that held the pieces of society together, the tangible method of connection. Tribes and clans eventually learned that intermarrying with each other could make an enemy an ally. No Sumerian is going to crack a lot of Hittite jokes (e.g., "How many Hittites doth it take to refill an oil lamp? It doth not matter—a Hittite could not pour oil from an amphora were the instructions cuneiformed on the bottom") if his grandson is half Hittite. Rival tribes or clans would marry off their leaders' children to each other. They would marry their gods to each other, then jointly worship the offspring of that union. They would ritualistically marry their leaders to their gods. The Queen of Athens was annually married to Dionysus, the god of the vine, in a ceremony designed to improve the harvest. In the Babylonian sanctuary of Bel, there was a bedroom in a temple where a mortal woman would lie to serve as consort to the gods, having nothing to do with mortal men. We've all known women

● ●

NOT RIGHT FOR YOU?

The *Kama Sutra of Vatsyayana*, a first-century Indian sage, lists the characteristics of a woman you do not want to marry.

"A girl who is asleep, crying, or gone out of the house when sought in marriage, or who is betrothed to another, should not be married. The following should also be avoided:

One who is kept concealed.

One who has an ill-sounding name.

One who has her nose depressed.

One who has her nostril turned up.

One who is formed like a male.

One who is bent down.

One who has crooked thighs.

One who has a projecting forehead.

One who has a bald head.
One who does not like purity.
One who has been polluted by another.
One who is affected with the bulma (enlarged glands).
One who is disfigured in any way.
One who has fully arrived at purity.
One who is a friend.
One who is a younger sister.
One who is a Varshakari (has sweaty palms).

In the same way, a girl who is called by the name of one of the twenty-seven stars, or by the name of a tree, or of a river, is considered worthless, as also a girl whose name ends in 'R' or 'L.' But some authors say that prosperity is gained only by marrying that girl to whom one becomes attached and that therefore no other girl but the one who is loved should be married to anyone."

like that. Marriage created harmony between people within a social group, between two societies, and between men and gods.

WHAT ABOUT LOVE?

Marriage did not, initially, have a whole lot to do with love. Parents chose their children's spouses. Marriage was performed to insure procreation—a man's duty to society, according to Plato, in whose ideal society a married man with children paid no taxes. In Sparta, according to the laws of Lycurgus, a childless wife could be forced by law to live with another man. Among the Israelites, if a man's married brother died childless, he was expected to marry the widow and father children by her. Back then the population of the whole planet was only a few million people—family lines were important. Whole chapters of Exodus are dedicated to nothing but the tracing of family lines, as anybody who's ever read them, trying to figure out where Cain and Abel got dates, will know.

WHEN DID LOVE HAVE ANYTHING TO DO WITH IT?

In our own not-so-distant past, marriage was seen as the only decent way for a woman to keep body and soul together, food in her belly and a roof over her head. Marriage was how a girl passed successfully from girlhood to adulthood, out of her father's home and into the world, or at least into her husband's world, beginning as soon as she was of breeding age. If she didn't marry, she could either stay home and become a spinster, or set off as an independent single woman, which meant she could work as a cook, a charmaid, a nanny, or a prostitute, and get paid pennies for her labor. By becoming a wife, she could cook, clean, tend the children, and have sex with her husband for no money at all. Sons could be put to work or kicked out of the house, whereas daughters were liabilities, mouths to feed; they were also desirable commodities while young and pretty, properties bought and sold, often as package deals. In some cultures, the groom purchased his bride from her father. In others, grooms expected (and got) her dowry as well, chickens and pigs and tracts of land, cash on the barrelhead and a player to be named later, a payment falling somewhere between bribe and blackmail. The bride herself was expected to bring with her a trousseau—from the old French word *trousse*, meaning "bundle"—consisting of linens and towels for the household, items single men, who apparently slept in their clothes and wiped their hands on their pants, did not yet possess. Men were usually already established as adult contributing members of society before they married, each with at least ten cows to his name, a mud hut, and a shoe for each foot.

Today, in this country, most marriages are self-arranged and transpire between consenting adults who marry for love, both of them established and contributing members of society. Yet traditions die hard. As late as the 1960s, marriage was seen as the best way for a woman to become fulfilled. There are still dowries, in the sense that the bride's parents are expected to bear the brunt of the wedding expenses. You may not hear the word *trousseau*, but the parties thrown with the intention of collecting household items for the couple's new home are called *bridal* showers, for her, not for you. The more things change, the more they stay the same. We mark the changes we fear with ritual, rites of passage that hold their general form from year to year and provide a sense of continuity, a way to deny the enormity of the change taking place, while simultaneously acknowledging its inevitability. Like funerals. In a way, marriage is like death—it's all around, but nobody really thinks about it until it could happen to them. It's not death we fear, Montaigne said, but dying, not the state but the stroke of it. Not marriage, but weddings.

WHY CAN'T WE JUST LIVE TOGETHER?

Living together has a certain history and tradition to it too. The Romans considered a couple who lived together for a year, without spending three consecutive days apart, to be married. Among the Eskimos, who depend on family structure for sheer survival in a land of bitter cold and scarce food, some groups consider it wise and perfectly acceptable for a couple to go through a trial marriage. Among what one nineteenth-century author calls "the lower classes of the Congo," young couples were required to live together for three years before they could marry, during which time the groom-to-be moved in with his bride and her parents. Persian and Bedouin people married, but only for an agreed-upon short term. Presumably if things worked out, they could renew the contract.

There are 2,588,000 couples living together today, as opposed to 1,529,000 in 1980, 523,000 in 1970, and only 439,000 in 1960 (*Boston Globe*, July 3, 1989). Cohabitation was once considered a trick men played on women, a way of getting free milk without buying the cow. Any man and woman who lived together were considered married by common law, or law comprising the collective wisdom of the courts, as opposed to statutes passed in the legislature. Common-law marriage was necessary to protect women, in the days when a woman who cohabited was considered *kept*, performing the duties of a wife but without the earning power of a man, entitled to alimony in case of a parting of ways, the same as any officially married woman. Now that women have equal earning power (well . . .) the best she can expect, in a state where common-law marriage is no longer recognized, is palimony. Common-law marriage is currently recognized only in Alabama, Colorado, Georgia, Idaho, Iowa, Kansas, Montana, Ohio, Oklahoma, Pennsylvania, Rhode Island, South Carolina, Texas, and the District of Columbia. More and more, cohabitation is seen as a legitimate nonmarital relationship, where both the man and the woman are getting their milk for free without buying cows.

It is not, however, the only way to find out if you're compatible, nor is it all that reliable an indicator. Couples who live together before marriage are 40 percent *more* likely to divorce in the first decade than couples who don't. Maybe a marriage needs momentum to get started, two people taking running leaps together instead of cautiously stepping off the edge. A quarter of all college graduates cohabit by the time they're twenty-five, versus a third for high-school graduates and half for high-school dropouts. You can test your compatibility by cohabiting. People who marry without cohabiting know it's also possible, just by dating someone and hanging around them long enough, to feel fairly certain you can live together, in which case a trial period of cohabitation becomes a waste of time.

CAN I AFFORD MARRIAGE?

Money is a bad reason not to marry. Poor people get married all the time. Two can live as cheap as one, though on a limited amount of money, only half as long. And don't forget that once you're married, if your wife works, you get to spend her money too. In 1960, only 27 percent of all married couples had dual incomes. Today 80 percent of all married men and 55 percent of all married women work outside the home. In 1987, an average wife made $13,245, a figure that includes many wives working part time. A full-time working wife earned $18,929. If you stay married 50 years, that's $946,450, enough to buy almost 30 BMW 525's. If you marry an above-average wife, or if your average wife gets a raise, you might even have enough money to service all those cars.

Of course, she gets to spend your money too. This will occur to you sometime before your wedding day. You'll be driving along with your sweetheart, slam on the brakes, pull over, and say, "Wait a minute—does this mean you get half my money?" She'll say, "Don't be silly. I get *all* your money." And she'll be right. If an emergency arises, it's hers. If an emergency doesn't arise, it's hers. It can be difficult to get used to opening your wallet to someone and saying, "Here, take what you need." Some men never do learn how. Pete Rose, for instance, while earning millions as a ballplayer, made his wife shop for their kids' clothes at K mart, arguing, "My money is my money." One reason why Pete Rose is inarguably one of the biggest horse's puds in history, at least where a man's family is concerned.

MAYBE BEING MARRIED WILL HELP ME SAVE MONEY

Maybe. Think of all the food you threw away as a bachelor because you never figured out how to cook for one, all the stuff you let rot in the refrigerator, until whatever it used to be looked and smelled like the surface of Venus. Think of all the stupid crap you bought on impulse because no one was there to tell you didn't really need it. There are numerous financial advantages to being married. It's easier to get loans. Credit card companies may flood you with offers for cards you applied for a hundred times when you were single and never got. In 1988 a single man earning $50,000 had to pay $12,014 in income taxes, but a married couple filing jointly for the same net income only had to pay $10,126. In the same year, a 45-year-old married man in Philadelphia paid only $1,893 in car insurance, whereas the 19-year-old single kid next door paid $6,039.

Marriage has other advantages. If you rob a convenience store, they can't make your wife testify against you. Being married doubles your chances of inheriting or finding money. On the other hand, if you both start spending money, thinking, "I couldn't afford this before, but now that we have two incomes I can," you'll go broke fast. At least you'll have company doing it.

WHAT ABOUT THE JOYS OF SOLITUDE?

Do you want to be like Thoreau, and live simply by the side of a gentle pond, pondering the mystery of life while gnawing on the occasional woodchuck? Good luck. Not even Thoreau gnawed on half the woodchucks he said he did. Most of the time he somehow managed to hop the fence to go visit Ralph Waldo Emerson just around the time Mrs. Emerson was ringing the dinner bell. Modern American hermits tend to be shack-batty old coots who roam the woods thinking UFOs want their pancreases, or ex-urban dwellers who suddenly discovered they were allergic to 90 percent of all the elements on the periodic table and moved to the mountains to live on brown rice and glacial runoff. Few people know how to do solitude.

Single men living in isolation, without close friends, are twice as likely to die prematurely as married men, according to a study conducted at the University of Michigan Institute for Social Research. Being lonely is as bad for you as smoking. Socially integrated people are less likely to commit suicide. Loners are more likely to eat, smoke, and drink too much, become depressed or schizophrenic, or suffer from ulcers, hypertension, pneumonia, or tuberculosis. Companionship encourages you to take better care of your health. You take your pills when somebody asks you if you've taken your pills. You get exercise when your wife comments that you're getting fat. Married people who have cancer get diagnosed earlier, having someone there to feel them for lumps, and have survival rates equal to single people ten years younger than them.

Furthermore, scientists now think companionship itself actually improves health, finding that the neuropeptides released in the brain when a man or woman is in love may actually stimulate the immune system. Even if you're sick, the natural opiates your body manufactures when you're in love may lessen the pain. Having a wife to take care of you and do all the things your mother used to do to make you feel better may lessen the pain as well. Affection is calming as well—dogs, cats, horses, and rabbits have reduced stress-related cardiovascular illnesses when petted regularly. Having sex stimulates the cardiovascular system. Your heart beats about 127 times during orgasm, and means every one of them. Sex also relieves depression. A monogamous marriage, obviously, greatly reduces your likelihood of picking up a sexually transmitted disease.

If you need solitude, when you're loved and trusted in a happy marriage, you can create periods of solitude within it, fruitful periods in which you're not worried about whether you're lonely or not. Periods in which you'll probably pound for pound perform the preponderance of your best pond pondering anyway.

I'VE BEEN A BACHELOR ALL MY LIFE— WHAT ABOUT MY NEW IDENTITY?

If it were easy to switch over from being single to being married, there wouldn't be such a universal custom as the betrothal period, when you're engaged and have a chance to get used to the idea, slowly change from being footloose and fancy free to having weightier responsibilities.

The first thing you realize, when you're engaged, is that you don't know why you do anything anymore. When you were single, you knew exactly why you did things, why you got dressed in the morning, why you went to work, why you ate dinner where you did, why you went to parties, why you bought cars, why you took a certain route home every night and not another, why you breathed or answered the phone or bothered to get out of bed.

You did it all to get laid.

Or rather, to increase your chances of falling in love. So you'd dress, hoping your clothes made you attractive. You worked to earn money to spend on dates. If you had a choice between eating in two restaurants of equal quality, you ate dinner at whichever one had more women eating there. You went to parties to meet women. You bought whatever car you thought could make your penis look bigger, or whatever car made you look smarter, or whatever car made you look like you didn't really care about cars as a macho symbol, if you wanted women to think you were blasé and didn't care about cars. You drove home a certain way because the route took you past the house of a woman you felt attracted to, and increased the likelihood of a chance meeting. Every time the phone rang, you hoped it was a woman calling. You got out of bed because today could be the day you meet the one woman you'll love all your life.

So the day comes, you meet her, she is the one, and you plan to love her all your life, but meanwhile, the phone keeps ringing, and when it does, you find yourself still hoping, out of habit, it's a woman, and not necessarily the one you're going to marry. It's confusing. You realize you don't know anything anymore. Why get dressed? You'll get arrested if you don't, but why look good? To impress your fiancée, but she's already impressed. Why go to a party? Just to talk to people and hang out with your friends, but you can do that anywhere. What if you see a pretty girl and want to talk to her? Why talk to her? About what—the weather? You're not in circulation anymore, but you're still circulating. Why? Why not eat where the food tastes best, drive home the shortest way, buy whatever car is the best deal and save the money you earn for the future?

Redefinition comes slowly. It's easier to know what you stand to lose than what you stand to gain, because the former is part of you, the latter only hearsay. Truer love? Better sex? Deeper commitment? Higher levels of understanding? Stronger emotions, more confidence, greater freedom? So they say. All you know is how to be a bachelor.

But bachelorhood is terminal, and always has been. In ancient Sparta, criminal proceedings could be instituted against those who did not marry. Old bachelors were stigmatized and ridiculed, forced to parade around the marketplace buck naked, singing self-deprecating songs. Plato felt that any man over thirty-five who was still single should be punished. Bachelorhood is still terminal. It's inconceivable to be married when you're fifteen. It's still acceptable and almost expected of you to date around and have neither commitments nor responsibilities when you're twenty. It's okay when you're twenty-five, though your parents start urging you to settle down. It's okay at thirty, though your parents keep asking how old the woman you're dating is. It's a little strange at thirty-five, because you find yourself doing the same things you've been doing for twenty years, telling the same stories, making the same jokes, still getting nowhere, though your parents are now delighted that you're dating younger girls as opposed to younger boys. If you're forty and have never been married, half the people you know start to think there's something wrong with you. Forty-five and it's three-fourths of the people you know.

The other thing to consider is that it's really not a new identity at all. New to you, but your dad did it. His dad did it. Lots of people do it. Idiots do it, misfits and malcontents, no-minds and ne'er-do-wells, would-be's and has-beens, bozos and boozers, big guys and little guys, rich men and poor men and beggars and chiefs. You've had examples all around you throughout your entire life, in and out of books, on and off the TV or movie screen. You can choose which ones you admire and imitate them. You can invent something all your own.

I MEAN, WHAT ABOUT, YOU KNOW . . . OTHER WOMEN?

Temptation? Infidelity? Divorce?

There is something of a myth men grow up with which says that once you find the woman of your dreams and marry her, you will not want other women. Someone you found attractive before you got married will not suddenly appear plain after you're married. In fact, you may find the opposite true, that you feel as if you've put yourself on a diet, believing you wouldn't be hungry, only to learn that deprivation increases want. Maybe that's why so many of the aphorisms concerning temptation seem to use food imagery. "Just because you ordered dinner," a married friend may advise you, "doesn't mean you can't still look at the menu." Or, "It don't matter where you work up your appetite so long as you eat at home." You may also find yourself feeling full.

The statistics for infidelity are generally not good, where men are concerned, studies reporting that anywhere from 50 to 90 percent of all married men are unfaithful. Most studies report women to be about half to two-thirds as unfaithful as whatever men log in at. In matriarchal societies, such as that of ancient Egypt, it's believed that the figures reverse, that whoever is in power cheats more than whoever isn't. Maybe we're more like mammals than birds after all. In China and Japan, and among Arabs and Eskimos, men acknowledged what they considered the *nature of things*, and had concubines, secondary wives subservient to their honored wives. Women in China and Japan saw concubinage as a job, a way to put food on the table, or did not accept the *nature of things* but were powerless to say anything. Polygyny and polyandry (in Tibet, a woman could marry a man and all his brothers) are both forms of nonmonogamous marriage that have been or still are widely practiced.

If fidelity is less than instinctive, it's certainly possible. You have impulses every day, for instance, to strangle the store clerk for refusing to take your check because your driver's license has expired, even though it's clearly you in the picture, but you don't always act on them. Ten percent of the people you see on the street are virgins, and another 10 percent would screw the first thing to fall off the next bus. Some people can control themselves, and some can't, or rather, some should try harder and some shouldn't try so hard. If you're thirty and have never been unfaithful to a girlfriend before, you probably won't be unfaithful to your wife. If you have a history of goatishness, you may have reason to expect more of the same, though it's also true that anyone is capable of change, and that marriage changes you. It can give you a strange new sense of empowerment, because when you're married you know exactly what the rules are, and you can hide behind the rules, the same as the store clerk who won't take your check. Rules are rules, you'll say to yourself, and feel invulnerable to temptation, able to walk down miles of crowded bikini-strewn beach without drooling once. Well, maybe once.

BUT RULES ARE MADE TO BE BROKEN— AND SO ARE MARRIAGES. HALF OF ALL MARRIAGES FAIL, DON'T THEY?

That 50 percent figure has been bandied about so many times it passes as common knowledge. The mistake is made in confusing ratios with rates. The divorce rate is a figure arrived at by looking at the number of marriages in a year and the number of divorces. If there are 2 million marriages in a year and a million divorces (close to the actual figures), then half of all marriages fail, right? But what are those 2 million marriages—new marriages or remarriages? There are 26,987,000 single American men over fifteen who have never been married (29.9 percent of all men over fifteen) and 22,509,000 single women over fifteen who've never been married (22.9 percent), representing the population of 49,496,000 men and women capable of marrying for the first time. There are about 58 million married couples in the United States, or 116 million people capable of getting divorced. If 1 million out of 58 million marriages fail in a year, why not say the failure rate is less than 2 percent instead of 50? There are 55,233,000 married men and only

5,771,000 divorced men in this country—doesn't that mean your odds of being a divorced man are only one in ten?

Two million marriages to 1 million divorces is a ratio that exists in two dimensions. Rates can only be understood in three dimensions, as ratios calculated over the course of time. If the odds of staying married a lifetime, when calculated in the first year of marriage, were 50–50, that would take into account all the things that could go wrong over the next fifty years. The odds of a couple who've been married for ten years staying together is 70–30. For twenty years, it's 86–14. To put it another way, if a freshmen class of a thousand people is told, during initiation week, that 50 percent of them are not going to graduate, these freshmen will think their chances of graduating are 50–50. But, if 300 drop out as freshmen, 100 as sophomores, 60 as juniors, and 40 as seniors, then almost 3 out of 4 freshmen make it, 6 out of 7 sophomores, 9 out of 10 juniors, and 12 out of every 13 seniors. The odds aren't that bad to begin with, and they get better every year. Besides which, we are human beings. We can learn from our mistakes and change the odds in our favor.

If you really need to continue living in a bachelorly fashion after marriage, you can do what a lot of young married couples do, which is to become pimps. As a bachelor, weren't you invited to dinner at your married friends' houses, where they extolled the virtues of connubial bliss and tried to talk you into it? How many times at those dinner parties was there, unexpectedly, an eligible young woman present, a surprise fix-up? Married people live the single life vicariously by inviting their single friends over and setting them up together, in the hope that if anything happens they'll be the first to hear the details.

WHAT ABOUT KIDS? I'M NOT SURE IF I WANT ANY.

I once tried explaining decaffeinated coffee to an elderly Swedish gentleman. I said it was coffee without the chemical in it that gives you the buzz and keeps you awake all night. He looked at me with an utterly baffled expression on his face.

"Then why drink it?" he asked.

You'd get the same look if you could go back in time and tell someone you want to marry, but you don't want kids. Marrying and not having kids would have made no sense at all. Marriage laws were, in effect, a kind of breeding control program, in which brothers couldn't marry sisters or cousins, fathers couldn't marry their daughters, mothers their sons, and everyone had to wait until puberty. Barren couples were pitied and whispered about. Offspring were the only shot at immortality anybody got, the idea of immortality itself only a figurative expression of the biological imperative to live on in successive generations.

Today we have DINKs (for Dual Income No Kids) who achieve immortality by making videos of everything they do. In the old days, they had NINKs (No Income Nine Kids). DINKs talk about being unwilling to sacrifice a certain measure of quality in their lives or shoulder the responsibility of bringing children into an already overpopulated world full of famine and strife. NINKs would have been too busy changing diapers and trying to get the cat's head unstuck from the toilet bowl to worry about such things.

BUT THE WORLD IS A MESS—WHY BRING KIDS INTO IT?

Maybe to a gloomy gus, the world is a mess. We have holes in the ozone, acid rain, horrible new diseases, unending wars, famine, earthquakes, insane terrorists armed to the teeth with automatic weapons and explosives, outgunned only by Uzi-toting neighborhood drug dealers selling preschoolers cocaine grown where the Amazon jungle used to be, enough nuclear weapons to obliterate all life on earth as we know it 10,000 times over, polluted seas, greenhouse effects, toxic waste dumps bubbling and boiling beneath our schools, satanic cults kidnapping our pets, Larry Bird sitting out entire seasons—even folk music is pretentious these days. The horsemen of the apocalypse are having a regular rodeo, and there's nothing anybody can do about it. Or there would be, if people just cared. The only hope is people who care. And as parents, you'd have the opportunity to create new people who care, brand-new people who could grow up to care, to be president, or host talk shows.

MY PARENTS MADE MISTAKES—WHAT IF I DO TOO?

You can correct your own parents' mistakes, or you can get even with them by doing the same things to your own kids. My father loved golf, and made me caddy for him, carrying his bags well over 200,000 miles before I was ten years old.

My kid is going to carry my golf clubs at least that far. And I don't even golf. I'm just going to get some clubs and make my kid carry them. Either way, the only way you can really make a contribution to the next generation is to generate, procreate, and take your chances.

It's true too that you don't even have to have world-shaking ambitions to have kids. You can just have them because they're fun. A bachelor begins to consider this when he calls up a married friend to play poker and hears in reply, "No thanks—I think I'm gonna just stay home and watch my kid." And not because anything's wrong with it. Just because watching your kid is fun. Kids give you reason to worry, because for the first time in your adult life you have people so important to you that you can't bear the thought of anything happening to them, but it's a small price to pay for having people that important to you. In that regard, NINKs could probably tell DINKs a thing or two about quality of life.

WHAT IF SHE ISN'T RIGHT FOR ME?

You're sitting with your bride-to-be watching television, and an ad comes on for some gigantic sale, truckload after truck-load of couch-sized art, and your bride says, "Oh, that one's nice—let's get it." Maybe you're a connoisseur of the Couch Size school, and have been following the movement since it was founded in a Burger King storeroom in Bakersfield, California, in 1979. Or maybe you're like me, and mutter under your breath, "Oh, my god—I hope she's joking," and cringe in terror at the thought that maybe she isn't.

During your engagement, you may see flaws in your fiancée you never noticed before, and blow them way out of proportion. You will realize, perhaps, that she isn't perfect. Most family therapists and marriage counselors agree that when one person who's perfect marries another who isn't, the union seldom lasts very long. Or if you can accept that fact that she isn't perfect, then you wonder how imperfect is perfect enough. When you're young, you think you'll meet someone who will fulfill 100 percent of your expectations. You also think you'll live forever and be a bazillionaire. As you get older you modify your expectations to bring them more in line with reality. You'll settle for someone who is 85 percent of everything you dreamed of—70. Some people say they'd settle for 50.

SO IN OTHER WORDS, I LOWER MY EXPECTATIONS?

You are not really lowering your expectations, just substituting realistic ones for fantasies. One person can't possibly give you everything you need from people. You'll be more able to talk about your work with someone who does the same job you do. You'll feel more familiar with someone who was raised in exactly the same kind of family situation you were. Someone will be funnier than her, or smarter, or have physical characteristics you find more appealing.

Where love is concerned, the whole is greater than the sum of its parts. The person who's funnier may be less considerate, the smarter person more neurotic. Choosing a mate is a gestalt decision, like buying a plaid blanket, an acceptance of the whole. You don't marry someone expecting or hoping they'll change either, because the parts aren't divisible, rose from thorn. Everybody's got good qualities and everyone has flaws, including you. Your fiancée is probably thinking the same things you are, that some other guy she knows is funnier or smarter or better looking. You are choosing each other as whole people, with histories and personalities and inadequacies. If she's only 85 percent of what you thought you'd ever want, in the end, the fact that she loves you and wants to marry you despite your flaws should make up for the missing 15 percent.

IS GETTING MARRIED A GOOD WAY TO SAVE A RELATIONSHIP?

Oh, that's *real* smart.

It's true that being married will get you through larger crises, but it will also create larger crises, even when you and your wife are truly compatible. If you're not compatible already, you'll probably scratch each other's eyes out. People do all kinds of diversionary things when their relationship starts to flag. They think, "We can save this thing by moving to a new town." Starting a business. Buying a house. It's like a doctor saying, "We can save this patient—quick, nurse—new bedsheets."

WHAT ABOUT PARENTAL EXPECTATIONS?

Another bad reason to marry, though you can hardly help but anticipate what your parents are going to think. In the days of arranged marriages, there was nothing else to think about, because your parents chose your wife for you and you had no say in the matter. Today you choose your own wife, and so you marry to please yourself. Whether you please or displease your parents is not exactly of no consequence, and will color your judgment, but should not cloud it.

Social scientists and family experts now have enough data to conclusively prove your parents come from another planet. Where they grew up, buildings that seemed impossibly high were called "skyscrapers," the second choice being "cloud pokers." No one knew why they didn't fall down. To your parents, landing a man on the moon was an incredible feat, whereas to you it was just a poor excuse to interrupt "The Beverly Hillbillies." Your parents had to walk fifteen miles through blinding snow to get to school every day of the year, since nobody built schools near houses in the old days, and students had to stay in school from sunup to sundown, doing math on sheets of slate and reading interminable poems by Longfellow. You, on the other hand, read one book a year and faxed your papers to your teachers on your dad's car phone. As a result, much of the advice your parents offer, while valid, has to be translated into terms understandable on your planet, because that's where you're getting married.

The odds are, your parents will be thrilled to hear you're

engaged, and will like your bride almost as much as you do. Both consciously and unconsciously, you grew up learning your values from your parents and will very likely admire the same traits in people that they do. But marrying just to please them, or choosing someone because you know they'll like her, would be a mistake, because you're the one who has to live with the person you choose.

WHAT ABOUT BIOLOGICAL CLOCKS?

A man's biological clock often starts ticking with a sports injury. You direct your body to do something it's always done, and your body responds by informing you it is no longer sixteen years old. You break an ankle skiing, your knee playing softball, or your wrist, catching yourself after a simple slip in the bathtub. You try on an old pair of pants you haven't worn in a few years and wonder how they could have shrunk, just sitting in a drawer. More and more hair clogs the drain after you bathe. You start jogging to stay fit, and realize that when you were a kid you felt like a gazelle when you ran. Now you feel like a cement block being pushed end over end up a hill. You can't imagine ever hitchhiking again. You make your bed because you *like* it that way. You hear yourself saying things like, "the President knows what he's doing."

Men have long consoled themselves knowing a man is capable of fathering children well into his later years, but it depends on what you mean by fathering. Having half a dozen or so viable sperm left, yes. Chasing a three-year-old around in play, maybe not, unless you want to end up like Marlon Brando in *The Godfather*, facedown in the tomatoes. And besides, when you're seventy-five years old, be realistic— what are the odds of some fertile young thing coming up to you in a bar, running her fingers through your hair, and saying, "Buy me a drink—I love a man with a hip replace-ment"? Very small.

SHOULD I MARRY BECAUSE IT'S A GOOD WAY TO GET PRESENTS?

No. You do get a pile of presents though.

I STILL DON'T KNOW. THIS IS MY THIRD SERIOUS RELATIONSHIP. YOU KNOW WHAT THEY SAY—THREE STRIKES, YOU'RE OUT.

There is nothing magical about the number three, or seven, or any number, unless you yourself imbue it with magical powers. Superstition is only self-doubt in disguise. Weddings are surrounded by superstitions, and always have been. In some societies, weddings were and still are occasionally called off because of bad omens. Horoscopes are still consulted to choose an auspicious day for the ceremony. The ancient Greeks sacrificed animals to the gods and then scrutinized the entrails for auguries. The tradition of carrying the bride over the threshold goes back to ancient Roman times, when a groom would do so as a way of presenting his new wife to the lares and penates of the house in propitiation. In America it's considered bad luck for the groom to see the bride in her wedding dress before the wedding day (ruin her surprise and see how lucky you feel). Putting a carpet down on the aisle of the church is supposed to deter the evil spirits below, who for some reason can't figure out how to go around it. Dressing the groomsmen and the bridesmaids to resemble the bride and groom is a kind of superstitious shell game, done to confuse any ill-wisher in the crowd trying to fix the newlyweds with the evil eye. Much of the wedding ritual as we know it today has its origins in primitive appeals to the supernatural for either guidance or lenience, placating or confronting powers greater than ourselves. Primitive in origin but current in application.

If love is a mystery, the wedding is its Mystery Play, and even the least superstitious of grooms can find himself caught up in it. You may find yourself worrying over fortune cookies, getting one that reads, "There Are Many Fishes in the Sea," and actually fretting over why you got that cookie and not another. You'll glance at horoscopes in the paper, even though you've never looked at them before. You'll think every headlight you see coming toward you on the highway is going to swerve across the centerline and kill you, just because it would be so ironic, just your fate, to die a month before your wedding. You may see a beautiful woman in a bar, someone who makes Kim Basinger look like the star of a Kibbles and Bits commercial, and instead of saying to yourself, "Oh, look—what a lovely human being," you will say, "This woman has been sent to me as a test."

There is a lot of poetry and pathos in superstition, as people struggle to find their place in the grand scheme of things, and see themselves in dramatic or mythic terms. When you marry, for a while, you feel like the center of the universe. But you're not. There are probably two tentacled Glorbs getting married in a simple 72-ring ceremony on some planet a jillion light-years from earth who think *they're* the center of the universe, and they're wrong too. The universe has no center. The universe doesn't care. Three strikes is bad in baseball but great in bowling. The only way superstition can bring you bad luck is if it makes you worry so much you say or do something dumb because of it.

SO IT ALL COMES DOWN TO
SELF-DOUBT THEN?

All of it. Fear of not having enough money, of being unfaithful, of parental disapproval, of being fooled or getting hurt,
of having kids, of not playing it safe, of change itself, comes
down to self-doubt, to not knowing what challenges lie ahead
or whether you'll be able to rise to meet them. Some people
never overcome self-doubt. John Steinbeck thought everything he wrote stunk. Michelangelo thought his last pietà
was so bad he smashed it to pieces. Both Glenn Hall, who
played goalie in 1,021 hockey games for Detroit, Chicago,
and St. Louis, and Gump Worsley, who played goalie in
930 games for the Rangers, the Canadiens, and the North
Stars, left their waffles in the locker room before *every game*,
throwing up from nervous stomachs—yet both men had long
successful careers. Steinbeck and Michelangelo did all right
too.

You can't know what challenges will arise, but you can
know whichever ones do won't be too different from any that
have arisen in other marriages, and there'll be people willing
to help you meet them, the first and foremost of whom will
be your wife. You can't really know how you'll react, but
you can look at your past and realize that if you could make
it through eighth grade, you can make it through anything.
Ultimately, marriage is a leap of faith, a blind leap into the
unknown.

A flying leap into the unknown is clearly an endeavor
best undertaken when you're panicked and numb. Fortunately, that's exactly the condition most marrying men find
themselves in on their wedding day. It's a fascinating process
to find yourself a part of, a rite of passage, growth and
maturation, like puberty, but not as drawn out, and without
the skin problems.

2

BUYING THE RING

That evening he carried away her picture in his eye: the thick blond plait, the longish, laughing blue eyes, the saddle of pale freckles across the nose. He could not go to sleep for hearing that ring in her voice; he tried in a whisper to imitate the intimate tone in which she had uttered the commonplace phrase, and felt a shiver run through and through him. He knew by experience that this was love. And he was accurately aware that love would surely bring him much pain, affliction, and sadness, that it would certainly destroy his peace, filling his heart to overflowing with melodies which would be no good to him because he would never have the time or tranquillity to give them permanent form. Yet he received this love with joy, surrendered himself to it, and cherished it with all the strength of his being; for he knew that love made one vital and rich, and he longed to be vital and rich, far more than he did to work tranquilly on anything to give it permanent form.

—FROM *TONIO KRÖGER*, BY THOMAS MANN

Once you've decided to take the leap, you may want to include your girlfriend in your plans. Let her know what you have in mind, just to sound her out on the idea and get her feedback. She is likely to have a thought or two.

The Latin origin of "propose" means to "place forth"—to lay on the table for further consideration and discussion. In most cases, you'd hope that the thrill of living with you for the rest of her life would be enough to convince her to marry you, but if not, you may want to have a bribe ready to lay on the table as well, in the form of an engagement ring, a symbol forged from diamonds and gold, our two most valuable elements, your way of saying, "If I weren't serious, would I have spent this much money?"

RINGS HISTORICALLY CONSIDERED

Rings have long been loaded with symbolic meaning, one of our oldest forms of jewelry. The very first rings are thought to have been made of straw or rope and worn by primitive peoples in the belief that girding a part of the body in a circle prevented the spirit from escaping. Getting an escaped spirit back into a body was harder than putting toothpaste back in the tube in those days. The earliest metal rings, brass and iron, come from the tombs of ancient Egypt, where a ring symbolized happiness without beginning or end. One of the oldest known rings bears the insignia of Cheops, builder of the Great Pyramid near Gizeh, around 2900 B.C. In the Bible, Pharaoh is said to have given Joseph his signet ring to serve as a passport during his travels throughout Egypt. Until the eighteenth century, European rulers often loaned their rings to messengers and emissaries as symbols of authority or veracity. King Solomon, known for his wisdom, wore a ring that was said to have the power to transport him to heaven, where he allegedly received the wisdom he used to amass a great fortune on earth. In the third century

A.D., the Roman Emperor Maximinus, judging from the moniker a very big guy, couldn't find a ring big enough to fit him, so he wore his wife's bracelet around his thumb.

Rings have been thought to have magical powers. The ring used in the wedding ceremony of Joseph and Mary once competed with pieces of the true cross for miraculous curative powers, and there were almost as many of each in the reliquaries of medieval Europe. A fourth-century physician and misornithope named Trallian was known to treat his patients by giving them a ring engraved with magic words that had the power to make bile leave the body of the wearer and enter the body of the nearest lark.

Certain stones were believed to have supernatural values. Diamonds could assuage the fury of one's enemies and frustrate poisons. Amethysts drew in vapors, or what scientists today call "germs." An emerald was supposed to break when touched by an adulterer. Opals sharpened your eyesight. Sapphires could ward off enchantments and, when combined with spiders, counteract poisons. Turquoise was thought to be able to reconcile husbands and wives who were angry at one another, though how much turquoise it took to redeem one cracked emerald is not known. Joan of Arc (1412–1431) was suspected of wearing charmed rings that gave her power over her enemies, but in the end, she wasn't wearing enough of them. Abbot Thitheim of Prussia (1462–1516) had a ring made out of something he called "electrum," which, he said, when worn on the left hand, rendered him invisible, which may have been true because a thief stole it and was never seen again.

TOKENS OF AFFECTION/ENSLAVEMENT

The ring as a sign of betrothal began with the Romans. The gladiators wore an early form of brass knuckles, rings so heavy they could kill with a single blow. As the empire declined and grew decadent, some Romans wore as many as sixty rings at a time, different sets of rings for summer and winter, an effective way, perhaps, to camouflage a wedding band at orgies. Wedding bands could be made of gold, silver, copper, brass, leather, or rush, but were commonly made of iron, symbolizing the strength and durability of the union. Slaves wore iron rings around their necks, and once freed, often wore iron rings on their fingers to represent their former state of bondage. The iron wedding band was a sign of voluntary enslavement. It also served as a deposit put down on the woman, a visible "Sold" sign to anyone wondering if she were still on the market.

Gold rings became prevalent in the Middle Ages, when gold itself became more readily available. Setting diamonds in gold to represent the value of the marriage became fashionable in fifteenth-century Venice, where the lapidary arts flourished. In 1477, Archduke Maximilian of Austria gave a diamond ring to Mary of Burgundy, thought to be the first diamond engagement ring ever bestowed.

At that time in Europe, wedding rings were worn on the fourth digit of the right hand, the hand on which popes and cardinals wore their religious rings and the hand considered closest to God. The fourth digit of the left hand became the annular finger after the Reformation, perhaps as a schismatic statement, or perhaps more a chauvinist revision, the right hand thought to be the masculine hand, having dominance over the left or feminine hand. It was also a common belief, one that persists to this day, originating from the work of ancient Egyptian anatomists, that the fourth finger of the left hand contained a nerve leading directly to the heart, a belief modified by Renaissance physicians who held it was not a nerve but an artery, the "vena amora," or vein of love. These, of course, were the same guys who thought you could fill passing larks with bile.

The practice of wearing the wedding ring on the fourth finger of the left hand became codified by the seventeenth

century. It was important to wear the wedding band on the
proper finger, to convey the appropriate message. A ring on
the fourth finger of the left hand meant you were married
or engaged. A ring on your index finger told prospective
suitors you weren't married and wanted to be left alone. On
the other hand, or actually, on the other finger, if you wore
a ring on your pinky, you were saying, "Hey, sailor—buy
me a drink."

We still wear our wedding rings to make public state-
ments, both to proclaim the love we share and to announce
to oglers in singles bars that we are now out of the game
and sitting on the bench. Today both husband and wife wear
wedding bands, which may have originated in the gimmal
ring, consisting of two or more separate loops joined by a
hinge or interlocking clasp mechanism, bride and groom each
wearing half of the whole ring, a practice popular in the
sixteenth century in northern Europe. As much as you wear
your wedding band to let the world know of your commitment, you wear it to let your spouse know you want the
world to know, a way of assuring her. It is thought to be
bad luck to lose your wedding band, and you don't have to
be Albert Einstein to figure out why. To lose it you usually
have to take it off first—you can't pretend the dog ate it—
and any spouse may reasonably be expected to ask why you
did; bad luck indeed unless you have a good excuse. In most
cases the ring is put on and rarely if ever removed, like a
tattoo.

Of course, men, being the possessive insecure little wieners that we are, want our brides to be more conspicuously
unavailable than us, just so nobody gets the wrong idea,
which may be why brides wear two rings to our one. The
engagement ring is commonly a diamond set in gold, the
gem as conspicuous as any found on the planet, able to
sparkle like a beacon in a dark bar. Some people use rubies
or sapphires, hard durable stones (though diamond is 86
times harder) in a ring that is worn every day. Soft gems such

as opals or emeralds are occasionally chosen. The diamond is nevertheless the stone of choice when tongue-tied Romeos want their rings to do their talking for them, popping open a jewelry box in lieu of actually popping the question. An acceptable custom, but not one to be entered into lightly.

THE NEED FOR CAUTION

Buying the engagement ring is often a marrying man's first encounter with the nuptial industry, or "Wedding Mafia"— an organized crime syndicate that most ordinary people are unaware of, until they get engaged and realize that the Wedding Mafia—caterers and florists and the rest—actually control all the money spent in America in the month of June. That means $27.8 billion annually (according to *Bride's Magazine*), a huge bloodsucking conspiracy of liars and thieves who lure you in when your brain isn't working and your defenses are down and soak you for every penny you have because they know you're going into your wedding believing it's a once-in-a-lifetime event wherein money, they will try to convince you, should be no object. Money no object? Imagine any industry in which the buyers have the same attitude. Okay, the defense industry, but name another. FBI listening devices planted in a New Jersey tuxedo rental store overheard the owner referring to the wedding industry as "*questa cosa nostra gioisa*," or "this joyous thing of ours."

The cost of an average engagement ring, again according to *Bride's Magazine,* is about $1,800. Jewelry families within the Wedding Mafia are currently seeking to establish a standard rule-of-thumb price for engagement rings, a prorated figure that should be roughly equal, they will tell you, to two months of your salary, assuming you really love and care about your intended, less if you don't like her that much. Two months, they hope, will sound like no time at all. A sixth of everything you earn in a year sounds like a much larger figure. If you work on commission as an air-conditioner salesman, maybe you can spend what you make in January and February, but for most people, two months' salary is going to add up to a lot of money. Maybe you have a lot of money. Maybe you don't want to spend any more than you have to, but end up spending it anyway. Either way, you will want to get your money's worth.

FINDING A GOOD JEWELER

There are plenty around, but it may not be easy to identify them. They may be in malls, but jewelry stores in malls carry a high overhead and have to make up for it by marking up their prices. Large discount stores with lots of loud advertisements on Top 40 rock radio stations sometimes try to sell the sizzle instead of the steak, telling you you can buy, for 250 bucks, a ring that would sell for $1,000 in another store, which, if you stop to think about it, makes no sense at all. What—they don't *need* the extra $750? If they could get it, they would. More likely they're selling a heavily flawed, poorly cut diamond set in 10-carat gold for twice its real value. Some stores actually give you the bum's rush if you appear to know too much about diamonds. Knowledge is your best defense.

The first thing to realize is that a diamond is not an element with an empirical value, like gold. A diamond is a *form* of an element, carbon. Carbon in the form of charcoal briquettes sells for 20 cents a pound. As it increases in purity and quality, crystallizing as diamonds, it becomes considerably more valuable. Variations in price are determined by subtle deviations in a number or characteristics, none of which a layperson can be expected to know. A reputable jeweler can be determined, first and foremost, by the amount of information he's willing to give you and the amount of time he's willing to spend with you. A reputable jeweler doesn't try to talk fast and skip over things you don't need to know. Ask if he custom-makes rings, casts his own gold, or sets his own diamonds—such a jeweler is bound to know more about his trade than one who merely orders and sells from a catalog. Ask if he's a certified gemologist. Try to find a jeweler in a small town, where he can't afford to rip people off because he has to live with them every day. The most important thing is to feel he or she is a person you can talk to and trust. Follow your instincts. If you think you're being jerked around, walk away, because you probably are.

WHAT TO SPEND

Should you spend all the money you have? Charge it and hope you'll be able to pay for it later? There will be large unanticipated wedding expenses ahead of you, but since you haven't even proposed yet, you probably aren't thinking about them.

There is the "Oooh Factor" to consider. Your bride's friends will all want to see her rock once she tells them she's engaged, an impulse that seems to overcome even the most ardent feminists from time to time, at a party or at one of her showers, when all thoughts of how many starving Ethiopians could have been fed on the money the ring cost will fade away. Your bride will be happier to have her friends "oooh" and "aaah" loudly than to hear them sigh or say, "Oh, what a dear *little* ring." A woman who has sworn not to covet a large rock on her finger to flash at her friends (and enemies) will suddenly find herself doing just that when an engagement looms, regarding such a stone as her birthright, conditioned to expect one ever since her daddy put a paper cigar ring on her finger at eighteen months. It's recompense for all the crap she's had to take from men her whole life. All the other married women have one. If all the other married women jumped off a bridge, would she jump off a bridge too? She'll still want a ring. Everyone wants to be "oohed" and "aahed" at least once in their lifetime.

DIAMONDS AS INVESTMENTS

You may also want to think of the diamond as an investment, though that's a strategy some less reputable dealers use to talk their customers into buying higher quality diamonds than they might originally have intended. Buying diamonds can be a legitimate investment, but not the kind of investment you'll see any dividends from in your lifetime. Your wife is not going to trade in her wedding rings just because you need a new washing machine. It is also a trickier investment than it would first appear. We've all grown up believing that diamonds never lose their value. It's true that they don't wear down, but they can chip. They're harder than anything, harder than learning German, and hold their value because they don't deteriorate. During times of war it's easier to smuggle diamonds out of a country than cash, and they don't melt until they reach 6,900 degrees, which means that, unless they take a direct hit (thermonuclear reactions take place at 180 million degrees), they'll survive the next nuclear war. Of course, you won't. Diamonds, as a stone, last.

As a purchase, results vary. A diamond bought in 1980 is, as of this writing, worth about a third of what it was worth then; at that time diamonds, gold, and silver all soared in value, until 20 percent interest rates pulled the rug out from under everybody and the markets crashed. Prices are rising now, doubling since 1985, due to heavy investing by the Japanese in top-quality diamonds, increasing demand against fairly steady supply, kept constant because the market is monopolized by the De Beers Company, the South African diamond giant through whose London-based Central Selling Organization more than 90 percent of the world's diamonds

● ●

POLITICALLY CORRECT DIAMOND BUYING

Because the De Beers Company controls so much of the market, owning both diamond mines and the organization through which diamonds are sold, it would be difficult for anybody wishing to boycott South African diamonds to completely avoid doing business with South Africa. Many jewelers wanting to accommodate customers' wishes not to buy from South Africa have been able to purchase diamonds directly from other independent sources, Angola or Brazil. You should feel free to ask where a diamond you might be interested in comes from, and to choose not to buy it if the policies of the country of origin are not to your liking. You'll have to take the jeweler's word for it, but then, you'll want to be working with a jeweler you can trust anyway.

● ●

are sold. Even with prices rising, you will have to lay out a considerable amount of money and wait a long time to see a return on your investment. A 1-carat stone that sold for a $1,000 in 1949 could be worth as much as ten times that today. The same could be said for houses or cars.

Furthermore, buying engagement rings is not the same as investing in diamonds as a commodity, because one is retail and one is wholesale. If for some reason you want to redeem your engagement ring (e.g., suppose she says no?), even though your jeweler has given you a written appraisal specifying the value of the stone and the setting, no jeweler is going to give you the appraised value. The appraisal is for insurance purposes, and estimates the replacement cost, or what it might be worth as collateral against a loan. When you try to sell a ring back to a jeweler, he or she will not care about the labor that went into it or the design, and will only look at it as gold that can be melted down or a stone that can be reset. A large-carat diamond with numerous impurities and poor color might have a high "Oooh Factor" and serve its purpose, because most imperfections are not obvious to the unaided or uneducated eye, but it won't bring much if you return it. A large perfect stone costing thousands of dollars will still be worth thousands of dollars, but a small ring featuring diamond chips, appraised at $450, might bring an offer of no more than $20. My own plain round wedding band, 5.65 grams of 18-carat gold, an element with empirical value, cost more than $200 retail and is worth $27 scrap. As a rule, jewelers have no interest in buying back used rings unless they are of high quality. Jewelers who will buy used rings are called either estate jewelers or pawnbrokers. The jeweler you buy your engagement ring from might be willing to give you a written guarantee to refund your money within a certain time period, but it's not required.

WHERE ARE THE FOUR Cs I KEEP HEARING ABOUT?

Knowing what to look for will familiarize you with what the diamond industry calls the four *Cs*—color, clarity, cut, and carat weight. The first two Cs describe what nature has done to the stone, the second two what man might do to it.

All diamonds come from the same source, the center of the earth, developing billions of years ago from carbon dioxide gas under high pressure as deep as 93 miles within the earth's molten core, at temperatures in excess of 2,600 degrees Fahrenheit, and are virtually the same worldwide. Six-, eight-, or twelve-sided diamond crystals were driven to the surface by carbon-dioxide gas eruptions through cracks in the earth's crust, something like a dry volcano, mixed in with a kind of consolidated rock known as kimberlite to form diamond pipes. Diamond is not only the hardest substance known but also has the highest thermal conductivity, which is why diamond points used in abrasives don't heat up from friction or wear down. Large quantities of diamonds are found on the ocean floor off Africa's west coast, and even in space—or at least in meteorites. The first diamonds were found in streambeds in India and Borneo in prehistoric times, mined in India over 2,800 years ago, found in Brazil in 1725, again panned from streambeds, and in 1866 a 21.5-carat bauble was discovered among the playthings of a small boy who had plucked it from the banks of the Orange River, near Hopetown, South Africa. Today Australia produces 33 percent of the world's diamonds, Zaire 23 percent, Botswana 15 percent, USSR 14 percent, South Africa 11 percent, and the rest of the world makes up the remaining 4 percent.

CLARITY

Clarity is the first thing to look for in a stone. As diamonds form, not all the carbon is crystallized. Some minute particles remain black, and, when found in a gemstone, are called inclusions. Flawless stones (rated FL) have no inclusions and are the rarest, therefore the most valuable. An internally flawless stone (rated IF) will have minor surface imperfections, and is second in value. Value drops as clarity worsens, from VVS (for very very slight inclusions) to VS to SI to I, until, in some diamonds, you can see the black specks with the naked eye. Your jeweler should encourage you to look through a microscope directly into the stone for inclusions, at a magnification of no less than ten, and show you the scale by which clarity is rated. A stone with a few inclusions at the edge, near the girdle, where the bezel may hide them, will be more valuable than a stone with the same number of inclusions in the table, the flat top of the gem, where they'll be more visible.

COLOR

Diamonds also vary in color. The clearest stones are the rarest and therefore the most valued. Your jeweler should have a master set of standardized stones, or sometimes imitation stones, color rated by the industry, against which you can compare the stone you intend to buy. Ratings range from D to Z (nobody seems to know what happened to A, B, or C), with D the clearest, called investment grade, and Z the yellowest. A 1-carat D flawless diamond could sell for as much as $25,000 or $30,000. An untrained eye may be unable to tell a G from an H, but you should be able to discern the difference between a D and an M. The stone should be observed against white paper in strong white light. The American Gem Society forbids its participating jewelers from using the term *blue-white* to describe stones that are not easily observed as yellow, because stones with actual blue coloring are as rare as true colorless stones.

CARAT WEIGHT

Carats measure the weight of the stone, 1 carat equal to 0.2 grams. There are 141 3/4 carats to an ounce. A carat is divided into 100 points, so if you hear someone refer to a 25-point diamond, they mean point 25, or a quarter of a carat, and not the number of apexes on it where cut planes meet. The average engagement ring stone is 30 points. The word *carat* comes from the seed of the carob trees, against which diamonds were weighed back when all they had to weigh diamonds with were carob seeds. Values increase exponentially according to carat weight. Where a 50-point GVSI brilliant cut diamond will sell for $2,985, a similar full-carat diamond, twice the size, with the same rating, will sell not for twice the price but more than three times the price—$10,290. The scale increases dramatically as the grade

of the diamond goes up—a full-carat D flawless will be far
more than three times the value of a half-carat D flawless.
Jewelers try to cut the largest possible unflawed stone from
a rough, carving the most value from it. The Cullinan diamond, the largest ever found, tipped the scales at 3,106
carats, or about a pound and a half, and was cut into 9
major stones and 96 smaller ones. The largest cut stone is
known as the Star of Africa, the largest cut diamond in the
world, at 530.20 carats and 74 facets; it is currently among
the British Crown Jewels. The largest diamond ever found
in the United States, in the Crater of Diamonds near Mur-
freesboro, Arkansas, is the Uncle Sam, weighing in at a
measly 40.23 carats in the rough. The Crater of Diamonds
is now a tourist trap.

CUT

The cut is one of the easiest ways to appraise the value of a
stone, simply because they don't let beginning stonecutters
cut high-quality rough diamonds. Fine stones go to master
gem cutters. A completely messed up cut indicates the stone
was probably of poor clarity and color to begin with. Cut is
also perhaps the easiest characteristic of a diamond to evalu-
ate. Still, it can be tricky, because it's something like looking into a house of mirrors, difficult to tell which line is
which or where. Here are some things to look for:

First, looking straight down into the stone through the
table, can you observe any double refraction? Do the lines
formed by the bottom facet junctions appear blurry or
doubled, two lines where there should be one? This could
mean the stone was improperly oriented when struck from
the rough crystal, and will not release or reflect as much
light as it should.

Second, is the girdle too thin or too thick? The girdle
is the narrow rim at the widest circumference in a stone,

where the crown (top) and the pavilion (bottom) of the stone meet. If there is no space between the crown and the pavilion, the two halves meeting instead at a knifelike edge, the prongs may chip the stone. Diamonds are hard but they're not tough, and they can splinter along certain crystallographic planes. If the girdle is too thick, the ring will appear clumsy. Its thickness should be 1 to 2 percent of its diameter.

Third, do the top facets align with the bottom facets? They should meet at the girdle. In some instances a culet facet is cut at the bottom of the pavilion, parallel to the cut of the table in a brilliant cut. The table facet should be a perfect octagon, the culet facet an exact reduction of the table facet.

Fourth, are there extra facets? A brilliant cut has 58 facets, no more or less. And are there junctions where a girdle facet and a crown facet overlap? Is the table facet parallel to the girdle? Is the circular plane described by the points where the star facets meet the girdle facets parallel to the table as well?

Finally, are the proportions right? If not, your diamond will not refract the maximum amount of light, and bozos in dark bars will be hitting on your wife for the rest of her life because her ring doesn't sparkle enough. A good jeweler will show you a drawing of what the ideal proportions should be. If the stone you're interested in doesn't resemble the drawing, keep looking. There are, of course, other cuts to choose from, but the brilliant cut (created by Marcel Tolkowsky in 1919 and sometimes called the Tolkowsky Cut, American Cut, or Ideal Cut) captures the most white light and allows for the greatest dispersion—the ability of the crystal to fracture light into rainbow spectrums, like a prism.

OTHER CONSIDERATIONS

What does your bride do? That is, what does she do with her hands? Some rings are high profile, stones set up on prongs rising as much as a quarter of an inch off the finger, which is fine if all your bride does is lie around in feather boas watching "All My Children" and eating Twinkies. You're a lucky man. If she works with her hands, then a high-profile ring will catch on everything and be a constant source of daily irritation, in which case a low-profile ring would be more appropriate.

Also consider her sense of taste. It's her ring to wear, and you should try to give her something that will please her esthetically. If she wears a lot of rings, you're in luck. One night when you're rifling through her drawers, you might be able to pilfer a few rings to show to the jeweler. If she wears only one ring, base your decision on the way she dresses or decorates her apartment. Is her taste simple or ornate?

FIT

You'll want to buy a ring that fits her. If she has an extra ring you can steal, take it in to the jeweler. If she has only one ring, you'll have to figure out a way to get it off her finger. Slyly trace it on a piece of paper when she takes it off to do the dishes, or if she doesn't take it off to do the dishes (or if she never does the dishes), suggest that she henna her hair and tell her henna will tarnish the metal. At a romantic candlelit dinner, play with a wad of candle wax until it's soft and then ask if you can play with her ring, and use it to make an impression in the soft wax. Or invite her to your place to help you paint something, use oil paint, and then ask her to clean the brushes—the turpentine will get under the ring and irritate her skin. When she takes it off to wash her hands, make an impression with it in a slab of window putty. Or play strip poker with her when you have friends over and cheat until the ring comes off, which won't take long because it's going to be the first thing she removes; then ask her to get you a beer and make an impression of the ring in the cheese loaf. Be devious. That's what marriage is all about. It's a skill you can use the rest of your life. Or just guess what her size is and don't worry about it, because most rings can be sized later.

WEDDING BANDS

It's easier to buy wedding bands than engagement rings, because gold is gold, an element (Au, atomic number 79), and you know what it is. It's also easier because it's common these days for a bride and groom to buy their wedding bands together. It's always easier to avoid being ripped off when you have someone to shop with. It can be the first of the many cute things you and your bride will do together as would-be newlyweds. There are standard jokes you will be expected to make. When you're being fitted, you're supposed to say "Make it loose so I can get it off quick." Trying it on, you are obliged to say, "It's too tight/it's suffocating me/ it's giving me a rash." You and your bride will laugh because you're giddy and nervous, but the jeweler has heard it all before. He'll smile to himself and say, "Yep, I'm in the right business."

ALL THAT GLITTERS

Gold is really amazing stuff. The Latin name for gold, *aurum*, means "glowing dawn." Ancient Greeks mined it from the earth and Egyptians buried their dead with it as far back as the Stone Age. It is one of the least chemically active metals, and does not tarnish or oxidize in the air, holding its sheen for hundreds of years. It is inert to acids and alkaline solutions. It is 19.3 times denser than water, and a cubic foot of it weighs 1,200 pounds. It is a good conductor of both heat and electricity, used in countless electrical circuits and connectors, including your telephone jack. It's the most malleable of metals. An ounce can be stretched into a wire 40 miles long. An amount the size of a pinhead can be hammered thin enough to cover Roseanne Barr. It can be thinned until, at a millionth of an inch, it's transparent, used to coat windows in office buildings to make them more energy efficient, or placed on the windshields of jet aircraft where it will still carry enough heat to defrost the glass. All the gold ever mined would comprise a cube 50 feet to a side, 75,000 tons, worth about $888 billion at today's price, which is roughly $370 an ounce. A nugget weighing 600 pounds was found in Australia. South Africa produces the most gold, followed by the USSR, Canada, and the United States. Three-fourths of the gold produced yearly is used in jewelry.

YOUR RING

The ring you buy will not be pure gold, which, at a tensile strength of 20,000 psi, is too soft for jewelry. Pure gold must be alloyed with another metal to give it strength, which is why the percentage of gold in an alloy is measured in karats, which have nothing to do with the carats used to measure diamonds. When you're talking about gold, "karat" means one twenty-fourth. If somebody tries to sell you 26-karat gold, there's a 110 percent chance you're getting ripped off; 24-karat gold is pure, but 12-karat is half gold and half something else. What that something else is determines both the strength and the color of the ring. White gold and yellow gold are by far the most

popular colors. Eighteen-karat white gold is 75 percent
gold and 25 percent platinum, or 25 percent palladium,
or 10 percent palladium/10 percent nickel/5 percent zinc.
Twenty-two karat bright yellow gold is 91.67 percent
gold, 5 percent silver, 2 percent copper, and 1.33 percent
zinc. Eighteen-karat yellow gold is three-quarters gold,
9.5 percent silver, and 15.5 percent copper. More copper
and less silver produces a rose-colored gold, which is sometimes used to decorate rings, as is green gold, which is an
amalgam of gold, copper, and cadmium. In fact, gold can
be alloyed in just about any color you want. Seventy-five
percent gold and 25 percent iron produces blue gold; 41.7
percent iron produces black gold, and I don't mean Texas
Tea. Twenty-five percent aluminum gives bright red gold,
whereas 16.7 percent gives you purple. Forging gold—
hammering it into shape—hardens it, and will make a
better ring than one in which the melted gold was poured
into a mold and then polished.

It's undeniably enjoyable to pore over a glass display
case in a jewelry store, examining gold rings, making your
selection. You think of all the other hopeful young couples
who've stood in front of such display cases before you, holding hands and giggling and swaying nervously at the knees.
It's corny as hell, or at least you always thought it was when
you saw other people doing it, but now you're doing it, and
you want to make the most of it. If you don't see what you
like, the jeweler might have catalogs for you to look through.
If you still don't see anything that appeals to you, you always
have the option, at least at a full-service jeweler, of designing
your own rings. You can describe what you want, or draw
a picture. Some jewelers will make you a wax sample and
paint it gold so you can see your design in three dimensions.
Custom rings may cost a little more, but you'll have the
satisfaction of saying you designed it yourself.

ALTERNATIVES

Another possibility is to give your bride an heirloom, the ring your mother or your grandmother wore. If you do, you should remember that an old ring, which has sentimental value to you, may be unappealing or silly looking to someone else, and again, it's hers to wear every day. You might also bear in mind that if and when an engagement is called off, it's customary for the bride to return her engagement ring, whereas in a divorce the heirloom has a good chance of leaving the family, or at the very least causing a nasty confrontation in or out of court. Heirlooms, particularly valuable ones, sometimes require prenuptial agreements if they are to be maintained in the family at all cost. You will be trusting that it will never come to that, which is, of course, what they all say.

It's also conceivable that your bride will not even want a ring. She might, quite legitimately, not relish the idea of wearing an emblem of voluntary slavery, or wish to convey the notion to others that she considers herself owned. Some people find that gold gives them a rash, sometimes from the residual radioactivity of contaminants in the gold. Other people find rings confining and just don't like them. If your bride doesn't wear rings, ask her why. Talk it over. Possibly she's a Puritan, who considers the ring "a relic of popery and a diabolic circle for the devil to dance in." Look on the bright side. You've just saved yourself a bundle. Take the money you would have spent and put it toward a honeymoon. If she doesn't like to go places, buy her clothes. If she doesn't like clothes, buy her a nice meal. Donate it in her name to her favorite charity. If she doesn't want any of that, check her pulse.

3
POPPING THE QUESTION

. . . One autumn night, five years
before, they had been walking down the street when the leaves were
falling, and they came to a place where there were no trees and the
sidewalk was white with moonlight. They stopped here and turned
towards each other. Now it was a cool night with that mysterious
excitement in it which comes at the two changes of the year. The
quiet lights in the houses were humming out into the darkness and
there was a stir and bustle among the stars. Out of the corner of
his eye Gatsby saw that the blocks of sidewalks really formed a
ladder and mounted to a secret place above the trees—he could climb
to it, if he climbed alone, and once there he could suck on the pap
of life, gulp down the incomparable milk of wonder. His heart beat
faster as Daisy's white face came up to his own. He knew that
when he kissed this girl, and forever wed his unutterable visions to
her perishable breath, his mind would never romp again like the
mind of God. So he waited, listening for a moment longer to the
tuning-fork that had been struck upon a star. Then he kissed her.

At his lips' touch she blossomed for him like a flower, and the incarnation was complete.
—FROM *THE GREAT GATSBY*, BY F. SCOTT FITZGERALD

Romantic enough, until you remember that Jay Gatsby had what could be the worst sense of timing in all of literature. "The course of true love," Shakespeare said, "never did run smooth." Gatsby shouldn't have waited. Romeo and Juliet should have waited. Popping the question is the *coup de grâce* of courtship, its final flourish, the point where courtship ends and betrothal begins. The problem is knowing when you're there, and what to say or do when you arrive.

Courtship was simpler in junior high school. It could happen without you having to lift a finger. You'd be sitting in the cafeteria, minding your own business, throwing food at your friend Jim, talking about the latest Beatles album (I'm dating myself, but then, I "dated" myself a lot in junior high school) when somebody taps you on your shoulder. You turn, and it's Mary Ellen Chase, a girl you hated from kindergarten to fourth grade, but sort of started to talk to in fifth grade. She's grinning.

"Do you like Kathy Barron?" she asks.

"I don't know," you say. "Who's Kathy Barron?"

"She's over there," Mary Ellen Chase says, pointing to a table of girls across the room. One buries her face from humiliation—that's Kathy Barron. Her friends tell her what's happening, point at you, and giggle. You wonder if you have a booger hanging out one or both of your nostrils. "She likes you, and if you give me a ring to give to her, I'll get a ring from her to give to you and then you can be going together."

The next day, Mary Ellen Chase facilitates the exchange of rings and presto, you're going together. Sometime that week, you might even pass Kathy Barron in the hall and actually say something clever like "hi." A week later you might find yourself at a make-out party, where since you're going together, you have to kiss each other. You get a boner the next day, just thinking about it. Usually in the middle of this boner, Mary Ellen Chase taps you on the shoulder in study hall and hands you your ring back. Kathy Barron thinks everything is going too fast and she just wants to be friends.

MODERN ROMANCE

Recent studies suggest adult women still initiate relationships twice as often as men do, though unlike junior high school, adult women act on their own behalf and not as go-betweens. A woman might introduce herself to you, suggest the first dinner, and at some point in the relationship say something like, "I love you and I want to be with you, but if you don't ask me to marry you sometime in the next six months, I'm going to have to start thinking about looking for someone else," which is in fact popping the question, or at least preempting the question. Modern or "progressive" women have always known it's just as much their right as a man's to be the one to propose. Still, it's more likely your bride will wait until you think it's your idea to actually speak the words.

In which case it gets more like high school than junior high school. In high school, boys are supposed to have caught up with the girls in maturity, and are therefore expected to call for dates. If the phone companies could figure out a way to bill clients for the time customers spend *thinking* about making phone calls, the amount they could rake in from fifteen-year-old lovesick boys would equal the gross national product. I knew a guy who waited so long to call a girl he liked that by the time he finally did, she was married with two kids and a mortgage.

OH, NO—I WAS A LOSER IN HIGH SCHOOL

Proposing marriage is slightly different from calling girls in high school, in that we all know *what* to say, those four little words, "Will you marry me?" We just don't know when, or where, or how. It can be on the tip of the tongue a hundred times and not come out. It is a pivotal moment. By proposing, you are making your pledge, and in a sense, from that moment on, you're already married. Preparing to repeat your pledge in public, before family and friends, is just the first thing you do, once you're already married. You can plan to do it, or you can do it spontaneously, but you have to do it. No one can do it for you. There are no Mary Ellen Chases to help you.

I told her I would get down on my knees if she wanted me to.

No, she said, that wouldn't be necessary.

She knew what was coming. After five years of sharing the same roll of dental floss, our relationship thrived on no surprises. Thrived and floundered. There had been a separation, a renewed courtship, and now, after six months of giving it another try, it was time to fish or cut bait.

I picked our favorite restaurant, a little jazz club next to the pier at Newport Beach, California. I started listing the problems.

"I don't suppose I'll ever have a lot of money," I told her.

She flipped her hand, as if to say money wasn't important. An easy thing for a doctor to say, but she didn't say it, fearing, perhaps, I would lose my train of thought.

"And we're in uncharted water," I continued. "We'll have to make up our own rules."

"Yes," she said patiently.

"Well, there it is," I said finally. "I love you and I want you to be my wife. Will you marry me?"

She leaned across the table and kissed me.

"I would be happy to," she said.

Later, we took a stroll on the pier. The fish weren't biting, so everybody was cutting bait. I was feeling good.

"Were you serious about the knees?" she asked.

—*Joe*

EMOTIONAL PRECONDITIONS

First, you should be enthusiastic about it. This is not to say you can't be matter-of-fact. Sometimes you've known each other for so long that marriage can be a foregone conclusion, in which case you might be eating dinner in a restaurant somewhere and say between bites, "So, do you think we should get married?" You probably don't want to talk with your mouth full, something your wife would remember and give you shit about for a long time. You don't want to give the impression that her answer doesn't really matter to you, one way or the other. I had a friend who tried to be nonchalant about it, even going so far as to give his bride $200, telling her to go buy a ring herself, since he had no idea what she'd like. A predictably short while later, she told him she wanted a divorce, and threw the ring at him. When he took it in to get his money back, the jeweler informed him the ring was cheap costume jewelry, not worth two bucks.

You want to be calm, not nonchalant. You will doubtless be full of anxieties, possibly goofy with excitement, and your bride will be able to tell, which should underscore your sincerity, but you don't want to look like you're scared to death at the idea of marrying her, or hyperventilate. In an excited state, you draw rapid shallow breaths, causing the ph level in your blood to lower, until hypo-alkalosis sets in, and you feel your extremities tingle and your muscles contract and your head spins and you pass out. You can reverse the progress of the attack by breathing into a paper bag, but your bride may have a hard time understanding your words through a paper bag. "Will I what? Will I *bury* you?"

You will want to be sober as well. Booze can have the effect of medicating and relaxing you, but it's easy to get too calm, and since the first thing alcohol does is affect your judgment, it's possible, when you're really nervous, to get toilet-hugging calm before you know it. If you're at all excessively artificially calm, your bride is not going to say, "Yes, I'll marry you." She's going to say, "You don't know what you're saying." You don't want it to be the whiskey talking, even though we all know we've meant every word of everything we've said, every time we've had too much to drink and said too much and had to apologize the next day and say we didn't know what we were saying. Inhibitions are there for a reason. An inhibited person is believable. You may feel the need to brace yourself with a snort, but you will have no credibility if you propose with a buzz on.

You'll want to make sure she knows it's her you're talking about too. There's the story of the couple who've known each other for years, sitting on the porch swing on a warm summer night, watching the moths beat against the screen. After a while, he takes a deep breath, lets it out, turns to her, and says, "You know, I think we should get married." She replies, "I think so too, but let's face it— who's gonna marry us?"

It was easy to deal with all the doubts about proposing again, thinking, "I'm older this time. Smarter. I know what I'm doing. Right?" Well, okay, maybe not, but once I paid the jeweler for the ring, it was past the time for screwing around. It winked at me from its little gray felt box, I tucked it into my sport jacket pocket, and the three of us—Debi, me, and the ring, which somehow seemed to weigh 10 pounds—drove to a restaurant Debi had chosen. By the shore, one of those restaurants where the walls are hung with copper stuff and all the woodwork is polished oak. I slipped the maître d' a five and whispered that I needed a booth. We ordered something vinaigrette, and since Debi almost never drinks, she was surprised when I ordered chardonnay. We sipped. We chatted. I said it was good that we'd lived together for so many months and things were working out, and she agreed. So I said I thought we'd try this for a while longer, and she agreed. So I withdrew the weight from my pocket and said, "Well, then, you ought to wear this." She cried a little, but of course, that was why I'd wanted a booth, and I'll be damned but the thing fit when I slipped it on her finger. Debi actually drank a glass of wine, and it occurred to me I hadn't actually asked her anything at all. What if she said no? All my confidence disappeared. I leaned across the table, careful to keep my cuffs out of the salad dressing, took her hand in mine, and as formally as I could, asked, "Will you marry me? I love you." She said, "Yes." Those seemed like the right words. Things were looking up, but I asked her if she was sure. She said she was. I felt very, very fine.

—Perry

NONVERBAL WAYS TO PROPOSE

An aboriginal tribesman in Australia would inform the woman he wanted to marry by poking her in the breasts with a sharp stick while she slept. She liked being poked by a sharp stick about as much as we would, but her suitor would keep it up, poking her with the stick and depriving her of sleep for months, until she finally gave in to him.

In other cases, it's the bride who wields the stick. Among the Mbuti people, a pygmy group of central Africa, young girls reaching puberty are educated in the ways of marriage in a special class that meets for several months. The older girls and women of the tribe impart knowledge of all things, including sexual practices, after which the girls venture out from the hut and put their learning to use. A girl who finds a boy she likes tells him so by beating the crap out of him with a tree branch. Then she takes him into the hut and beats the crap out of him again, after which, if he still can, they make love. If they like each other, he seeks to pay a return visit, but first the mothers of the tribe get a chance to pelt him with rocks and stones.

One tribal people in the Neilgherry region of India developed a kind of Eastern version of drawing straws, in which maidens hoping to marry enclosed themselves behind an opaque brush fence. Prospective grooms would thrust sticks through the fence, and the maidens would each grab onto a stick, marrying whoever was on the other end.

By the time we decided to get married, we'd been together for three years, and had lived together for half that time. It was clearly a relationship that had all the qualities needed for the long haul. Don't get me wrong— I think an element of anticlimax is good in a marriage. Better a sense of happy inevitability about a lifelong commitment than an aura of suspense. But it became obvious to both of us—in the way that things become simultaneously obvious to two people who have come to understand each other's habits of mind, that I was going to pop the question on her upcoming birthday. A surprise was out of the question. Instead, I just tried to make the context as memorable as possible. We went out to dinner, the fanciest place I could think of. Over coffee, following a great meal, I simply took the diamond engagement ring out of my pocket and put it on her finger without a word. It would have felt dumb and artificial to have done it any other way. Why say anything when there was nothing words could have added?

—*Bill*

POETRY

You can say it in writing. Everybody alive has written at least one poem. Some people keep their poems hidden in a box in the closet, whereas others publish theirs. You know where yours are. If you don't have any yet, now might be the time. In ancient Japanese society, a suitor was expected to announce his intention to the woman of his choice by writing her a *tanka*, a thirty-one-syllable poem. She'd write him a *tanka* back, and if he liked it, he'd sneak into her bedroom in the middle of the night, where it would be slam-bam-*tanka*-ma'am until dawn. Then they would both write morning-after poems, expressing the evanescent and transitory nature of love. One might write:

Kimi ya koshi	*My mind is dazzled.*
Ware ya yukiken	*Did you come to visit me?*
Omoezu	*Did I go to you?*
Yume ka utsutsu ka	*Was our night a dream? Reality?*
Nete ka samete ka	*Was I sleeping? Or was I awake?*

The reply might come:

Kakikurasu	*Through the blackest shade*
Kokoro no yami ni	*Of the darkest heart I wander*
Madoiniki	*In bewilderment—*
Yume utsutsu to wa	*You who know the world of love decide:*
Yohito sadameyo	*Is my love reality or dream?*

Apparently, if things didn't work out, both parties could claim to have dreamed the whole thing. At any rate, Japanese society still places a great stress on education and literacy, two areas in which American society, some say, lags behind. If you want to use the ancient Japanese approach, here are two thirty-one-syllable poems you can use:

> *Roses are red*
> *Violets are blue*
> *Life is too short*
> *To waste time counting the syllables it takes*
> *To say I want to marry you*

or in limerick form:

> *There was a young man, namely me,*
> *Who is not good at poetry.*
> *I feel like a jerk,*
> *I can't make it work,*
> *But tell me, will you mar*

If you don't want to write a poem, you could write a letter. This would carry with it a certain amount of weight and formality, and give you a chance to say exactly what you want without worrying about fumbling for words. It might also seem cowardly to say in writing what you can't say face-to-face. If you and your girlfriend have a long-distance relationship, however, a letter might be more romantic than a phone call. She's bound to telephone you, after all, once she gets your letter, and that way, she'll have to pay for the call. Unless she proposes to you in a letter first.

> *She had a good job at a department store. I was doing*
> *bank examining for the state of Iowa. That week in*
> *April 1934, I was "doing" the bank in Keosauqua and*
> *staying at the famous Manning House, a luxurious hotel*

with beds right in the rooms. I came down for breakfast one morning and found a letter from Jean saying, "When you get back to Des Moines this weekend, I think we should go out to Adel and have Judge Dingwell marry us. It's time—I'm not preggers or anything; I just think we know each other well enough to get married and ruin our lives." Since there was a competitor in the offing, and since we had been in love off and on since the seventh grade, I accepted. I wore a Donegal tweed suit and was literally supported by Judge E. W. Dingwell, the father of my best college friend. "Marry in the church," he said. "When you want a divorce, then come to me." We were married in the Methodist church, by a parson whose name I have forgotten. We had dinner at Grace Ransom's Tea Room, went to a movie—I have no idea what movie—and started a marriage which lasted another forty-three years, until death did us part in 1978. Some of it stormy, not a moment of it regretted. Judge Dingwell, I remember, shed a respectful tear, but we never did go back to him for a divorce. Kept putting it off.

—Norman

SURPRISE PROPOSALS AND OTHER ALTERNATIVES

If your proposal is to be a surprise, then you'll have to decide when and where. If you take your girlfriend somewhere extremely expensive for dinner, she may think something's up. If you take her to the International House of Pancakes for breakfast and ask her there, she probably won't be expecting it. It was, in fact, at an IHOP that Harry and Leona Helmsley hooked up. Going someplace you've always gone, the diner you hit for burgers whenever you can't think of where else to eat, will have the advantage of allowing you to begin by saying, "Think of all the changes in our lives that we've talked through, sitting in this very booth." There would be something romantic in the familiarity of the place, but then again, although it's special, it's not unique.

It might be hard to think of a way to propose that hasn't been done before. You may want to rent a billboard to write "Sarah, will you marry me? Bill." Where I live it costs $400 a month, one month minimum, for a 6' X 12' poster on a medium-trafficked road, or as much as $5,000 for a full-size billboard off the interstate, with a four-month minimum. Then again, you might not be the only Sarah and Bill in town, and you could be getting somebody else named Bill in big trouble. A banner towed behind an airplane costs between $150 and $175. More visible still would be to hire a skywriter, who will spell your proposal at 10,000 feet, legible for 15 miles in any direction, for about $650. You'll have to make sure that your girlfriend is around to see your message. There is a computer-generated form of aerial advertising involving five jet planes flying in formation called skytyping, in which the entire message appears in as little as 20 seconds, but at a cost of around $5,000. At that price, you might want to just take your girlfriend on a picnic, lie on your blanket, point to the sky, and say, "Don't you think that cloud looks like a wedding chapel?"

I didn't propose to my wife, my wife proposed to me. Teri and I were sitting on the sofa in her parents' living room. This was my first visit to her relatives. Christmastime. We'd known each other since early November. Already we'd discussed the possibilities of moving in together. Teri's parents were out for the evening, we were necking, but Teri seemed reluctant for the proceedings to migrate from the living room to the bedroom, as they would've any other time, any other place. Freud. Oedipus. Pope John Paul II (her hometown is 90 percent Catholic). Teri in her white communion dress, age six. I think you could say they were all present, inhibiting her, but also nudging her in an altogether different—and not necessarily opposed—direction. That's when she asked me to marry her—partly, I suppose, so she wouldn't have to go to bed with me under her father's roof. I think I said yes. We passed out drinks to the visitors. Drank a toast. They've been frequent guests of ours since.

—Chuck

Most planned proposals take place in fancy restaurants. Expense shouldn't matter. If she says no, you're going to be annoyed at spending all that money to get rejected, but then again, you're not trying to bribe her. It's going to be a place where you'll eat on your anniversaries, so if you're really cheap and don't want to spend all that money every year, you might want to pick someplace trendy and likely to be out of business in a few years.

WHAT TO SAY

You're reasonably certain you won't be rejected, and you don't care what you spend, because this is your big night. You get dressed up, get to the restaurant, have a predinner cocktail at the bar, eat your salad and your main course, and are now nibbling at your dessert while the waiter pours the decaf. The moment has arrived.

For economy of line, directness, and clarity, nothing beats "Will you marry me?" It's easy to understand, quick to say, a yes-or-no question. "Will you marry me?" She can't say, "Who, you?" She can't say, "Who, me?" She can't say, "Will I what?" In high school, after staring at the phone for an hour, you finally realized all you really had to say is, "Will you go out with me Saturday night?" The same policy holds true. Don't be fancy, don't be cute—just say what you mean and wait for an answer. You can get in trouble, trying to be creative. Suppose you say, "I'd like to marry you." She could reply, "Oh, you would, would you? And what makes you think I'd like to marry you?" She may well want to, but you've given her a chance to make you squirm a little first. "I'm going to marry you," will certainly make you sound self-confident, but even if she's for it, you've ignored her feelings on the matter. "Would you like to marry me?" asks the question but fails to demand a simple answer—she could knock the ball back in your court and say, "I don't know—would *you* like to marry *me*?" "Can we get married?" might bring the reply, "Well, of course we *can*, but the proper way to phrase that is *may* we get married?" "Marry me and I'll give you five bucks," makes you sound cheap. Offer at least a hundred. "Please don't marry anybody but me" puts the question in the negative. "Please don't not marry me" is a double negative. "Let's get hitched" makes you sound like Jethro Clampett. "Let's get married" is okay, but it's still not as good as, "Will you marry me?" which carries with it the weight of tradition, a measure of dignity, which, when you're trying to be serious, can't be beat.

FALSE STEPS AND SECOND GUESSES

I said the wrong thing myself.

At the start, we weren't supposed to get serious. She told me the day we met that she was moving to Australia and was only waiting for a work visa. Thanks to the America's Cup and Paul Hogan (or was it Hulk Hogan?) Australia suddenly became a popular place to go, and visas became scarce. Joking about marriage, once Diane realized she wasn't going abroad, became the way in which we kept our distance while continuing to see each other. "Will you marry me?" I'd say. "What? Marry you," she'd say, "you pencil-necked geek?" "Will you marry me?" she'd say. "Not if I was starving and the only food to eat was a wedding cake," I'd reply.

Then we started to realize we were a lot more compatible than we'd thought, beginning with a 10,000-mile road trip across Canada and back, 600 straight hours together. We'd made all kinds of preparations in case we got on each other's nerves. If worse came to worse, we'd flip a coin, the loser would get on a bus, and we'd rendezvous a few days down the road. Our precautions were entirely unnecessary. Six hundred hours without a hitch, laughing all the way. It only became strange once we tried to get used to being apart again. We were better together than apart. Gradually, we realized we weren't making jokes about marriage anymore.

If men have biological clocks, then a medical emergency is the alarm going off. Mine was a false alarm which, nevertheless, scared the shit out of me. The specifics of my medical nonemergency is of a delicate and somewhat embarrassing nature. Let's just say that I had something in common with George Brett and Portnoy's father, an ailment that can afflict men in their early thirties, causing them, when walking in public, to duck into doorways and scratch themselves where they are the least tan. If the ailment goes untreated long enough, those afflicted will eventually see blood in pretty much the last place you want to see blood, and immediately assume the worst.

In some cases a relative or friend dies suddenly and mortality approaches indirectly. In other cases, mortality makes house calls, a lump under your arm, an odd blotch on your skin, a thundering in your chest, or blood in a small clean room. It happens to everyone sooner or later, but it's still a terrible shock. Cancer, I thought. A tumor. Something is really wrong.

I found Diane at the shop where she works and tried to be calm, but when I told her what I feared, my voice broke. We went back to my place. She called the health clinic for me, described my symptoms to the triage nurse, who made a simple diagnosis. I felt overcome with relief, but beyond that, gratitude. I told Diane I never wanted to go through anything like that alone again. She swore to me I'd never have to. I held her in my arms. I'd already known she was the one for me, but I wasn't sure if I was ready for marriage. Now I was ready. She could be the judge whether or not I was the one for her.

"Would you marry me?" I said.

"Of course I'll marry you," she said. "I'm already married to you."

A week later, once the scare had passed, I tried to weasel out of it, make a joke about it, put a little distance between what I'd said and the enormity of commitment it signified. I didn't want to take back my words, just loosen the hold they had on me, so I could breathe. I was not entirely certain what we'd done. Had I really proposed? It was almost like in the Japanese poems, a confusion of dream and reality. I asked Diane what it was we'd done, one night when we were sitting on the couch, watching television.

"Are we engaged? We are, aren't we?" I said. "I don't remember."

She said she remembered.

"You haven't told anyone, have you?"

"What are you trying to say?" she said.

"I just mean, you know, I said, '*Would* you marry me.' Not '*Will* you.' I was saying *would* you, *if I were* to ask you."

She slugged me and called me a worm. I eventually proved I meant what I said, but I never should have said "Would you" in the first place. I should have said "Will you?" No ambiguity, hidden or double meanings. Direct and to the point.

We'd met at a New Year's Eve party, so I thought it would be romantic to propose on New Year's Eve. My plan was a Broadway show, then dinner, and then Times Square to watch the ball drop. I was going to propose at midnight.

Dinner went fine. We finished around seven, and

I started trying to get a cab. I tried for an hour. I stood there with a twenty-dollar bill in my hand. It was bitter cold. I saw a police car, and tried to explain to the cop that I was going to propose, had to get to the show. I was sure my wife was thinking, "This guy can't do anything right." Finally, I saw a big stretch limousine across the street, waiting at the curb. I explained the situation to him, and he said he was free until midnight and would be glad to give us a ride. I was so flustered I got in the front seat while Cindy got in the back. By the time we got to the theater, the show had started, and they weren't letting anybody in, but they made an exception for us, assuming we were somebody important, since we'd arrived in a stretch limo.

The show was They're Playing Our Song. *Afterward we went to Sardi's for drinks. When midnight approached, we made our way to Times Square. We were back from the crowd, standing by the statue of George M. Cohan. I pulled out the box from the jewelers. There wasn't a ring in it—you don't want to flash a ring in Times Square on New Year's Eve—but there was a folded-up piece of paper with a poem on it, asking Cindy to marry me. Suddenly, we found two champagne glasses thrust toward us. A British couple had been standing nearby, watching us. They'd gotten engaged on the same spot, five years earlier, and were there drinking champagne to celebrate their anniversary. We drank a toast.*

—Jay

Many proposals are not planned for but stumbled across. The words come out unexpectedly, because the time and the place feel right, a method preferred by men who know how well-laid plans can go astray. You might set yourself a deadline to propose by, or say you'll propose the next time you see two convertibles in a row, and let the laws of random chance determine when and where you propose. Flip coins. Throw the I Ching. Deal seven hands of poker for each day of the week and propose on the winning day.

• •

TEN THINGS TO SAY IF YOU POP OPEN THE BOX AND SHE LAUGHS AT YOU

Look what I found yesterday when I was jogging.

Look what they're putting in Cracker Jack boxes these days.

Aw nuts—the squirter didn't work. Goddamn cheap novelty stores.

Like it? My dad asked me to pick it up for my mom—they're going to renew their vows.

Great—I just wanted to see your reaction. It's for a play I'm writing.

Not bad, eh? Tenth prize in the Publisher's Clearinghouse Sweepstakes. Wonder where I can hock it.

I was thinking of opening a jewelry store—what do you think I could get for this? I made it in the garage.

Will you hold this for a few days, just until the heat is off?

My mother died this morning—I forgot to tell you. Anyway, she wanted you to have this.

It's a collar. My uncle raises show mice.

• •

NEXT STEPS

Okay—you've plithed troths. You are to be congratulated, because you've taken a bold first step, but you're not out of the woods yet. You're not even *into* the woods yet. The woods begin at the point of no return, which is the moment you pick up the phone and tell somebody *else* you're engaged. Some couples prefer to wait before making any public announcements, to get used to the idea, the way art galleries will let you take a painting home and live with it for a while before purchasing. Other couples find their joy uncontainable, and immediately tell everyone they see, bag boys at the supermarket, telephone operators, bartenders, highway tollbooth cashiers, and automatic teller machines.

According to etiquette, you're supposed to call your parents first. If you feel that's too big a step to take right away, you can practice by calling friends long distance, friends who live too far away to spread the word, don't know your parents, and aren't likely to talk to anybody who does. You don't want your parents hearing of your engagement from somebody else. Still, you might need time, because you have to say words like *engaged* or *fiancée* twenty or thirty times before they sound natural, and you don't feel like you're ordering off a menu in a language you don't speak. Sooner or later though, you have to call your folks.

ASKING HER FATHER FIRST

Some men still feel that as a courtesy, the groom should call the bride's father and explain his intentions. It's not required, but it might not hurt. If you know him to be a particularly formal person, or if you're afraid he'll object or have questions, or if you simply get along well and can chat easily with him, there's nothing wrong with calling him before you propose, unless, of course, you think your bride might object. Calling the father of the bride first harkens back to the days when brides were commodities young men acquired from old men, a conceit that might not sit well with a modern bride, who could see that more as an insult to her than as a sign of respect to her father. If he's the type who would somehow expect you to inform him of your intentions, and be angry with you if you don't, but your fiancée would be angry with you if you do, you'll have to decide who you want angry with you. (*Hint:* You're going to be living with one of them.)

Once you decide to make the call, your fiancée's parents are customarily the first to be told, which may also be seen as part of the patrilinear tradition, in which case you can always flip a coin.

HOW TO CALL

The proper way to call is to dial the first six numbers and then put down the phone. What are you going to say? You can call simply to announce you're getting married, or you can call with more information than that. The call you make is the first determinant of the kind of wedding you're going to have. It sets the tone.

There are only two kinds of weddings to choose from, the kind that gets out of control, and the kind that gets *completely* out of control—that is to say, out of *your* control. A wedding that simply gets out of control is the one you plan yourself. A wedding that gets *completely* out of control is the one where your families, usually your mothers, do all the planning and you just show up. It can be a relief, and save you time and trouble, to let your folks shape your destiny, but it can also make you do things you said you'd never do, beginning with being fitted for a turquoise tuxedo and ending with dancing a Strauss waltz played on the accordion at a reception in the Regatta Room of a 100-year-old hotel where the halls smell like urine.

WHAT YOU HAVE TO KNOW BEFORE YOU CALL

The more information you supply in the initial phone call, the more in control you will be. The first thing you and your betrothed have to talk about, then, is how much time you can devote to planning the wedding, and how much money you can afford to spend. There are four ways to divide up the labor and the costs: (1) you can do all the work and foot all the bills yourself; (2) you can let the costs be allotted traditionally, where the bride's parents bear the brunt of the financial and organizational burden, again, going back to the days before women had earning power, when a girl's parents figured they owed it to the groom, since he'd be supporting her for the rest of his life; (3) you can split the cost and the work evenly three ways—between you, your parents, and her parents; or (4) you can split the cost and the work unevenly three ways.

Second, you have to have plans to announce. You have to decide *when* you're going to be married. An engagement should, according to custom, last three to six months. A shorter engagement, and you may appear impetuous. It also won't give the people you want to invite enough time to make travel arrangements, especially those who live far away, or who will be required to take time off from work to attend the festivities. It may not give you time to prepare properly. Then again, it's a little like having a tooth pulled—the sooner it's over with, the better. A longer engagement might disperse the pressure and pain of doing all the work and making all the arrangements, or it might just prolong it. The Wedding Mafia, hoping to lengthen the amount of time they can milk you for cash, is advising that the engagement period last a year or more. Much depends on what month you get engaged, because most people want to have their weddings when the weather's good. If you get engaged in Duluth in October, you may want to wait for the spring thaw, sometime around July, unless you prefer getting married indoors, at a hockey rink or in an ice-fishing house. If you get engaged in April and want to marry in June (the most popular month for weddings), you may not have much luck reserving the chapels and reception rooms you want on such short notice. You'll want to avoid marrying on holidays, when the people you want to attend might have other plans, although it would help you remember your anniversary. Other people's birthdays or anniversaries might not be a good idea unless you want to share the day with them for the rest of your life. You can consult the long-term weather forecast, or even see what *The Farmer's Almanac* has to say. If you want to marry during the baseball season, you could see when the home team is going to be around in case any out-of-towners want to take in a ball game. You don't have to pin down the day exactly, before you call your parents, but a rough estimate will help them start making plans, scheduling vacations, or reserving hotel rooms.

Third, once you have an idea when, you'll want to tell them *where*. You might avail yourself of this opportunity to have your first premarital fight. The convention holds that a wedding marks the passage of a woman from the home and caretaking of her father to the home and caretaking of her husband, in which case the act of leaving, the ceremony, takes place on her turf, at the church or temple she attended as a child, or even in her parents' home. If her father foots the bill, he can be reasonably expected to assume that if he's paying for it, then he can call the shots. If you and your bride decide to have your wedding someplace other than her home turf, do it your way, you should be prepared to shoulder the expenses yourself. Having the wedding on your turf might give your parents cause to consider themselves guests and not hosts. They can and probably will want to contribute to the celebration, financially and otherwise, but they don't have to. If you live close to your parents but far from your fiancée's parents, you might argue about how fair it is for

who to make whose relatives drive farther. Other problems
can arise. You agree to marry on her turf, but her father
lives in Cleveland and her mother lives in Cincinnati, and
she doesn't want to favor either of them. Or she despises her
stepfather, but he owns a country club and would throw the
reception for free. Or she has her heart set on getting married
in Keokuk, but you have $300 in unpaid parking tickets in
Keokuk. Or her folks live in Toledo, but so does your father's
other wife. If you don't live in the same town as either of
your parents, and if you've been living independent of them
for some time, and want to marry on your own turf, then
the town where you live should be an adequate compromise.
If not, you should try to find some sort of neutral territory—
an inn halfway from everyone concerned, a state park, someplace both you and your bride find meaningful. Again, for
the purposes of the initial phone call, you needn't know
exactly where you'll marry, a rough idea will do.

WHAT YOUR PARENTS WILL SAY

Once you've determined when and where, you can pick up
the phone and finish dialing. You might even consider a
conference call. Some people invite their parents over to dinner, but that's not always practical. As the phone rings, even
if you know her parents fairly well, you'll still have reason
to be nervous. It can happen that her parents won't approve
of you, or of the idea that she get married just yet. Some
parents have unshakable convictions as to what they feel will
be best for their daughter, from the school she attends to
what she does for a living, and especially as to who she
marries. Doctors and lawyers are often high on the list of
preferred spouses, because it's common knowledge that the
more money you have, the more caring and compassionate
it makes you. You may find yourself suddenly being grilled
as to your financial situation, what your religious beliefs are,

how many children you want to have, if you are now or ever were a member of the Communist party.

There's nothing new about this. Prospective grooms have always been put to such tests, required to complete tasks, bring back big deer, scar themselves with knives, or watch whole episodes of "thirtysomething" without vomiting. While you're being interrogated or tested, it begins to dawn on you that you are asking permission to enter someone else's family, for which there may not be free admission. If the worst happens, and her parents decide they can't support your marriage, you can say, "We're sorry you feel that way, we think your feelings will change with time, we hope you can respect our decision even if it's not one you'd make yourself, and we'd like your blessing." Or you can say, "Well, in that case, you can both bite a big one." You shouldn't though. This call sets a precedent for future relations, assuming you intend to defy her parents' wishes and marry anyway, and you don't want to damage chances for reconciliation.

Not to overemphasize worst-case scenarios. The call should be and almost always is a joyous occasion, full of laughter, blessings, and good wishes. You can still be a little nervous, because any dad who's a wise guy, hers or yours, is going to know he has you over a barrel and use the advantage to make jokes like, "Well . . . I don't know, sweetheart, I mean, the guy hardly has a job . . ." or, "Gee, son, you're thirty-six years old—do you think you're ready?" They will have fun with you because they can, and because it's one of the moments in life a parent looks forward to. They can hear how uncertain and excited you are, and remember how uncertain and excited they were, and know the pleasure of watching history come full circle. Their parents put them on the spot, so now it's their turn. They will have fun with you because out of nowhere they will suddenly find themselves saddled with a large, unexpected debt in the very near future, about which there's nothing they can do but laugh.

They will have fun because they will be feeling that their babies finally made it. You will have fun because it's ineffably gratifying to hear your parents tell you you finally made it.

AWKWARD SITUATIONS

There are rules of etiquette to follow if either parents are divorced. It's mostly common sense. If she was living with one of her parents and not the other before leaving home, you generally call that parent first. The same holds true if your parents are divorced. After you've spoken to all parents involved, the groom's parents are supposed to call the bride's parents and arrange for everyone to meet, whenever possible, so you will need to give your parents her parents' names and phone numbers, the divorced parent you or your fiancée lived with making or receiving the first call. Somewhere in here, it may begin to occur to you that not only are you merging your life with someone else's, joining another family, but your families are intersecting too. It is as much a merging of clans as anything that ever happened in the Scottish Highlands. Your families are different from each other. What if your mom makes risqué jokes and her mom's a prude? What if her dad hates George Steinbrenner, and your dad *is* George Steinbrenner? If your parents haven't met yet, you might want to offer a brief description of their opposites before you put them in touch with each other.

After that you should call your grandparents, then your siblings, and then your close friends. Everyone you tell is going to tell everyone they know, usually sounding surprised, saying, "You'll never guess who's getting married," since nobody ever believes anybody is going to get married until they do. Your nuptials will become a hot gossip item. Given that, you should try to call whoever you think is going to be upset if they hear it from someone else and not from you. This can include an ex-girlfriend you're still friends with who may have reason to fleetingly (or relievedly) think it could have been her, or feel put off, wondering why you're ready for marriage now when you weren't before. Without owing her an explanation, if you think she'd rather not be the last to know, a call or a card might be considered courteous. On the other hand, if she dumped you like a sack of garbage and left you on the curb for the dogs to rip apart, you don't have to call. Word will reach her eventually. Living well is still the best revenge.

ENGAGEMENT ANNOUNCEMENTS

When all the calls have been made, you need to have one last fight over whether or not you want to place an engagement announcement in the newspaper. The practice of publicly announcing an engagement goes back to the custom of proclaiming or publishing banns, from the Anglo-Saxon word *bannan*, which means "to summon." The banns were either spoken aloud on three consecutive Sundays in church by the minister or priest, or posted in written form on the church bulletin board or in the town square, notices apprising the community of the intended wedding and summoning forth anybody to speak who might show cause why the wedding should not take place. What constituted showing cause varied from place to place. "She's passive aggressive and he's inattentive" probably wasn't enough. Previous wives, husbands, or arrest warrants outstanding were taken more seriously.

The purpose of public announcements today is to inform total strangers who couldn't care less of your plans. Some people who you know won't learn of your wedding plans via word of mouth—distant acquaintances, your old third-grade teacher, your pediatrician's assistant—will benefit from a public announcement. Even without one, people you've never met before will come up to you and say, "So, I hear you're getting married." For the most part, public announcements serve mainly to allow your parents to brag about you, or rather, her parents to brag about you both, because it's customarily the bride's parents who place and pay for the announcement. Many newspapers have forms for applicants to fill out with the useful information, and then the newspaper's society editor determines which ones to publish, often according to the status and social prominence of the families involved, at least in competitive places like the *New York Times* or the *Washington Post*. You never see:

> *Harriet Henderson, beautician, daughter of Mr. and Mrs. Jack Henderson, unemployed, of Teaneck, to marry Jon Carpenter, unemployed, address not given, son of Marianne Carpenter and some guy she met during the war . . .*

You see pedigrees, parents' occupations, what prep schools the groom attended or in some cases even graduated from, what Seven Sisters college the bride got her equestrian degree in, before becoming a vice president in her father's brokerage. Some announcements list what the bride will wear, who her attendants will be, who the officiants will be, or even that the ring bearer will be a child from a previous marriage. If you and your bride wish to have your engagement publicized, you'll have to decide how much you want the world to know. If you do want to put an announcement in the paper, it's now quite common for both the bride and the groom to appear in the photograph. You'll probably want to put on a shirt and tie and play it fairly straight for this photograph, though anybody who reads the society page would agree it would be pretty funny if both the bride and the groom were wearing pearls.

4

DISTANT PREPARATIONS

I f you want to get along, go along.
—SAM RAYBURN

There was a section on your kindergarten report card where your teacher graded you on how well you got along with others. Did you share your toys, or did you punch your classmates and take their toys from them? Did you try to boss them around? Did you sulk all alone in the corner and refuse to cooperate or join in? Hog the crayons? Hold the door for the other kids at recess? Look around you to see who wasn't being included, or choose only your friends when picking sides for team sports?

You didn't think the play skills you learned in kindergarten were going to matter in your adult life, but you were wrong. It's essential to organizing and planning a wedding that you get along well with others. Even if the wedding is completely out of your hands, agenda dictated by your mother-in-law, you will still be required to act gentlemanly in a variety of situations where you don't want to. If you are a perfect Zen master, able to sit in serene contemplation while events whirl around you, you will still be surrounded by people who aren't Zen masters, who are in fact half-crazed with frenzied planning and need your input. You cannot remain aloof. You will have to get involved, and when you do, you will have to get along well with others.

SKILLS YOU WILL NEED

Beyond cooperation, you will need *linear reasoning skills*, the ability to grasp complex mathematical structures without losing sight of the small details, because planning a wedding is an enterprise in which you need to know everything first before you can know anything next. You can't call the caterer before you know the guest list, but you can't know the guest list before you know the room, and you can't know the room until you know what's available and whether or not you'll have to rent chairs and tables, which you can't know until you know the caterer, who can't tell you until she knows how many guests there will be, which you won't know until you set the date and send out the invitations and get your responses back, which you won't get until you have them printed, which you can't do until you know how many and what they'll say, which you can't decide until you know where and when the wedding is, which depends on whether or not the band you want is available, who won't know until they talk to their booking agent, who's getting married himself and can't say when he'll know anything at all. The pieces of the puzzle start to fall into place one by one, eventually, but unless you stay on top of them, you can tell two different people two different things, give the florist the wrong address, forget to call the minister back, and find your flowers delivered to the minister's house while he's in Hawaii for two weeks.

You need *communication skills.* You have to speak extra carefully and be excruciatingly clear and concise to everyone you deal with, or someone will misunderstand you. You have to say everything at least twice, and ideally, in writing, and make everyone who says anything to you repeat themselves and/or put it in writing. All the same, you will tell the photographer, "I loathe wedding videos, do you hear me— I *loathe* them," and he'll show up with a video camera anyway, saying, "I thought you said you *loved* them?"

You need *managerial skills*, and must know how to delegate responsibilities as well as have responsibilities delegated to you. You have to know how to say no. How to say yes. You have to know how to say both yes and no at the same time, and how to simultaneously convey the idea that something both matters to you a great deal, and that you really couldn't care less. For instance, suppose your bride wants to know whether or not you'd like her to wear a veil. "I don't care," you say. She says, "You mean it doesn't matter to you?" You say, "Of course it matters to me—it's very important to me. I just don't care. I mean, I want whatever you want." "Oh sure," she'll say, "just wash your hands of it."

Finally you have to learn to *accept and welcome failure*, and give up on the idea of having a perfect wedding, or learn to redefine perfect. Like a raiku pot, admired for its imperfections, a wedding is only perfect if it has five or six major screwups for you to laugh about later. If you don't fight tooth and nail with your bride two or three times, something is wrong. If you don't shed at least a quart of tears between the two of you, somebody is sandbagging. If you don't come close to calling the whole thing off, it won't be a whole thing—it will be incomplete. A wedding should be a trial, with everything at stake and peril on every side. Like Ulysses returning home, there have to be delays, catastrophes and recoveries, obstacles to overcome, near-death experiences. It's a test of your relationship, the first big one, and the harsher it is, the more strongly you'll be bonded once it's over. Like war buddies.

GREAT EXPECTATIONS—HERS AND YOURS

The first person you have to get along with is your bride. You may have an idea what you're like together under stress, but the stress of planning a wedding is greater for her, because she has different expectations and associations. Men and women approach weddings differently, not the same way at all.

That's because the odds are, your bride has been brought up to believe her wedding day will be the most exciting day of her life. Her mother told her it would be, because *her* mother told her it would be, because *her* mother told her it would be, back to the days when it really was the day a girl became a woman, left home, and started having sex and preparing for motherhood, her other reason to exist, in addition to being a wife/housekeeper. Today only 36 percent of all brides (according to *Bride's Magazine*) are virgins or have had sex with one partner. Women are not limited to maternity or housewifery as reasons to exist. Even so, your bride will find it difficult to shake the notion that her wedding day is supposed to be the most exciting day of her life, her coronation, the day she gets to wear the same size dress queens wear, and a crown of flowers on her head, and be the center of attention, something she's had images of since she was a little girl. Maybe she and her friends staged mock weddings after school, if not among themselves, then with their Barbie and Ken dolls, carrying things all the way through to the honeymoon, taking Barbie's and Ken's clothes off and letting them enjoy the pleasures of the plastic. All girls did this. An anatomically correct Barbie and a transformer Ken might even have had children.

Fathers don't tell sons their wedding day will be the most exciting day in their lives, because *their* fathers didn't, because *their* fathers didn't. Little boys don't play wedding, unless the game is called something like, "The-Wedding-Party-Versus-the-Killer-Mutant-Invaders-from-Space" ("THEY'RE STEALING THE WEDDING PRESENTS! PUT DOWN THAT FONDUE POT, YOU DIRTY ROTTEN MUTANT! TAKE THAT—RAT-A-TAT-A-TAT! LOOK OUT! THERE'S A BOMB IN THE CAKE! KERPLOOOOEEEEEY!! RUN EVERYBODY, RUN! AIIYYEEEEE!!!"). Adolescent boys think their wedding day will be no more than a highlight, like winning the high-school football championship or being elected class president. In the end, it's an event with primarily emotional content, and since we don't like to talk about emotions, we play it down.

PROBLEM SOLVING

Men and women don't approach basic problem solving in the same way either, and wedding planning is nothing if not cooperative problem solving. If you have eight tasks that need completing and give them to two men, they are likely to each take on four tasks. Give the same eight tasks to two women and they will each do half of each task. Men don't want anybody criticizing us for the way we're completing the task, or correcting us, when doing it wrong will get the job done anyway, if less efficiently. Even if we're doing it entirely wrong, we want to find out on our own, so we'll learn, and so we won't be embarrassed. Women *like* cooperating, learning from each other, talking things through, getting other opinions, and aren't embarrassed when they don't know something.

Either two men or two women can finish the eight tasks assigned them adequately and in roughly the same amount of time. But, try to give the same eight tasks to a man and a woman. He'll tell her what to do, she won't like the way he says it, he'll get mad and do something by himself, and do it wrong because he's mad, while she stews because he's left her alone when she wanted to have fun doing things together, so she'll do something alone just to show him she can, and he'll change the way she did it even though she did it right, and he'll know she knows there's no difference between the way she did it and the way he did it, so to save face he'll say he wants it one way and not the other because that's how his ex-girlfriend did it, until the woman has no choice but to come after him with a hatchet.

MEET ED AND GAIL

Imagine what might be a typical night in the planning of a typical wedding of a typical couple, Ed and Gail. They're trying to get their invitation mailings together. Included in the mailing will be an invitation, a reply card, a map, and a list of nearby hotel accommodations for out-of-town guests. It should be simple enough to organize. Ed and Gail argue for only ten or twenty minutes over which way to phrase the invitation itself, hashing out a compromise by choosing a standard form given them by the stationery engraver:

Mr. and Mrs. Norton Whetherhill
request the honour of your presence
at the marriage of their daughter
Gail Elizabeth
to
Mr. Edward Fournier
Saturday, the 10th of June
at five-thirty o'clock
Saint Paul's Church
Macaroni, New Jersey

Ed has a little trouble with "five-thirty o'clock," but he lets it go, and considers himself noble for doing so. Gail owes him one. He suggests a simple postcard would suffice for a reply card, and cost less than an engraved reply card with a separate envelope. Gail agrees, though she really wanted an engraved reply card. She thinks Ed owes her one. Ed wants the postcard to read, "Yes I can come / No I cannot come," with a "yes" box and a "no" box for the guest to check, and then, "Number of persons in party." Gail says, " 'Number of persons in party' sounds like you're organizing a fishing trip," and prefers, "Number of guests." Ed says that sounds like they're asking how many guests their guests will be bringing, in addition to themselves. "How many will you be?" No. "Are you bringing anybody and if so, how many?" No. "Number of people?" No good. "Number of persons in your car?" Uh-uh.

"Just tell me what you want it to say," Ed says.

"Number of persons in party," Gail says.

"Don't patronize me," Ed says. Gail stomps out of the room. It's one of those weird fights where you both end up switching sides and practically strangling somebody to convince them you agree with their original position.

While Gail calls the local hotels and motels to get prices to include for the out-of-town guests, Ed sets about drawing up the map, directions to the old New England mill where their reception will take place. An hour later, Gail comes in to apologize, but changes her mind when she sees what Ed's up to.

"What are you doing?"

"Drawing the map," Ed says. Gail stomps out again. Ed pursues, asking what he's done wrong. Gail wanted to draw the map too. She wanted to help. Ed tells her she did help—she called the hotels and motels for prices, while he drew the map. Drawing a map, Ed argues, is not a task requiring two people. Whether it required two or not, Gail says, she resents the fact that Ed did it alone. What, Ed asks, did she want to do—hold one end of the Scotch tape while he held the other? It gets ugly after that. Neither one of them really wants to fight, but neither one can drop it, though both know it's silly, because both suddenly realize they're not just talking about how an invitation should be worded or how a map should be drawn—they're talking about *the rest of their lives.* They're like two warring nations, fighting tooth and nail, down to the last twelve-year-old soldier, over the last four blades of grass in no-man's-land, because they know a cease-fire is going to be declared soon, territory divvied up and new boundaries drawn, and neither one wants to back down, give ground, establish a precedent, or look bad.

Ed apologizes, and so does Gail. Ed tries to explain.

"Maybe I just don't know how to work with people. I got bad grades in Citizenship in kindergarten. I work alone."

"There are two of us now," Gail points out.

"I'm trying to figure this out," Ed says. "I love you. I just want to be right."

"I guess you do," she says.

"For you," he hastens to add. A Freudian pause. "I just want to be right *for you.*"

"I think you had it right the first time," she says.

MOTHERS-IN-LAW

If you're not planning the wedding yourself, then the second person you'll have to learn to get along with is your mother-in-law, who, sometimes in league with your mother (sometimes not) will be doing all the work for you, whether you want it done or not. The domineering mother-in-law is a stereotype who exists in real life but not in the numbers you might assume from watching sitcoms or listening to old Shelley Berman records. Mothers-in-law just want to have fun too, don't mind the trouble, don't want to be any bother, and are glad to do it because they have the time. Usually you'll already have some kind of relationship with your mother-in-law and know what to expect, whether the tastes on the planet she's from differ significantly from the tastes on your planet. If your bride and her parents get along, and if your mother-in-law is a reasonable person, then with a small amount of guidance from you, lists of your favorite foods to give the caterers, cummerbund colors you're allergic to, putting the wedding together should be no problem. If your fiancée and her folks somehow don't get along, and have arguments you find yourself in the middle of, as a rule of thumb, you will be expected, by your wife-to-be, to take her side. You should be alert to "hey-will-you-please-help-me-out-here" looks, because it's you and her against the world, until further notice.

● ●

WEDDING RECORDS FROM THE *GUINNESS BOOK OF WORLD RECORDS*

The smallest brilliant cut diamond weighs 0.00063 of a carat, is 0.02 inches in size, and is owned by Gebroedeus van den Wouver, of Antwerp, Belgium.

The country with the lowest average age for marriage is India, with 20.0 for males and 14.5 for females. The country where people marry the latest is Ireland, where males are 26.8 years old and females 24.7.

There are 1006.7 men in the world, for every 1,000 women. In the USSR, there are 1,132 females for every 1,000 males, the country with the largest shortage of men. Pakistan is the worst place to meet women, with only 906 women for every 1,000 males.

Sheika Dena Al-Fassi sued her husband, Sheik Mohammed Al-Fassi, of the Saudi royal family, for
divorce in a Los Angeles court, and was awarded
$81 million. It is rumored that Soraya Kashoggi, wife
of arms dealer Adnan Kashoggi, divorced him for
$800 million. Mrs. Anne Bass, ex-wife of Texan Sid
Bass, rejected a settlement of $535 million as inade-
quate to supporting herself in the style to which she'd
become accustomed.

The most expensive food you could serve at a wedding reception would be Saudi Arabian truffles,
which, in a market in Riyadh in 1985, sold for $2,160
a pound. But then, a pound goes a long way.

Sir Temulji Bhicaji Nariman and his wife, Lady Nariman,
of India, were married in 1853, at the age of five, and
were married for 86 years, until Sir Temulji died. Lazarus
Rowe and Molly Webber, of Greenland, New Hamp-
shire, were both born in 1725, married at eighteen, and
died in 1829, another 86-year marriage.

Octavio Guillen and Ariana Martinez of Mexico City
were engaged for 67 years.

In the monogamous world, the record for marriages
belongs to Pak Awang, a Malaysian witch doctor,
who was married 80 times. In this country, a Mr.
Glynn de Moss Wolfe, a Baptist minister, was married 27 times, first marrying in 1927. One Giovanni
Vigliotto was arrested in Panama City in 1981 on 104
counts of bigamy between 1949 and 1981.

A wedding in Abu Dhabi, in May of 1981, between
Mohammed, son of Shaik Zayid ibn Sa'id al-Makh-
tum, to Princess Salama, cost $33 million.

The largest recorded dowry was that of Elena Patino, daughter of a Bolivian tin millionaire who bestowed $22 million on the newlyweds.

The oldest bridegroom was Harry Stevens of Caravilla, Wisconsin, who married at 103, to Thelma Lucas, a fox of only 84. The oldest bride was Winnifred Clark, who married the day before her 100th birthday to Albert Smith, 80, in Yorkshire, England.

The oldest divorcée was Ida Stern of Milwaukee, who divorced her husband Simon Stern in 1984. She was 91, and he was 97.

Jack V. and Edna Moran of Seattle have married and divorced each other 40 times.

The tallest married couple was Anna Hanen Swanm of Nova Scotia, and Martin van Buren Bates of Kentucky. She was 8 ft. 1 in. and he was 7 ft. 2½ in.

Nigel Wilks married Beverly Russell in 1984. He's 6 ft. 7 in. and she's 3 ft. 11 in.

Jon and Jeannette Minnoch married in 1978, and had two sons before he died, in 1983. His wife weighed 110 pounds and he weighed more than 1,300 pounds.

THE SECRET TO PLANNING A SUCCESSFUL WEDDING

In the end, if or when you find yourself pinned down and pressed to give your opinion on something, or find yourself butting heads with your bride, locked in an argument where you switch sides, or just confused, it would be wise to remember the single most important rule a marrying man needs to know, a skill you can work on and perfect with time, more important than any managerial or communication skills you could learn, and something you'll benefit from for the rest of your life: THE SECRET TO PLANNING A SUCCESSFUL WEDDING IS LEARNING TO ADMIT YOU'RE WRONG WHEN YOU'RE NOT.

If your mother-in-law tells you, "We hired a polka band because that's what the kids are listening to these days," all you need to do is smile and say, "Well, that's true." If your fiancée doesn't want to rent coat racks because "No one wears coats in August," agree, even though you know for a fact men who wear suits to the wedding will have suit coats they'll want to remove on a hot August day, after the ceremony is over.

Admitting you're wrong when you're not will let you glide past innumerable controversies which, when you think about it, really aren't worth arguing about, though when you're tense and stressed out, you'll feel the urge to. It will also cover you when you think you're not wrong but in fact actually *are* wrong, which will be about a third of the time. Another third of the time, you'll *both* be right, but instead of fighting to see who's more right, if you admit you're wrong first, your fiancée can say, "No, you're right," and you'll get your way without an argument. If she doesn't say you were right, it doesn't matter because she was right too. There will be times when you'll feel you have to hold your ground and not give in, insisting there be absolutely no prom balls at the reception, or fountains with little cherubs pissing in the punch—the more you admit you're wrong when you're not, the more weight it will carry when you take a stand and say you know you're right.

As soon as you get engaged, sooner if possible, you might want to practice admitting you're wrong when you're not. Practice with waitresses who tell you you didn't order a side of bacon, when you orderd a side of bacon, or with people who cut you off in traffic, until you feel comfortable with your new skill, because before you know it, your fiancée is going to say, "We need to talk about the wedding." You should be ready for her. You will hear her, or her mother, or yourself, say, "We need to talk about the wedding," about once a week—more often than that as the day approaches.

When you do start talking about the wedding, you need to begin by talking about the size, the guest list, where you're going to have the ceremony, and where you're going to have the reception.

CONTROLLING THE SIZE

The first thing you have to decide is how big a wedding you want. Traditionally, the bride wants a wedding roughly twice as big as you do, and her mother wants one twice what her daughter wants. The father of the bride wants something midway between what your fiancée wants and what his wife wants, unless he throws up his hands and says, "Go ahead, invite everybody in the world." People you're related to, who are special to you, who you don't know but like, who you don't like but know and owe somehow, and the people who you don't know, don't like, don't owe, but who somehow end up at your wedding anyway. In theory, you and your bride should act in concert and have the last say on how large a wedding you want, but in practice everybody and their dog has a story about how they wanted a small wedding but it got out of hand, how both sets of parents invited twice the number of guests they were told they could invite, how extra guests kept getting added at the last minute any- way, and then twenty people who weren't invited showed up, along with twenty more who were invited but said they couldn't make it and then changed their plans. There are a few things you can do to control the size of your wedding, but there are no guarantees.

LIMITING SPENDING

If you're running the entire show yourself, you can tell your parents you can afford about 100 people. The whole thing, you hope, will cost about "three thousand dollars." Depend- ing on how extravagant you want to be, a wedding can cost very little per person, for a potluck barbecue in someone's backyard, to $50 a head or more for a catered affair, more if you want to serve everyone a five-course sit-down dinner in a fancy restaurant with full table service and a complete bar, less if you want a simple wine-and-cheese reception in someone's home. The average total cost for a wedding, including rings, flowers, attire, trimmings, fees, and honey- moon apparel, with around 200 guests, is about $13,000 (according to *Bride's Magazine*), or what somebody earning $6.25 an hour, working a 40-hour week, makes in a year, before taxes. The reception alone costs about $4,500.

It's a lot of money.

Talking about money can be an uncomfortable experi- ence, but it's necessary. If either your fiancée's parents, or your parents, or both, say they'd like to contribute to the cost of the wedding, you can give them a rough estimate of what the total should be and tell them any help they can give would be appreciated. Nobody thinks it's rude anymore for the groom's parents to offer to help pay for the wedding, but you don't want to ask them to help, and you don't want the bride's parents to have to ask. If you suggest a three-way split, both sets of parents may wish to give more than a third. If her parents are considerably wealthier than yours, or vice versa, equal contributions would not be fair and might not be possible. Keeping the amount you want to spend low can be one way to avoid a situation where one father ends up trying to match the other father when he can't really afford it. If the fathers work it out between themselves and end up sending you more than you need, you can either increase the size of the wedding, upgrade the extravagance, or just leave the money in the bank and offer to refund it if you don't spend it all. Setting a spending cap is one way to keep the size down. If you say you can only spend $3,000, and can't possibly go a penny over, then with luck, you'll only spend about $4,000.

LIMITING THE SPACE

You can keep the size down by picking a small room, for the service, for the reception, or both. It's not uncommon to have guests who are invited to the reception but not the ceremony, so to control the crowd, a small reception room is better than a small ceremony site. A restaurant with a limited seating capacity would give you a built-in excuse. It makes for a better party to have a crowded small room than a cavern with a few people collected in one corner anyway.

CONTROLLING THE GUEST LIST

Tell each family how many people they can invite. Do so as graciously as possible and as soon as possible. If you wait three weeks after your engagement announcement to tell your mother, "We were thinking that each family can invite twenty people," she's liable to say, "Oh, dear—I already invited at least forty of our friends by word of mouth." She can't disinvite her friends, and you shouldn't put her in a position where she has to. The guest list then grows further, because if one family gets to invite forty people, the other family should have the same right. This makes eighty people, all of whom are asking their friends, people more distantly acquainted with your parents, "Are you going to the wedding?" Out of the uninvited people who get asked, "Are you going to the wedding?" half will find a way to call your folks for no particular reason and say, "So, I hear your baby is getting married." To be polite, your parents may have to invite them too. That makes 120 people, up 80 from your original limit. At $50 a head, that's already $4,000 more than you counted on spending.

One of the greatest things about a wedding is the fact that for the first time in your life, you can summon your friends from all over the country and ask them to come to a party, with reasonable expectations that many of them will show up. The only other time is your funeral. You may enjoy the wedding more. If you've lived in five or six different towns in your life, for the first and only time, you can see your entire history connect and form a circle, as your best friend from one town meets your best friend from another, or your childhood pal meets your college buddies. People you sat up with, into the wee hours of the night, sipping wine and pondering the vagaries and vicissitudes of romance, people you've talked to over the phone about love gone sour, people you've bored to death for years over beers in bars bemoaning girlfriends who dumped you—they all finally get to meet the one you've chosen to marry, and sanction your decision. You get to introduce everyone you've ever wanted to introduce to everyone you've ever wanted to introduce them to. At an ideal wedding, where money really is no object, you could invite everyone you could possibly want to see again, and have them all come spend the weekend.

Unfortunately, when money is a factor, the guest list has to be curtailed. It's a difficult task, and something you should start working on as soon as you're engaged. There are several kinds of people you'll want to consider.

PEOPLE WHO ARE RELATED TO YOU

Parents, brothers and sisters, grandparents, cousins, aunts, uncles, great-aunts, great-uncles, and anybody who ever pinched you on the cheek growing up. Weddings are, first and foremost, family affairs, a true gathering of the tribe. To be absolutely correct, you should even send invitations to fringe relatives, black sheep, outcasts and ne'er-do-wells, weirdos the rest of the family talks about, your second cousin Ferdie who collects empty soda cans, your great-aunt Frieda who's worn the same dress for the last sixteen years. If they come, they come. Hey—it's a wedding. It's supposed to be awkward. It can get awkward too when your parents are divorced and remarried, particularly if they no longer get along with one another. There are no rules to consult, when every family is different and only you know how hostile parents are going to relate to each other. You can't expect them to cheerfully leave their new husbands or wives or boyfriends or girlfriends behind (if there are any), but you can ask. Maybe they'll be jealous about who got invited first, or try to compete to give you the biggest gift. All you can do is express your feelings and hope they'll try to honor them. If you want both of them there, tell them you want them both there because you love them, and let them work out how to do it.

PEOPLE WHO ARE SPECIAL TO YOU

Your close friends, the ones you couldn't imagine not invit-ing. It's very easy to begin this list, but harder and harder to know where to stop, because by the end, you get into a gray area where you start running into . . .

PEOPLE WHO AREN'T SPECIAL ENOUGH

These are people who are in fact special to you. You like them fine and think they're swell, but not swell enough to be included, if you want a wedding for the proverbial "just a few close friends and family." You like them, but you have to draw the line somewhere, and you have a feeling they're on the other side of the line. People whose first name you've known for years, but you still don't know their last name. The guys you play softball with, or your poker buddies. Someone you shared an apartment with, years ago. Old school chums. Former colleagues.

Some arbitrary rules can be drawn up to sort out these acquaintances. You can say you'll only invite someone you've seen in the last year. You can say it has to be someone both of you know, and/or have seen in the last year. Someone you know from more than one venue, both a softball player and poker buddy, but not only a softball or poker acquaintance. Someone who's invited you over to their house. Often you'll feel obliged to invite someone to your wedding if they invited you to theirs, even if your bride doesn't know them or you haven't seen them in a year. You may also have to bend the rules when one of these borderline friends invites him- or herself to the wedding. It can happen when somebody asks, innocently, "When's the wedding?" If you tell them the exact day, June 20, they might say, "Hey, I'm not doing anything on June twentieth," and then you have to ask them. You might make a joke and say, "I wish I weren't doing anything on June twentieth," but they'll know you're not inviting them because you've passed up the obvious chance to do so.

PEOPLE WHO KNOW THEY AREN'T SPECIAL BUT WHO WILL BE PISSED IF THEY AREN'T INVITED AND WILL GET BACK AT YOU SOMEHOW

This group consists primarily of your employers, your bride's employers, and occasionally your parents' employers. Sometimes they're people you actually like. Other times you don't like them, but you have to invite them because if you don't somebody won't get that raise they've been hoping for. It can also be people who aren't necessarily anybody's boss but whose business you need. People your family has been feuding with for years, but it would only make the feud worse to omit them. People who, for whatever reason, you just plain have to invite because you can't afford to have them mad at you.

PEOPLE YOU DON'T KNOW WELL ENOUGH BUT THINK MIGHT BE SPECIAL

In this case, you are inviting people not from the past but from the future, a couple you've only met or had over to dinner once or twice, but who you really hit it off with and hope to see again. The only danger here is that if you invite someone you just met, someone you've known a long time but didn't invite will be miffed. You'll never be able to please everyone, but you'll have to decide who you want to miff. You can partially unmiff the people you don't invite by sending them formal wedding announcements after the wedding is over, to let them know you were thinking of them but couldn't include them. Even so, it's not the same as getting invited.

PEOPLE WHO USED TO BE SPECIAL

Do you send an invitation to an ex-girlfriend? It depends, of course, on whether or not you're on good terms with her. More than that, it depends on how your fiancée might feel about it. If she thinks you want to get back together with your old girlfriend, then an invitation to her is counter-indicated. Surprisingly, you can be marrying a person, making a public permanent spiritual statement of your willingness to live with her and love her for the rest of your life, the biggest commitment you'll ever make, and she'll still think you want to get back together with your old girlfriend. Go figure.

The best way to make a guest list is to write down everyone you want to come, or have to ask, without discriminating, and then cross off names. As you do, you will also want to note which people you will invite but who you know won't come. Family etiquette will require you to invite Uncle Ernie, the ranting lunatic from Alaska, but you can cross your fingers and feel fairly certain he won't show up. If everyone you invite actually shows up, you'll have too many, but usually not everyone will.

Before you cross off names, you should settle with your bride on the number of vetoes you're each allowed, and the number of veto overrides. When you're done making the list, you should call your parents and ask them who they'd like to invite, because it's their party too. When you've gotten the total number of guests, add a few more gate-crashers to get a rough idea how many people you'll have; as the wedding nears, however, your conscience will get to you and you'll put back on the list another handful of people previously crossed off. When you've taken down the names and addresses, you're ready to start shopping for invitations, but until you know the exact day, time, and place, you're not ready to do much more than price them.

DAY OF WEEK

The Romans considered it inauspicious to marry on the ides, the nones, or the calends of any month, or on any day in February or May, the month in which women abstained from bathing. Today, for some people, any summer Saturday is the obvious choice (though for Jews, Saturday is the sabbath). No one has to take off work or go to work the next day, except possibly the officiant. Out-of-towners have time to drive or fly in and can make a weekend of it if they wish. Some wedding celebrations last an entire weekend. Unfortunately, Saturday is such an obvious choice that most people make it, and depending on where you plan to have the wedding or reception, you can run into booking problems. Some of the popular places may host two or three weddings in a single day, and if your heart's set on one particular place, and the day is already locked in, you may have to take whatever slot is available. At some receptions held at country clubs or catering halls, the guests are suddenly given the bum's rush by the help because they have to get ready for the next reception, which is no way to end what should be the best bash you've ever thrown.

Sunday can be the second choice, but it takes somewhat more careful planning, because certain businesses are closed on Sundays. You can't make an emergency run to the liquor store if they forget to deliver the champagne, and if a sudden thunderstorm blows in and your reception is outdoors, tent rental places might be closed. Friday evening is a swank time to get married, but you'll cost your out-of-town guests a day's work and force everybody to fight rush-hour traffic if the service is early in the evening. The same is true for weeknight weddings, and few guests will be able to stay late at your reception. It's a tradition in many Eastern cultures to cast a horoscope to decide what day is most propitious for a wedding ceremony. It isn't known whether or not Nancy Reagan consulted her astrologist before marrying Ronnie, but she's done all right by her decision—at least from her point of view.

TIME OF DAY

The time of day you have your service and reception can affect the kind of wedding you'll have and the cost. A morning wedding will leave you the rest of the day to socialize or play an interfamily game of softball, but if you have a wedding before noon, remember that only half the musicians you hire are going to show up. A noon wedding suggests you intend to feed your guests, whereas a one or two o'clock wedding doesn't necessarily imply a sit-down meal. Between four and seven o'clock, you'll have to feed 'em. Eight o'clock or later and you can get by with cheese and crackers. Guests will compensate for any savings by running up a larger bar bill at an evening reception. If you have a seven o'clock wedding and then try to get by with cheese and crackers, guests (who may not have eaten anything all day, anticipating a feast that night) are going to get hungry and bolt like rats leaving a ship, or else think you're cheap and steal something to get even. Evening services and receptions will be cooler in the summer, and sunsets make for nice photographs. Afternoon ceremonies in the winter will be better for grandparents who don't like walking or driving in snow, and the sun will illuminate the stained-glass windows, if the service is held in a church or synagogue. Again, much depends on where you have the wedding. If guests have to use back roads and country lanes to get there, you might want to give them some daylight to navigate in.

LOCATION OF CEREMONY

Weddings can take place practically anywhere, on mountain-tops at sunrise, in hot-air balloons, on boats or beaches, in cars or caves, nude on horseback, or nude on a horse in a cave near a beach at sunrise. It's hard to imagine what hasn't been tried. People marry where they met, where they got engaged, in their gardens, in diners, anyplace that holds special meaning for them. In my town, a couple got married at the local mall, right in the atrium between the Benetton's and the Arthur Treacher's Fish n' Chips, and took out an ad in the paper inviting the general public. I had no idea who they were or where they were from, so I had to take out an ad in the same paper to tell them I couldn't make it.

Even though more brides and grooms today are having their receptions and ceremonies at the same location, traditional wedding ceremonies still take place in churches or synagogues. The wedding has been considered a religious ceremony by the Jewish people for more than 3,000 years, more recently so among Christian religions. In the Middle Ages, among Christians, only rulers and community leaders were officially married in religious ceremonies, whereas the peasants were left to negotiate whatever arrangements suited them. It wasn't until 1563, when the Council of Trent ended, that the Catholic Church required religious ceremonies for all its members. England had long recognized civil ceremonies for its populace and religious ceremonies for its rulers, though Henry VIII did a lot to undermine the credibility of both. When the Puritans took over, party animals that they were, wedding ceremonies were stripped of all "Popery" and became strictly civil events, occasionally blessed afterward with a solemn prayer in church. Civil ceremonies, consequently, have been institutionalized and recognized as legal in this country since it was founded. Secular marriages are recognized in most countries, and in fact may be the most common form of marriages in the world. Yet even where marriages are secular events, there is still ritual and celebration, and a kind of religious feeling present, prayers, or simply reverence toward the past and a faith in the future.

If you are marrying in a church or synagogue, it will most likely be in one where you or your bride have attended services, though sometimes people who do not regularly attend church feel they want a church wedding "with all the trimmings." Few churches or synagogues will let you use their facilities if you don't believe in what they stand for but just want a church wedding. If you're marrying in a place of worship you're unfamiliar with, you may encounter new ideas and customs.

Catholic Cathedrals

The best thing about the Catholic Church—or the worst thing, depending on your temperament—is that you know who you're dealing with and what to expect. They have traditions extending back almost 2,000 years, edicts and bulls and guidelines and rulings and laws and helpful hints covering just about everything you need to know and every question you could think to ask. The Catholic Church is, if nothing else, structured, with a hierarchical chain of authority no other church has. For that reason, services and ceremonies from church to church and diocese to diocese won't vary as much as they might in other churches. That isn't to say the Catholic Church doesn't change. One friend who describes himself as "a former Catholic who now fly-fishes" was surprised, for instance, to be informed by a priest that they don't have *limbo* anymore. "What, Father?" he asked the priest—"did it go condo?" For the most part, the foundation of Catholicism is solid and changes little.

To marry Catholic, you must marry in the *church*. This is not the same as marrying in the *Church*. It's a mistake a non-Catholic might make, upon hearing someone say aloud, "You must marry in the church," presuming the word *church* is capitalized, meaning you must marry within the Catholic tradition, according to Catholic laws, as a Catholic and to a Catholic. In fact, "in the church" simply means *in the building.* No outdoor weddings. Some dioceses will allow you to be married in an ecumenical chapel or catering hall, but only if the diocese finds the chapel or hall dignified enough. Mixed-faith weddings are perfectly acceptable, with a minister or rabbi sharing the bill with the priest, though the priest does the vows, when the ceremony is in the cathedral, and only after he's received a dispensation from the diocese to perform an interfaith marriage. If a priest is to serve as a sub-officiant in another faith's service, he has to obtain a "dispensation in form." A Catholic who wants to marry in a parish outside his or her home parish has to get a dispensation from the home parish, and both the Catholic and the non-Catholic may have to present affidavits or "letters of freedom," demonstrating that they're not already married. A Mass is expected if the wedding is between two Catholics, but is often omitted at a mixed service.

The couple meets with the priest several times before the wedding, to go over technical details, choose the readings, and square away the paperwork; and they may be expected to attend Pre-Cana classes as well—marriage seminars where, with other engaged couples, you discuss things like sex, finances, communication skills, what the parts of the ceremony mean, and basically what to expect from marriage. In some Pre-Cana sessions, the couple might be expected to promise to procreate and raise the children Catholic, but, as someone who went through such a session explained, "They seemed pretty willing to fudge it," and allow you room to change your mind later. If you want to convert to Catholicism, it takes about a year. Services haven't been conducted in Latin since 1968, and cannot be performed without a special dispensation from the bishop, no matter how much "trimmings" you had in mind. Most churches charge a nominal fee for the use of the chapel, and there's an extra charge for the musical director. Some dioceses do not allow weddings on Sundays. Many Catholic churches can't accommodate wedding services past about 1:30 or so on Saturdays either, because it interferes with confession and Saturday Mass.

Protestant Churches

Protestant churches are, by definition, varied and unaligned, often founded by troublemakers and radicals like Martin Luther, who protested the sale of indulgences by posting his 95 theses on the door of the Palast Church in Wittenberg in 1517, or Roger Williams, an assistant pastor at a Puritan church in Salem who leaned a bit too heavily on the concept of individual choice in his sermons and got his malcontent butt kicked out of the Massachusetts Bay Colony in 1636, to go on to found the Baptist Church in Rhode Island. Every religion or denomination, in some way or other, organizes around the principle that it knows the proper way to worship, believes what ought to be believed, and the Protestants are no exception, dividing into Presbyterians, Methodists, Episcopalians, Baptists, Lutherans, Congregationalists, and so on. Some, as the old joke goes, disapprove of making love standing up because it looks too much like dancing, while others are quite progressive and liberal. Some fundamentalist churches in the South can't meet more than three times without a monthly schism, where one side tells the other it's going to go to hell and splits off.

Interdenominational rivalries can occur in even the least fervid of religions. The various synods of the Lutheran Church in this country have recently united, but when I was growing up in the American Lutheran Church, full of stoic Scandinavians, if you were on vacation and the only Sunday services you could find were in the less stoic churches of the

Missouri Synod, well, maybe you went fishing instead. Each church provides its members with a sense of community and continuity and adds a spiritual dimension to their lives, but between churches, you may encounter conflicts arising from semantics, methods, liturgical styles, strict or broad scriptural interpretations, political orientations, and what have you, to the point where, in all seriousness, some little old Norwegian lady raised in the ALC might consider an American Lutheran Church–Missouri Synod wedding to be a mixed marriage. Therapists and marriage counselors have found that one of the most difficult problems to overcome in a failing marriage is religious incompatibility. Maybe it's easier to base a country on the principle of religious tolerance than a marriage or a family. It might be worth talking over with your bride just exactly how far apart or close together your views are.

What you have to do varies from church to church. Some will want to have several counseling sessions with you over a period of months, whereas some will ask for only a few short meetings. In general you will pay a fee to the church to rent the space and pay for candles, as well as for the services of the sexton or custodian, both for the wedding rehearsal, the night before the wedding, and for the service itself. If you plan to have your reception in the church basement, that will often require a larger cleanup staff and cost more. Arrangements with the music director or organist have to be made separately as well. You should book well in advance, at least three months.

Quaker Meetinghouses

Friends meetinghouses are often available for rent, but you cannot contract a Quaker minister to do the ceremony because there aren't any. The Society of Friends, founded by George Fox in 1648, operates on the principle of "inner light," a divine presence within everyone, so that although they meet once a month, no one is in charge. Two people wishing to get married in effect marry themselves, which is why Quaker marriages were not recognized as legal in England or in this country for some time. When a couple makes their wish to wed known to the meeting, a "clearness committee" is appointed—two men and two women who meet with the couple during the next few months and ask them questions, or answer any the couple might have, about sex, setting up a household, balancing a checkbook. If the clearness committee recommends that the marriage should take place (it's rare for one not to be recommended), then an overseer's committee is appointed to arrange for licenses, civil requirements, and to plan the party. At the actual wedding event, the society meets in silence, until the couple feels married ("You mean until they feel bored and trapped?" someone asked me), whereupon the couple stands to speak their vows, short and sweet. After another period of silence, members of the meeting rise to give their congratulations, their thoughts on marriage, their feelings about the bride and groom, and to offer them their best wishes.

Unitarian/Universalist Societies

The Unitarian/Universalist Society is one of the most liberal churches in America, and one of the first to perform mixed marriages. In New England, where both the Unitarians and the Universalists flourished in the days of Emerson, Thoreau, and transcendentalism, the Unitarians are known as much for their coffeehouses featuring folk music as for their worship services, and can often be found prowling airport corridors hitting on unsuspecting travelers, trying to sell them Pete Seeger tapes. The recent best-seller, *All I Really Need to Know I Learned in Kindergarten*, is by Robert L. Fulghum, a Unitarian minister who has written down his philosophy, which, in a nutshell, could be called good plain common sense. The Unitarians like good plain common sense, and will feature it on the bulletin boards outside their chapels whether it comes from Martin Buber or Katharine Hepburn. They enjoy sharing their facilities and resources with the community, and may be the place to go if you want to be married by a woman minister.

Synagogues

Jewish wedding traditions predate the Bible. The Old Testament was written from Jewish oral lore and teachings. The idea of Eve springing from Adam's rib, metaphorically expressing the belief that men and women are not complete without each other, which in the final analysis is what weddings are all about, can be found in Genesis. The custom of a bride wearing something blue can be traced to the Israelites, whose brides wore blue ribbons symbolizing purity and faithfulness. Tying shoes to the bumper of the newlyweds' getaway car might be traceable to Deuteronomy, chapter 25, verses 5–10, where shoes are described as symbols of male domination in a marriage. The bridal veil might be a smaller version of the *chuppah,* or canopy, beneath which Jewish weddings take place.

Tradition is identity, to anyone, but especially to a people whose struggle to preserve their identity, through exile and diaspora, Inquisition and Holocaust, is historically without equal. Isolation and adversity forced the Jews to preserve their Jewishness, a proposition which has, ironically, in some ways become more difficult since the founding of the Jewish state of Israel, which is now old enough to have full-grown citizens who are both Israelis and Arabs. Who, then, is an Israeli? As isolation (and, as a consequence, the apparent urgency of maintaining traditions) has lessened in the last forty years, the question being debated now is, who is a Jew? Are you a Jew if you say you are? If your parents were Jewish, but you know no Hebrew and don't attend synagogue or keep kosher or honor Jewish traditions, are you still a Jew? And who has the right to say who is or isn't a Jew? Sez you.

On one level, it matters if you want you or your children to have access to Israeli citizenship. On a more metaphysical level, it matters to you if you want to know yourself as a Jew, and have others know you as one. What is more personal than having your identity challenged? It can matter to either a Jewish or non-Jewish marrying man, because different congregations and/or rabbis will have different requirements, depending on how they define you, may ask you to fulfill certain obligations, or may not sanction the wedding at all.

Again, this is nothing new. Cultures and tribes throughout history have regulated marriage as a way of preserving identity, where a groom of one social unit, totem, tribe, clan, or caste, can marry only a bride of another. It's obvious that if two separate groups intermarry and have offspring, they will eventually no longer be two separate groups. Children will be half of each, their children a quarter, and so on, until the original identities become watered down and dissolve, at least to those who see such a dispersion as a loss rather than as gaining something new to add to the culture. To prevent such a loss of identity, some Jews do not recognize the offspring of a Jewish father and a non-Jewish mother as Jewish, in which case two people who were raised Jewish and consider themselves Jewish may be forced, because one's mother was a Gentile, to consider either "converting" to what they already think they are, or submitting to a "mixed" marriage. Synagogues will allow a non-Jew to convert before marriage, but an Orthodox rabbi may not recognize a convert as a Jew if he's been converted by a Reform rabbi.

Orthodox congregations are the most conservative and traditional, won't allow mixed marriages, and will probably have more Hebrew in the service than a Conservative congregation. A Conservative rabbi may offer more extensive English translations and explanations than an Orthodox rabbi, if there's a large number of Christians at the wedding, but won't perform a mixed ceremony either. Both Orthodox and Conservative rabbis are bound by Halacha, Jewish traditional law, which strictly prohibits mixed marriages. Reform Jews are the most liberal, and some Reform rabbis will perform mixed ceremonies. Many Jewish boys and girls, contemplating an unknowable future, hear the names of such rabbis and make a note of them, just in case. Other Reform rabbis will perform wedding ceremonies following the rules that satisfy Conservative or Orthodox definitions as to who is a Jew. You can get a list of Reform rabbis willing to perform mixed marriages from the Rabbinic Center for Research and Counseling, 125 E. Dudley Avenue, Westfield, NJ 07090. Even then, Reform rabbis may have their own personal requirements. Reform rabbis may not require a Jew wishing to remarry to obtain a Jewish divorce from his or her first spouse, whereas Conservative or Orthodox rabbis won't consider a civil divorce adequate, in which case the ex-husband has to commission a scribe to write a 12-line divorce document called a *get*, which is then delivered to the ex-wife. Easier said than done, sometimes. A *get* must be gotten no matter how long ago the civil divorce took place.

The wedding ceremony is rich in time-honored usages. The ceremony itself takes place under a *chuppah*, a four-cornered canopy of cloth or occasionally flowers that symbolizes the bridal chamber. Unlike Christian weddings, where the couple's parents sit in the front pews and observe the joining of their families, the bride's and groom's parents in a Jewish wedding walk them down the aisle and stand with them under the *chuppah*, where they take part in the service, passing the wedding wine to their children. Then the *ketubah* is read in either Aramaic, Hebrew, or English. The ketubah is one of the oldest forms of prenuptial agreements, originally spelling out such things as what the husband will do for his wife, what her rights are, what his rights are, what he'll pay her if he divorces her, and what she'll forfeit if she divorces

him. Today's ketubah may simply express the couple's senti-
ments. After the ketubah is read, seven marriage blessings
are recited over the wine, which is then drunk again by the
couple, who symbolically ingest the blessings through the
vehicle of the wine. The vehicle, of course, passes through
a few hours later, but the blessings are presumably retained.
When the glass is empty, it is placed under the groom's
heel, and he stomps on it. The breaking of the glass has
been said either historically to symbolize the destruction of
the temple, the frailty of life, the destruction of the hymen,
the damage a broken marriage can do, or to remind those
assembled to stay sober. Today you do it for good luck.
Nervous grooms should remember to wait for the rabbi to
get his hand out before stepping back on the glass, but a
firm stomping is in order, because it's bad luck if the glass
doesn't break. When it breaks, the congregation shouts
"mazel tov," or congratulations, and the couple is pro-
nounced husband and wife. The couple is then led away for
a brief time, into some chamber or anteroom where they are
left alone, a time during which they symbolically consummate the marriage. Remember, this time can be as short as
a minute, so keep it symbolic. They are led back to the
congregation, who applaud and congratulate them, and then
the party begins.

Islam

The wedding ceremony in Islamic countries is usually a civil
affair. However, the marriage won't be considered official
until after the completion of various celebrations and rituals,
which usually take place in the home. Frequently two parties
are going on at the same time, one for the men and one
for the women, parties requiring constant demonstrations of
hospitality, exchange of gifts, feasts and coffee, and conversation. A fish is sometimes used as a fertility symbol in wedding rituals, where a bride might be required to walk seven

times around a platter of them. Eggs may be thrown against
the door of the bridal chamber. In some places, it's forbidden
for two people who suckled at the same breast to marry,
which would rule out brothers and sisters but also unrelated
people who shared the same wet nurse as babies. In rural
Tunisia, a groom may, a week or so before his wedding,
allow himself to become unshaven and degenerate looking,
to protect himself from envious powers, though he cleans
himself up for the big day.

Eastern Religions

In the caste system in India, it is of great advantage to marry
up. Traditionally only women may do so. Girls may marry
as young as eight or ten years of age. Many marriages were
and still may be arranged by the parents. The process of
marrying could involve several days of making oblations,
taking seven steps in various directions, and pouring clarified
butter over each other's heads. A rainy wedding day was
considered bad luck, and seeing a snake on the way to the
wedding was enough to call the whole thing off. For a
groom, it was good luck if a bluebird were to fly past on
his left. It was also a fortuitous omen if one felt a pulsing
in the right eye.

In China, girls were taught to strictly obey first their
parents and then, upon marriage, their husbands. Marriages
were arranged by the parents, who would betroth their children at the age of ten or twelve. Wives were commonly sold
or pawned. Usually the bride and groom didn't meet until
the wedding day, when the bride would be bathed and
dressed, her hair cropped short in the style of married
women. She was then taken in a covered sedan chair to her
husband's house, accompanied by musicians and firecracker-
throwing relations bearing her belongings, her clothes, furniture and, at the head of the procession, something called a
"thunder box," a device which, whatever it was, is said to

have preceded modern plumbing. The groom, upon his bride's arrival, would open the door of the sedan chair and behold his bride for the first time. If he didn't like what he saw, he would close the door. If he did like what he saw, he would lead her and her thunder box into his house. A priest would cut the head off a chicken and sprinkle blood on the lucky couple, and in the crowd, somebody would turn to the person next to them and say, "Well, I guess the head's off the chicken now."

Arranged marriages are not uncommon in Korea and Japan as well, often contacts between families forged to create business ties or propitious social bonds. Ceremonies are usually not religious. The name for the officiant at Korean weddings (where thousands of couples sometimes marry in the same ceremony) translates as "Master of Ceremonies." In Laos, newlyweds may not be allowed to consummate their marriage for three days, to prove their discipline. In Tibet, young brides and grooms were often not told of their arranged marriages until the very day of the wedding, when their parents would lure them to the temple under false pretenses and surprise them.

Nondenominational Chapels

Nondenominational churches may be listed in your phone book. You may also wish to contact university or college chapels, although it's possible that a college chapel won't rent space to you unless you're an alumnus or have some connection to the school. Some colleges have religious affiliations, but many do not, having instead chapels able to accommodate any religious, civil, or self-created ceremony, with, for example, some kind of covering that can be lowered to conceal the cross if the chapel is to be used for a Jewish service, or nonspecific floral or geometric stained-glass windows. They may have chaplains available to officiate, or you may have to find your own. You can also find nondenomina-

tional chapels in places like Las Vegas or Tijuana. At the
Chapel of Love in Las Vegas, you can get married by either
an ordained minister or a justice of the peace, hire witnesses,
rent taped music and a chauffeur who'll pick you up at your
hotel, take you to the courthouse to get a license ($27 at
the courthouse), bring you to the chapel and back to your
hotel, all in an hour, for only $49, not counting a tip for
the driver. The photo package is also extra.

City Hall

For the absolute least fuss and bother, you can always go to
your town hall and be married by a justice of the peace. JPs
are listed in the phone book and frequently double as town
clerks, which is why you can find them in town halls. JPs
make good officiants because that's actually all they do, as
glorified town clerks. A justice of the peace can marry people, administer oaths of office, take depositions, or serve as
a notary public. It would be possible for somebody you
know, a relative or close friend, to become a JP and marry
you him- or herself, but it could take awhile for them to be
commissioned, by the governor or by whoever commissions
JPs in your state.

Other Sites

You can marry in planes, trains, or automobiles. You can
marry on a boat, but a ship's captain can only marry you in
international waters, at least twelve miles offshore, and only
in time of war, or under other such urgent circumstances—
suppose, for example, your ship runs aground on a desert
island, where cannibalism is illegal except among married
couples. In most cases, you would use a yacht or cruise ship
like any other hall or function room, and would have to
supply your own officiant. Prices vary according to the size
and location of the yacht. A 130-foot luxury motor yacht,

able to hold up to 150 people, for four hours, not including food or beverages, rents for about $5,000. If the seas are high on your wedding day, you may need to ask the ship's cooks to whip up a nice Dramamine punch. Some charter agencies can arrange trips to places like the Virgin Islands where a couple can hire a boat, marry on it, and then tool around on it for a week, for about $2,000 a person.

You can marry in restaurants or social clubs, which, like renting a yacht, will allow you to have the ceremony and reception in the same place. Restaurants, as a rule, don't like to lose money, and will charge you at least whatever they'd stand to make by staying open for regular business, or else shunt you into a back room. Elite social organizations with names like the University Club or the Atheneum Historical Society will probably require someone in the family to be a member.

Finally, you can marry in fresh air. Outdoor weddings seem to be more common every year, and can be the choice for people who want to celebrate life wherever life celebrates itself—in parks, gardens, fields, mountaintops, beaches, or with the whole party wearing hip boots standing knee deep in the groom and bride's favorite trout stream.

FINDING AN OFFICIANT

Whatever religion or nonreligion you get married in, you need to find an officiant you get along with and can feel at ease with. Sometimes when the wedding is being held at the bride's church, it isn't always possible to choose the officiant. If you don't feel comfortable with the officiant you have no choice but to use, you can ask that someone you know participate as well. Even a justice of the peace may feel like he or she is presiding at an important event in your life and consequently wish to get to know you before proceeding with the service, maybe ask questions you don't feel comfortable answering. You want to feel comfortable with whoever it is, because when the time comes to actually do the deed, you'll be so nervous trying to remember your lines and not drop the ring or stammer or swear or spit up or faint that you end up a helpless quivering mass of Jell-O in a tux, at which time all you want is a capable officiant who will speak clearly, make you repeat after him or her, and take you through the ceremony, leading you out of it like a horse gets led out of a burning barn.

Who's going to pay for all this?

Traditionally, the groom pays the officiant's fee. The bride's parents pay for the sanctuary fee, the organist, the soloist or choir, the sexton or janitor, and any decorations for the chapel such as carpets or extra candelabras. The groom will be expected to throw a coin into the baptismal font for good luck as well.

PLACES FOR THE RECEPTION

Once you book the ceremony site, the next step is booking a place to hold the reception. You may have to juggle things a bit and reschedule the former to coincide with the latter. Most people think of the reception as the fun part of any wedding, the second half of the ceremony, no less rich in symbolism or tradition. You'll want to choose your site with care.

Outdoors

On a warm summer evening, a rosy sunset chased with a cobalt twilight and then a starry night sky, there's really nothing as romantic or as pleasant as an outdoor reception, where voices waft out across the lake, above the gentle melodies of a six-piece swing band, and everything is dreamily perfect. Dream on. Going on the assumption that perfect weddings are the exception rather than the rule, all you can do is try to anticipate whatever problems may arise and then keep your fingers crossed. The convenience of having a reception in the backyard or on the lawn may be offset by the extra effort involved, as well as the extra expense of renting everything you need. In the end it may not be any cheaper than hiring a hall.

What to Consider

The weather. Midwestern farmers are likely to say, in the middle of a drought or after a prolonged rainy spell, "We must not be paying the preacher enough." Offering the clergyman an extra fifty to pray for good weather (the groom would pay for this) may not be preparation enough, in which case you will want to have a tent on hand. Tents can cost from $110 for a 20 × 20 foot canopy to $450 for one 20 × 60 (frame tent). (All prices are from Taylor Rentals' 1989 Price List.) The rental agency will set up the tent for you, but may charge extra if a long drive is required. You have to put down 50 percent for a deposit, which may not be refundable. The experts figure you need 10 square feet per person for a sit-down dinner and about 8 for a buffet, which means a 30 × 60 foot tent will hold 180 for a sit-down and 225 for a buffet, fewer if everybody is fat. Tents will not protect your guests from rain if they have to walk to and from their cars. Lightning striking you after the minister asks for anyone with objections to speak now or forever hold their piece would be very difficult to explain away or laugh off. If you rent a tent for an evening reception, you'll also need lights, which cost $10 for a 100-foot string.

Parking. There may be regulations regarding parking on the street, if the reception is held in a backyard. Sometimes the local police department will cut you some slack, but not always. You may even need to rent a cop to control parking or watch cars during the festivities. You should also call the highway department and ask if there are any plans to tear up the streets near your reception or dig new sewers alongside them on or before the day of your wedding.

Neighbors. Will there be loud music? Do you have cranky neighbors? You should discuss your plans with them in advance. The easiest thing to do, if they object, is invite them.

Clothing facilities. Guests will need places to put their coats or purses. If you are having the ceremony at the same place as your reception, your bride may need a room in which to change clothes.

Bugs and critters. Is the site near standing water, swampland, or deep woods? In spring and early summer, mosquitoes can be more than annoying. In northern Minnesota at an outdoor wedding, two mosquitoes were seen actually carrying off an unsuspecting bridegroom and dragging him into the woods. After a rainy spring and heavy mosquito infestation, spraying may hold them off for twelve hours or so, but it stinks. Citronella candles smell better but don't work as well. You can keep undiluted diethyl-m-toluamide on hand, but it's going to make everybody greasy. Your reception could also be spoiled the first time a bridesmaid screams out "ticks!" and runs for the house. Skunks are, of course, always welcome at wedding receptions, and usually come properly dressed. In Florida, a 20-foot python was recently removed from under a house, an animal large enough to swallow most flower girls whole. Bats love weddings as well, but although they are perfectly harmless, may not be particularly attractive hanging from your bride's veil.

Power. Normal house current may not be enough to handle strings of lights in addition to band amplifiers or whatever other electrical needs you might have. Will the band members electrocute themselves and then charge you for it? A 3,500-watt generator rents for about $40 a day, and a 5,000-watt generator is $50 a day.

Kitchen facilities. Caterers need three separate places, to prep food, serve it, and wash dishes. A garden hose will suffice for the latter. They will need someplace to put the trash.

Sanitary facilities. Portable toilets rent for about $85 a day. You'd need at least one unit for each sex, for an average-size four-hour wedding, two per sex if you have a large wedding, 500 guests or so.

General layout. Will everyone be able to see the ceremony, if it's held in the same place? Is there a place for a receiving line? A place for guests to leave gifts, where they'll be safe from the weather but inconspicuous? Anything dangerous where children might hurt themselves, quicksand pits, steep precipices, or busy highways nearby? Barbed wire or electrified fences?

Miscellaneous rental. Here are some things you may need:

Portable bar	$15.00
Candelabras	$20.00 pair
Chairs (white Samsonite)	$ 1.00 each
Coatrack	$12.00
Dance floor	$ 7.00 3′ × 3′ section
Grill	$50.00 2′ × 5′ propane
Tablecloth	$10.00 90″ round white
Table	$10.00 72″ round (seats 10)
Lattice arch	$25.00
Gazebo	$50.00
Chuppah	$75.00

Not included in this list are the costs of renting all the silverware, dishes, glasses, warming trays, and whatever else the caterer may need. It can add up to about $3.50 a place setting. Some caterers own their own tableware, but many do not. Usually you make a deposit, and pay the balance upon return.

Indoors

If you rent a hall, you may not have to rent anything extra, or worry about parking, or the weather, or sanitary facilities, but you may have to settle for a less than desirable room.

The best places will be expensive. Places like the ballroom at the Helmsley Palace in New York, the Augusta National Country Club in Georgia, where the Masters golf tournament is held, the ballroom at the Beverly Wilshire Hotel, in Los Angeles, the Petroleum Club in Houston, or K-Paul's Louisiana Kitchen, in New Orleans, could all cost as much as $100 a person or more—or much more, depending on the menu. In April 1988, the Metropolitan Museum in Manhattan hosted a wedding rumored to have cost in excess of $2 million, with as much spent on flowers alone as most people pay for a house. "The rich," Fitzgerald said, "are different from us." No kidding.

A step down from there are the less elite country or social clubs. Universities often have faculty clubs that can be rented, and many service organizations such as the Elks or the Rotarians may have rooms available to the public, certainly available to members. Nice restaurants often have back or basement rooms available for wedding receptions, but somehow the food you get at a reception is never as good as what you get just ordering off the menu. Quite a few function rooms have adjacent kitchen facilities in which a caterer can operate. Historical houses or mansions can be nice, with beautiful rooms and gardens, but if they're old, they may not have adequate wiring or plumbing. Prices for such places will be in the $500 range, give or take a few hundred.

Or you may want to consider professional function rooms, catering halls, or banquet facilities, those buildings that exist primarily as wedding processing plants. They are often given names like Briarcliff or The Glades or 401, in structures formerly called Tony's Billiards or Carpet World or Danny's Dirty Den—Exotic Dancers Nightly, now stuccoed white with rhododendron all around the outside and red-and-green colored floodlights to provide nighttime illumination. Inside, you can identify them by their flocked velvet wallpaper, faux Greek pillars and balustrades, plastic chandeliers and plants, paisley carpeting you could ground an oil tanker on and not see the spill, and a general malodorous ambience commingling room fresheners and stale cigar smoke. The kitchens are able to vulcanize chicken for up to 500 people an hour. The "wine cellar" is two stainless steel tanks on the roof, one labeled "red" and one "white," though the wine steward will gladly run the white through a carbon-dioxide infuser if you want champagne or mix that with red to make sparkling rosé. The bartender is an ex-bookie's collection agent named Vinnie who's kept his nose clean since getting out of the slammer, but if you ask him what single malt scotches he has, he's likely to say "Yukon Jack." Function rooms will often have a house band as well, featuring a piano man who's sleepwalked through the same songs every week for the last forty years and can now read Russian novels while playing; a seventeen-year-old bass player who quit high school to be a professional musician; a drummer who's got two basic beats, "on" and "off" and mutters "oh yeah!" a lot; a guitar player who used to sub for Mel Bay and whose taste of the big time came when he helped Charlie Parker stagger into a cab in 1948; and a trumpet-playing master of ceremonies with a phony smile and an even phonier tuxedo who thinks his job is to run the entire affair, talk about what a lovely institution marriage is, "But who wants to live in an institution?" (rimshot—"oh yeah!"), make bedroom jokes while getting the names of the bride and groom wrong, and cajole Gramma into getting up and dancing even though she's a week out of hip-replacement surgery. Such bands may charge extra to exclude accordions.

Some banquet halls, it must be admitted, will do a completely satisfactory professional job, with up-to-date facilities, tasteful decor, and good food, but some can be disappointing. The problem with any kind of room is that you can't exactly crash somebody else's wedding just to see what yours might be like. What you can do is ask for the names of people who had their weddings in whatever room you finally choose and call them up and ask them how they liked it. You should also visit the place where your wedding or reception is going to be at least four times, once while you're shopping around, once after you've shopped around and in broad daylight, once at night if that's when your reception will be, and once again a week before the wedding to make sure they're not redecorating or putting in a new septic tank. You should ask, when you book the room, if any such undertakings are planned or anticipated, because once you've mailed out your invitations, it's hard to change sites, and the people booking the rooms know this. Even if they swear remodeling will be completed in time for your wedding, strikes or work stoppages can move back deadlines and ruin your day. You have to book well in advance, and most places will require a deposit. Catering halls charge by the head, from $15 to $50 a person.

Who's going to pay for all this?

Traditionally, you're not all that involved with the reception expenses, which will be picked up by the bride's family. Your family does pay for the rehearsal dinner (if there is one), usually at a nice restaurant, the reservations made well in advance. Needless to say, any of these expenses can be shared by those involved. More will be said about expenses in the next chapter.

PNS

PNS, or "Prenuptial Syndrome," is a painful and embarrassing stress-related nervous disorder that can affect either men or women. Some sufferers begin to show signs of it as soon as they're engaged, whereas others may seem to be perfectly fine, as close as a week before the wedding. Onset occurs halfway through the engagement period and grows progressively worse as the wedding day approaches. It's the body's way of protecting the brain from overloading, as the brain is increasingly called upon to both remember wedding details and ignore the massive future ramifications of getting and being married. The result is a desperate but fogged and mindless state, which can sometimes last for months after the wedding is over. Some symptoms are:

Losing your keys or eyeglasses, things you may have lost before, as well as losing things you've never lost before, such as coats, shoes, even your car.

Numerous stupid arguments over trivial details.

General ditziness. Missing freeway exits, putting your underwear on backward, leaving wash at the Laundromat.

Visual innumeracy. Having difficulty reading or understanding numbers correctly, writing the wrong date or amount on a check, setting the alarm clock wrong, and so on.

Episodes of *déjà vu*, the feeling you've been some-where before, when you haven't, or *presque vu*, the feeling you can get, in a familiar place, that you've never been there before.

Loss of sleep, or sleep interruption, waking every morning at exactly 4:29. Waking with the cold sweats or sleepwalking. Really weird dreams, populated by Star Trek characters or Smurfs.

Increased superstitiousness. Finding yourself on the lookout for omens, or for signs of PNS.

Denying you have a problem.

Loss of appetite or sex drive. General wistfulness.

Under no circumstances should a person who is pre-nuptial try to operate heavy machinery, make long-term commitments, work on a computer, or attempt to do your tax return.

5

THE
WEDDING
MAFIA

. . . W*ine maketh merry: but money*
answereth all things.

—ECCLESIASTES 10:19

You've picked a day and a place for your wedding. Go out
with your fiancée and have a nice dinner. Buy each other
presents. Send a card to your gramma, visit people who are
hospitalized, write a check or two to your favorite charities,
to build karma for the days ahead. You'll need it, because
now all you have before you is the simple task of getting a
mere 200 or 300 people from all over the country to show
up in the right place at the right time, including all the
help you hire, who not only have to be in the right place at
the right time but bring the right stuff with them and do
the right things with the stuff they bring, in the right
sequence. If you have an entirely homemade wedding, a few
friends at a potluck in a backyard with flowers from the

garden and a good radio for music, then you may stay out of trouble, but if you intend to have an elaborate affair, you have no choice but to deal with the Wedding Mafia.

HISTORY

The Wedding Mafia's story begins, naturally enough, in Niagara Falls, in the year 1872, the day in October when the *Cornucopia* arrived, a cutty sark out of Glasgow carrying a load of immigrants. The captain and his men had been put in a dingy in the mid-Atlantic after a mutiny on the high seas, in which the ship was commandeered by a Bayreuthian wedding band led by a man named Giuseppe "Schlomo" Muldoon, a sousaphonist of uncertain origin. The wedding band was wanted in Prussia for playing "Wir Haben Erst Angefangen" at a royal wedding, in a key too high for the Kaiser to sing along. They fled to the new land, but fearing they'd be arrested at Ellis Island, Muldoon and his men took over the ship and its passengers. Muldoon managed to steer the *Cornucopia* down the St. Lawrence by cover of night, reaching the mouth of the Niagara River around midnight of the fourteenth. Muldoon and his men were gathered on the bridge, playing a polka as the ship neared the precipice, the music drowning out the roar of the falls. The *Cornucopia* went over the edge, killing everyone aboard except Giuseppe Muldoon and his bass player, an escaped slave named Blind Whoopee John Robinson, who'd run away from a plantation in Georgia, boarded the wrong train on the Underground Railroad, and ended up in Warsaw. The two managed to float ashore, clinging to Robinson's bull fiddle.

Muldoon soon put together another band, "The Castaways," and rented a local barn for receptions. A few months later, the only other local banquet hall burned down in the middle of a drenching rainstorm. By 1883, Schlomo Muldoon had the entire wedding services industry of Niagara Falls to himself.

He succeeded because he gave people what they wanted. Soon, other immigrants seeking employment made their way to Niagara Falls to work for Schlomo Muldoon—tailors, caterers, florists, and photographers unable to find work in New York City. Robinson found drunken clergymen willing to come work in Muldoon's chapels for a bottle of rum a day. In 1904, Muldoon commissioned a Norwegian carpenter named Svenson to make the first heart-shaped bed. In 1920, Muldoon applied for a patent for the first water bed, a crude contraption fashioned from the ballast-bladder of a sperm whale. By 1929, Muldoon's bakeries made more than 600 three- and four-tiered wedding cakes a day. Couples were regaled by 200 bands, served by 150 caterers, photographed by 300 photographers; clubs were opened in Detroit, Chicago, and Kansas City.

Then the stock market crashed.

Muldoon lost everything. He died in 1931, a broken man. Blind Whoopee John Robinson's son, Albert "Swiss Family" Robinson (from his penchant for wearing lederhosen), tried to pick up the pieces, but found that the people formerly loyal to Giuseppe Muldoon had dispersed to start businesses of their own.

Today, America is dominated by the descendants of Muldoon's wedding syndicate. The police are helpless to stop them, both because they're vastly outnumbered, and because most of the activities of the Wedding Mafia today are perfectly legal. They can charge $5,000 for a dress your bride wears *once*, or $1,000 for a cake—a *cake*—or $3,000 for a ring you can't return, and the authorities can't touch them. John Q. Public and Ms. Average Citizen have learned to look the other way, to say, "It's like this everywhere," or, "What can one individual do?"

The sad thing is, in a grade school in Flat, Texas, a teacher recently discovered a group of second graders using

Monopoly money to put on their own playground wedding, paying out $6,000 to the caterer, a grand to the florist, tipping the waiters with play fifties. They even had a make-believe videographer charging $200 an hour.

Second graders.

Sure, they're just kids. And sure, it's only play. But where does it stop?

INVITATIONS

As soon as you know how many guests to expect, as well as the time and place of your ceremony and reception, it behooves you to apprise the former of the latter, the sooner the better, at least four to six weeks before the wedding. You will want to give your guests as much advance notice as possible, and you'll want the fights you and your bride have about the invitations to die down quickly so you can move on to other things.

You may fight over the need for invitations at all. When a friend in high school got married, his invitation consisted of a piece of notebook paper with the words:

> *I'm getting married Saturday at St. Mary's at one o'clock. My friends can come but you other guys stay away. You know who you are.*
>
> *Murphy*

in Bic pen; the note was left on the bulletin board in the pool hall where everybody hung out. To many men, this would seem sufficient. Tell them where, tell them when, and as long as the information is clear and unambiguous, it shouldn't matter what the invitation looks like. Why go to any trouble on something everybody is just going to throw out anyway? Why not just type something up and photocopy it?

The Wedding Mafia knows this is how men feel, so they try to convince your bride that only scum photocopy wedding invitations. For an occasion so important, only the finest engraved invitations will do. Guests may decide not to come if the invitations aren't fancy enough. Women probably throw away old wedding invitations too, but when it's time to print their own, they start thinking in terms of mementos for the wedding album. Again, the Wedding Mafia encourages extravagance by putting up mottoes and slogans in bridal boutiques and florist shops:

IF YOU'RE GOING TO DO IT, DO IT RIGHT

YOUR WEDDING—A ONCE-IN-A-LIFETIME AFFAIR

MAKE ← IT ← A ← NIGHT ← TO ← REMEMBER

WHEN THE GOING GETS TOUGH, THE TOUGH GET GOING

Wait a minute. That last one was from my high-school football locker room.

You get the idea. If you agree that if you do it, you should do it right, then you have to have invitations printed up. You do this by getting in the car with your fiancée and going down to your neighborhood copy center, where somewhere on a counter, near the self-serve copying machine, you will see one or more enormous loose-leaf notebooks, thick as books of wallpaper samples, from which to make your selection.

The first thing you notice is that the general wedding esthetic seems to imply that you're not entering a state of matrimony so much as *The Magic Fairyland of Eternal Wedded Happiness*, where smiling red-cheeked cupids flit from cloud to cloud eating cotton candy while lilies bloom in treacly abundance. The majority of invitation forms are floral, lacy, dainty, and sugary. You can get a buzz by just looking at them. If they were scented (and perhaps somewhere they are), they'd smell like urinal crystals and cherry Kool-Aid. They are feminine, designed to appeal to brides and mothers-in-law. Another spat, then, may ensue over just how candified you want your invitations to be. There are usually a few plain unembroidered forms to choose from.

After you've chosen the style of paper, you have to choose a typeface and ink color to match it. You can have some really bizarre arguments over typefaces, something most people never give a moment's thought to. Suppose you want:

Mr. and Mrs. Norton Whetherhill
request the honour of your presence
at the marriage of their daughter Gail . . .

"I hate sans serif," she says.

"You never told me you hate sans serif," you say. Obviously this is something you should have talked about on your first date. "All right, then. What do you want?"

She proposes:

Mr. and Mrs. Norton Whetherhill
request the honor of your presence
at the marriage of their daughter Gail . . .

"I will not have my invitations go out with little curlicues on the letters," you tell her.

"Those aren't curlicues," she says. "They're flares."

"They're not flares—they're curlicues."

"They are too."

"Are not."

You also have to decide how many different kinds of forms you want. The Wedding Mafia encourages you to send:

Engagement announcements. In case the wedding is in the distant future. An engagement announcement does not necessarily imply that an invitation is forthcoming, but one may be expected from you.

Invitations. They also want you to send them in lined envelopes, for the "enhanced elegance of color coordination." The wording of the invitations is standardized according to modern rules of etiquette, different forms for different situations, where, for instance, one parent is deceased, or one has divorced and remarried, or where the marrying couple is announcing their own wedding. You may find yourself fighting with your bride over whether or not you want to say "hon*our* of your presence" or "hon*or* of your presence" (by no means should your invitation read "honor of your *presents*"), but the easiest thing to do is just pick a form. The envelope containing the invitation goes inside the one you put the stamp on and mail. Whoever you list on the invitation envelope is who you want to come. If, for example, you want Mr. and Mrs. Brady, but not the entire Brady Bunch, you print "Carol and Mike Brady" on the envelope containing the invitation. You don't write, "Carol and Mike Brady (please, no Bunches.)"

Reception cards. You include these only if you want a big ceremony but a small reception, in the envelopes you send to the people you want at both. Being invited to the wedding but not to the reception is bound to annoy somebody, but sometimes you have no choice, and it's better to spell it out than make anyone wonder.

Response cards. Some kind of RSVP cards, whether formal or just return-addressed postcards, are essential, because you need to be able to tell the caterer exactly how many guests you're expecting. Formal response cards are accompanied by their own envelopes, which may have your address printed on them.

Wedding announcements. You send these to the people you didn't invite, after the fact, to let them know. Usually you mail them, or have someone else mail them for you, the day of or the day after the wedding.

"At home" cards. These are change-of-address cards you slip in with the invitations. It's also a way for your bride to let people know whether or not she's keeping her own name or changing it. One might read:

Ed and Gail Fournier
will be at home
after the tenth of June
100 Main Street
Macaroni, New Jersey 19181

The only problem is that it makes it sound like you have no hopes of ever going anywhere after you're married.

Thank-you cards. These can save you time after the wedding. If you really want to save time, send them with the invitations, and write "Thank you for the lovely gift we know you're going to give us. We look forward to seeing you."

Miscellaneous. This includes personalized items like napkins with your monogram on them, matchbooks, place cards for the dinner, pew cards for in-church seating arrangements, or thank-you scrolls to leave at each place setting. Some stationery suppliers will also furnish you with monogrammed ashtrays, party favors, the bridal garter, the ring bearer's pillow, an engraved set of toasting champagne goblets, a matching plumed pen set, an engraved cake knife and server set, and an album for your guests to sign. None of any of this is really necessary, which is why they call it "trimmings." If you really want to trim, you could order monogrammed tissues for the rest rooms, specially printed "Ed and Gail" sun visors for the dads, "Ed & Gail—Good Luck" pencils, and maybe a "Newlyweds on Board" yellow sign to stick on your rear windshield.

If you're having a wedding for 100 people, your costs will break down roughly as follows:

100 fancy invitations	$70.00
100 lined envelopes	$14.00
100 reception cards	$30.00
100 response cards	$39.00
100 return addressed envelopes	$20.00
100 thank-you notes	$34.00
postage for invitations	$25.00
postage for return envelopes	$25.00
postage for thank-you notes	$25.00
100 thank-you scrolls	$29.00
100 rice paper engraved napkins	$23.00
100 souvenir matchbooks	$17.00
garter and hanky	$10.00
ring bearer's pillow	$12.00
plumed pen set	$8.00
engraved silver goblets	$49.00
silver plated cake knife set	$17.50
guest book	$23.50
	$471.00

You might have to leave a deposit upon ordering, and pay the balance upon delivery.

You are also encouraged, the Wedding Mafia will tell you, to order twenty-five extra of everything you need, in case your guest list unexpectedly swells, as it so easily can. You may misaddress an envelope, or spill coffee on them, or change your mind, tear one up and then change it back about somebody (do not send a torn invitation you've taped back together), in which case ordering extra may not be a bad idea. You should allow time for reordering in case you find misspellings in your invitations. Depending on whose fault it is, reprints owing to misspellings may be free, or you may get to pay double.

Along with the invitations, you will want to include any maps your guests might need to find their way, as well as a list of nearby hotels or motels, specifying costs and amenities when possible, a pool for the kids, kitchenettes, and such.

Who's going to pay for all this?

Traditionally, the bride's family pays for the invitations, announcements, and mailing costs. The groom's contribution, then, is to lick stamps, which can mean, if you're having a large wedding, lubricating a thousand stamps or more, enough to make your food taste like the ink from a leaky pen for a week. The groom should also help address envelopes, which involves hours of making phone calls to make sure you have all the correct addresses, hours of actually writing the names on all the envelopes, and another hour or two of standing at the post office, looking up zip codes in the directory.

Average cost for invitations, etc.: $286.

PHOTOGRAPHERS

You will definitely want to have a lot of pictures of the wedding to bore your friends with for years to come. As a rule, slides are more boring than prints, but they aren't nearly as portable. Videos, the latest in wedding photography, are twice as tedious as slides, but are even less portable, requiring a VCR to be effectively ennui-inducing. Even then, if you offer to bring your videos or slides with you when you visit your friends in their own homes, they can always claim their VCRs or slide projectors are broken, whereas no one can pretend to be blind to get out of looking at your prints.

A still photographer will cost anywhere from $500 to $1,500, depending on what you need and for how long. The price includes materials, developing, prewedding interviews, and the finished photo album. Prints and wall portraits cost extra, $500 to $750 for a 40″ × 30″ portrait, about $20 for an 8″ × 10″ print, wallet sizes for $2.50 each, more if you want your portraits or prints to look romantic and fuzzy, the way the *Magic Fairyland of Eternal Wedded Happiness* looks. A standard shoot includes formal couple and family portraits, usually taken either before the ceremony or between the ceremony and the reception, pictures of the ceremony, candid pictures of the reception, and whatever corny traditional pictures you ask for—you removing her garter, both of you cutting the cake, stuffing cake into each other's mouth, dancing with your mother while your bride dances with her father, and so on. A photographer billing by the hour may charge about $100 an hour, and may expect to be reimbursed if he has to drive a great distance or stay overnight in a motel.

Some people try to save money by hiring a friend with a good camera to take pictures, figuring an amateur taking thirty rolls of film is going to supply as many good pictures as a pro taking five. Most regret it. Apart from making mistakes with apertures and exposures, amateurs won't have the best equipment, won't know what shots marrying couples traditionally appreciate, and won't have either the pro's charm to get people smiling or the temerity to get close up and be obnoxious for the sake of a good picture. Some brides and grooms get so annoyed at the flashing of strobe lights they tell the photographer to stop, but as often as not, they end up loving the pictures and wishing they'd let him continue. Pros know how to use light, how to freeze a dancer or let her blur, when to change lenses or when to use filters. A pro knows to bring extra batteries and flashes, enough film to shoot the wedding twice, how to tell when a camera is misfunctioning, how to label film and not lose it. He buys film from a refrigerated photo-supply house and not from a drugstore. He knows what shots to anticipate so he can be there before they happen, and he can tell what's missing at the end of a wedding shoot that he might have forgotten— a picture of the bride with her sisters or you with your brothers. A talented amateur is simply not likely to know as much as someone who does it every day for a living.

Photographers will tell you you need pictures because most brides and grooms are so busy and/or spaced out on their wedding days that they don't remember what happened, which isn't quite true. At the same time, your attention is going to be diverted in so many directions that you'll never really get a chance to spend as much time with any one person as you'd like. You can spend that time with a photograph of someone. It's not the same, of course, but then, photographs aren't going to bore you by telling you soporific stories about when they got married, or give you useless advice about what to do with your life, the way some wedding guests can.

Which isn't true about videotapes. Videography is the latest trend in wedding photography. Ever since hand-held camcorders became widely available and almost affordable, people have taken to them the way they took to Super 8 home movies in the fifties, only more so, because you can plug a home video right into your TV and watch it two minutes after you've taped it. As a result, people now tape themselves doing something, and then stop doing it to watch themselves do it on tape. Instead of actually having a birthday party or Christmas celebration, we get together to watch a tape of what we did last year. Sometimes we tape ourselves while we watch, so that next year, we can watch a tape of ourselves watching a tape of two years before. Try going back in time and explaining that to anyone.

One thing to consider when contemplating making a wedding video: the camera's presence may change the way both you and your guests behave. Some people find it intrusive or irritating. Although a videotape can jog your memory by recording events you're too distracted and spacey to notice, having cameras (and lights, in the case of old equipment) pointed at you may distract you more than you'd be distracted anyway. Then again, you could be in such a state of shock after the wedding that you're not sure if you're really married at all, in which case you can watch yourself on instant replay to make sure no one omitted an "I do" or stepped out of bounds before the whistle.

About a quarter of all weddings are videotaped these days, 500,000 last year. Costs can range from about $300 for unedited master tapes of the ceremony and reception to $1,500 or more for a superslick Hollywood job. A state-of-the-art wedding video might have computer animated titles, a montage blending childhood snapshots (or childhood videos) of the bride and groom leading chronologically to the present, a shot of the place where the bride and groom first met, maybe the college they attended together with voice-over narrations. It could have interviews with the groom's friends at his bachelor party, interviews with the bridesmaids, pictures from the rehearsal dinner, footage of the bride and her bridesmaids getting ready for the ceremony, of the groom and his father trying to tie their bow ties, the bride leaving her house, the groom leaving his, guests arriving at the church, the limousine pulling up, an up-close-and-personal shot of the minister. Then the ceremony, the minister with a wireless mike, individual readers, soloists in full song, a tear running down your mother's cheek, a close-up of the rings being placed on your fingers, the pronunciation of man and wife and then the kiss, freeze-frame, a pan down the receiving line outside the church, cut to the reception, pan down the buffet, a close-up of someone saying grace, then toasts, the first dance of the newlyweds, the bride and father dance, groom and mother, cutting the cake, throwing the bouquet, interviews of guests as they reminisce about their own weddings, cross-cut with pictures of the groom's zany pals sabotaging his car, cut to a montage of babies sleeping, old guys smoking cigars, the maid of honor looking tired, Gramma looking crabby, the proud but exhausted parents, and fade out as the happy couple emerges in street clothes and departs in the sabotaged car, unless, as has happened, the videographer is invited to come along and film the honeymoon. You can have special effects, in which the image flips over like a page being turned in a book, inserts, titles superimposed telling the viewer the name of whoever's on the screen ("Vicki—bridesmaid"), subtitles if somebody is speaking a foreign language, a sound-track featuring the band at the wedding and/or the bride's and groom's favorite songs, their theme song, if they have one, matte shots, animation, splices of other movies or TV shows, final credits, and whatever else they can do on MTV. A wedding used to be a coronation, couples thinking of themselves as king and queen for a day. Now brides and grooms get to think of themselves as TV stars.

A good videographer should have cameras that can operate in low light, professional television-quality cameras, and should know how to operate inconspicuously. This person should have full editing capabilities as well. You may be charged separately for shooting and editing, perhaps $100 an hour to shoot and $150 to edit, and in the case of most filmmaking, it takes longer to edit than to shoot. You can be charged an additional fee for music, graphics, or titles. You should ask for references and credentials as to education and experience, and make sure the person you hire does video for a living, either working in television or at some private video lab, and isn't just some palooka who bought a fancy camcorder hoping to cash in on a trend.

You'll want a photographer, whether you have a videographer present or not, because it's easier to hang a photograph on the wall than it is to leave the TV on 24 hours a day with your wedding video on freeze-frame. Many wedding videographers started out as still photographers, and can do double duty and take your family portraits for you, but not all are qualified. Some are fresh out of film school, studied only video techniques, and may not know an aperture from an aperitif. Ask, when shopping for a photographer or videographer, to see samples or demo reels in as varied a sampling as you can get—candid shots, formal shots, group shots. Does he know how to use light? Are the compositions attractive? If you like his work and want to hire him, give him the addresses of your ceremony and reception sites, and a rough itinerary of what's going to happen where and when, so he'll be there ahead of time, taking light readings and setting up. Tell him if you don't want flash pictures during the ceremony. You might also wish to give him a list of the people you want photographed, aunts and uncles and whoever else is special to you, and assign some family member to point them out to him. Get everything and put everything in writing.

Finally, you should consider how you want to store your wedding memories. Photographs will bend when loose and fade if left in direct sunlight, but protected in an album, will last for generations. Videos begin to deteriorate after about 100 viewings (as does your brain, watching your own wedding 100 times), so you may want to have a master copy and a viewing copy. Videotape can be damaged by airport metal detectors, the ones that sound an alarm when you have too many keys in your pocket, but won't be harmed by X-ray machines. So feel free to bring one to show your dentist.

Who's going to pay for all this?

Traditionally, her family. You will also receive copies of pictures taken, developed, and paid for by all the camera-wielding guests you've invited. Once you get your pictures back, you will pay for framing and sending copies to close relatives or whoever else you think might appreciate a print.

Average cost for photos/videos: $908.

FLORISTS

Flowers have probably been a part of weddings for as long as there have been weddings, because for as long as there have been weddings, weddings have served as occasions to celebrate the fertility of life, and there's no more obvious fertility symbol to celebrate with than a flower. A flower is both a beautiful thing grown from seed, like a child, and the sex organs of the plant itself, the male stamens surrounding the female pistil, centered in a corolla of petals, each flower a self-contained microcosm of a wedding ceremony, if you want to be cute about it.

Brides everywhere have decorated themselves with flowers. Roman brides wore wreaths of verbena. Brahmins closed their wedding ceremonies by presenting their guests with flowers sprinkled with sandalwood dust. Chinese brides were carried to their grooms in floral chairs. When Buddhism found its way from China to Japan in the sixth century, it brought with it the practice of decorating the altars of the temple with flowers, which the Japanese developed into an art form called "ikebana," in which flowers are assembled and arranged to represent a harmonic balance between opposites, strong and weak, masculine and feminine, dark and light. We decorate our churches and temples with flowers for nearly the same reasons. In the West, certain flowers have taken on symbolic meanings.

The *rose* is well known as the flower of love, pure and innocent. It wasn't always so. Roses were disfavored by the fathers of the early Christian church, to whom the rose stood for the debauchery of the Roman Empire. The rose was the flower of choice at Roman orgies, worn in wreaths and crowns, petals sprinkled on the tables and floors and beds. The word *subrosa* comes from the practice of not discussing or repeating anything said or done beneath the roses decorating Roman banquet halls. Nero supposedly spent the equivalent of 16 million donkeys on roses for a single banquet, or $4.8 billion, in current U.S. donkeys. In the Middle Ages, an Anglo-Saxon leech named Bald thought you could cure a sore maw by drinking a potion of ground-up roses and black peppers and then sleeping with a fat child on your stomach.

Today a red rose means "I love you," a tea rose means remembrance, a white rose stands for secrecy and silence, and a yellow rose for jealousy. Giving someone a withered white rose says "You made no impression on me." Roses find their way into the majority of wedding ceremonies, in bouquets or boutonnieres.

Iris was the goddess of the rainbow in Greek mythology. She was said to lead the souls of dead women to the Elysian fields, and as a consequence, the iris is the flower often found on the graves of women. Perhaps it's not an appropriate flower for weddings if both of you are of French origin; it's thought that the iris was the flower upon which the French fleur-de-lis is modeled, after King Louis VII saw one in a dream and adopted it as the emblem to lead him into the Second Crusade.

The *lily* has stood for female goodness and purity for thousands of years, originating on the island of Minos, where the lily represented the goddess Britomartis. When Greek culture assimilated Minoan culture, the lily became associated with Hera. It's said that when Zeus wanted to deify his favorite illegitimate son Hercules, he drugged Hera and bade Hercules to suck at Hera's breast. Hercules, being Hercules, didn't know his own strength, got carried away, and ended up spilling drops of Hera's milk all over the place. Those that fell in the sky became the Milky Way, and those that fell to earth became lilies. Later the lily became the symbol of the Virgin Mary. In China it's the emblem for the mother.

Daisy is a contraction of "day's eye." Like many flowers, the daisy was thought to have medicinal powers and was considered useful in the treatment of eye ailments, warts, and insanity. Give a lunatic a daisy and it will keep him occupied for hours. It's a flower commonly used today to determine if someone loves you, as when a young girl plucks the petals one by one, saying, "He loves me, he loves me not . . ." After determining whether or not she's loved, the young girl can then mutilate a second daisy to find out who she's going to marry, reciting, as she plucks, "Rich man, poor man, beggar man, thief." For both these reasons, you may not want daisies at your wedding, should your bride have misgivings or second thoughts and turn to daisies for answers. On the other hand, it's a plain and simple flower, not terribly ostentatious or expensive.

Choosing flowers for your wedding depends primarily on when and where it is, as well as what color scheme you or your bride or your mother-in-law may have in mind. There's no one single traditional wedding flower, though white is obviously the most common color flower used. Myrtle, verbena, ivy, peonies, or stephanotis have been considered wedding flowers in the past, but no one's going to take you to court if you use something different. There are some flowers you definitely do not want to use—those with scents that attract insects by imitating rotting flesh, such as skunk cabbage. Stinking nightshade is not only malodorous but poisonous. Monkshood, daffodils, and poinsettias are also poisonous, and could, if used to decorate a wedding, be mistaken for the edible flowers on the cake. Ragweed is out. The flower of the anthurium is an extremely phallic-looking thing, which would be in keeping with the fertility theme, but may not be appropriate staring at Aunt Henrietta from the centerpiece while she's trying to eat her chicken Kiev.

Traditionally, grooms don't get involved in selecting the flowers, leaving it up to the bride and her mother, since they have to decide what the bridesmaids are going to wear, in order to make the occasion best resemble the *Magic Fairyland of Eternal Wedded Happiness.* Still, a groom who says he doesn't care about the flowers had better be prepared to not care when he's asked to wear a turquoise tuxedo because it matches the color scheme. If you want to be involved, make an appointment to see a florist—more than one, obviously, if you intend to comparison shop. When you agree on a color scheme, look at what kinds of flowers fit it. The florist will tell you which of them are likely to be in season at the time of your wedding. Many flowers can be forced to grow out of season, or shipped up from South America or New Zealand, but if someone insists on having flowers that are out of

FLOWER SYMBOLISM

Other flowers have been assigned symbolic meanings over the years, by poets, Victorian gardening club presidents, and other people without jobs who had time to sit around assigning symbolic meaning to flowers. Some are:

Acorn	Nordic symbol of immortality
Aster	love, daintiness
Bachelor button	single blessedness
Bittersweet	truth
Pink carnation	remembrance
Crocus	cheerfulness
Daffodil	unrequited love
Forsythia	anticipation
Geranium	stupidity
Holly	domestic happiness
Ivy	wedded love
Larkspur	fickleness
Marigold	cruelty, grief, jealousy
Narcissus	egotism
Orange blossom	marriage and fruitfulness
Peony	happy marriage, or gay life
Poppy	sleep, oblivion
Spider flower	"elope with me"
Stephanotis	happiness in marriage
Sweetpea	good-bye
Tulip	good lover
Violet	modesty
Zinnia (white)	goodness

season, you may find yourself paying $3 a sprig in December for lilies of the valley from Brazil, which grow wild in June. If the place where your reception is going to be held doesn't have flower or bud vases for the tables, you might have to rent or buy them. You can't buy flowers directly from cut-flower suppliers to save money, but you might find a local greenhouse cheaper than a florist, but then you'll have to do all the arranging yourself. If you have a large garden, you might be able to grow your own flowers from seed, but depending on the growing season where you live and factors such as rain, drought, pests, or late frosts, you may not have anything ready in time. Once you make the initial arrangements with the florist, you should go back about two weeks before the wedding, when your florist will have a better idea what flowers will be available and what the prices are going to be. It's customary to leave the flowers decorating the church behind, and to give the flowers at the reception to members of the wedding party or to special guests.

Who's going to pay for all this?

According to tradition, the groom and his family pay for the bride's bouquet, the mothers' corsages, and the boutonnieres, whereas the bride's family pays for the church and reception decorations and the bridesmaids' bouquets. Some brides will have two bouquets, one to throw and one to keep.

The average cost is $478.

HAIRDRESSERS

Hairdressers are among the minor Wedding Mafia families, and apply more to the bride and her bridesmaids than to you. Your bride may make an appointment for herself and her attendants to have their hair done sometime shortly before or on the day of the wedding, in order to effect the unified look so key to deceiving evil wishers, as well as to insure that no one shows up looking like Loni Anderson, or

for that matter, looking better than the bride. In the early
sixties, brides and bridesmaids tended to look like Sandra
Dee. By the late sixties and early seventies, brides and their
attendants wanted to look like Cher, though no groom ever
wanted to look like Sonny. In the eighties, brides and their
attendants tended to resemble Barbara Mandrell, with big
hair, full of highlights and curls, hairstyles created with a
"sing heavenly mousse" and devil-take-the-split-ends attitude. Through it all, bridesmaids have been required to wear
frilly strapless taffeta the-Supremes-on-acid/Dixie-whore
dresses that cost a fortune and can't be worn again, often
accessorized with humiliating straw hats. No one knows what
the wedding look in the nineties will be, possibly bridesmaids resembling Robert Palmer's backup band. The groom
is expected to get a haircut, wash and comb his hair before
the wedding, and shut up when anyone mentions how much
the bride and her party spent at the hairdresser's, somewhere
around $50 to $75 each, depending on degree of braiding
and price of styling gel, as set by OPEC.

Who pays for all this?

*Your bride, unless the money comes from a general wedding
fund, in which case you will contribute to defraying expenses.*

THE BAND

Music is a time-honored tradition too. Paleontologists dig-
ging in Africa's Olduvai Gorge, near where Dr. Louis B.
Leakey discovered the oldest known human remains, uncov-
ered a more recent Cro-Magnon burial site where they found,
in the grave of a pair of newlyweds, a stone tablet with
markings carved in it. The tablet baffled scientists until
1987, when one finally realized the markings were in fact a

crude primitive musical score, which, when played upon a modern piano, to the astonishment of the scientific community, turned out note for note to be Paul Stookey's "Wedding Song."

Everyone wants music at a wedding celebration. Popular bands can book as much as a year in advance. The best way to begin looking for one would be to sneak into a lot of weddings and listen, but since you can't do that, the second best way is to ask around. Any band ought to be willing to send you a demo tape and/or a song list, but that won't necessarily tell you what they sound like in performance. You can ask people you know who've recently been married, or people who've recently attended other weddings. You can ask anyone you've already spoken with who is a member of the Wedding Mafia, because many florists or caterers do weddings with the same bands several times during the course of a summer. Photographers know bands because they always end up eating together in the kitchen. You can attend wedding shows and look at the promotional videos the bands at the show run in their booths. You can ask radio DJ's who are hip to the local club scene. You can also ask a club owner, if you know one, to recommend a musician.

Sometimes you can go to the club and actually hear the band you're thinking of hiring, but some groups play nothing but weddings, sometimes three a day on a good day, for more money than club gigs. A well-known wedding band can easily play more than 100 "society gigs" in a year. Because it's so lucrative, many bands are in fact put together solely for the purpose of playing weddings. They are sometimes put together by booking agencies, which often consist of one guy in a grungy smoke-filled office who drives a powder-blue Cadillac and knows all the wrong people. He has the names of 100 musicians in his Rolodex who he can call on a moment's notice, combining anything from a trio to a twenty-piece big band, as need be, often people who've never met or rehearsed or even played together before, who then fake their way through a set list of jazz standards and wedding chestnuts and go home, with the booking agent taking 15 to 20 percent off the top. You can, in some instances, find truly good or even great musicians in wedding bands. In some cases, quality jazz or rock musicians who prefer to work in other more purist forums will form their own generalist combos strictly for receptions and social functions—"rent gigs." You can also find burned-out old geezers and union hacks whose idea of chops is pork or karate.

You might already know of a good band whose music you like, but keep in mind that the requirements of a wedding band are unique, in that no other band is likely to be asked to play a wider range of music, in as great a variety of styles, to satisfy as great a variety of listeners. For this reason jazz elitists disdain playing weddings, because they have to play hard rock, and rock bands disdain them because they have to play jazz, whereas pop bands love them because they get to play both rock and jazz. In an evening, a wedding band can be expected to play a quiet dinner set, then switch to dance music and get progressively more contemporary as the older guests leave. They need to know at least one polka, one Irish tune, one Italian, one Jewish, a fox-trot, a Latin rumba, swing tunes, waltzes, and so on, in addition to big band music, jazz standards, a few classical tunes, rock-and-roll oldies, contemporary Top 40 music, and anything the bride and groom might specifically request.

You can hire any kind of band you want, thinking, "It's our wedding and we want our favorite kind of music," but you also want to have the best possible party you can throw, which means everyone should be involved in the dancing. You might personally want to hear only jazz, and the band might want to play only jazz, but if guests who can't relate to jazz (or agree with Frank Zappa, who said, "Jazz isn't dead—it just smells funny") hear only jazz from the band, they're going to leave early. Guests want to hear songs that mean something to them, songs from their past or from their heritage. There was a wedding where the bride and groom instructed the band to play absolutely no polkas, no matter how many times anybody requested them, even though the parents of one of the newlyweds and most of the guests were Polish. The band complied, until the newlyweds drove away. The band then relented, and the party immediately turned rowdy and fun, once all the polkaholics and polkamaniacs got what they'd come for.

A truly great band will be able to create a truly great party no matter what they play, if they play with skill and, more important, enthusiasm. The first thing to look for is a

NATIONAL ACTS

You *might* be able to get the following bands for the following fees, as estimated by knowledgeable industry insiders.

Queen Ida	$5,000
Asleep at the Wheel	$5,000
Dr. John (with band)	$7,500
Count Basie Orchestra	$7,500
Dizzy Gillespie	$10,000
Mercer Ellington Orchestra	$10,000
Bobby Short	$10,000
George Winston	$12,500
k. d. lang	$12,500
The Neville Bros.	$15,000
Jimmy Cliff	$15,000
Oscar Peterson	$20,000
Fabulous Thunderbirds	$20,000
B. B. King	$25,000
Merle Haggard	$25,000
Randy Travis	$25,000

Wynton Marsalis	$25,000
The Allman Bros.	$30,000
Ella Fitzgerald	$50,000
Frank Sinatra	$100,000 plus respect
Dolly Parton	$100,000 plus awe
Prince	your first child
Michael Jackson	your first male child
The Rolling Stones	no amount of money
The Beatles (reunion)	twice that

We had Elvis at our wedding. An impersonator would have been cheaper, but we wanted the real thing. When we found him, he was up to over 400 pounds, working as a referee at high-school wrestling matches in Attleboro, Massachusetts. The dinner set was a little weak, but once he got cooking in the dance set, we could see why he's still The King.

• •

band that really loves to play weddings, a band that, despite the travel, the cold food served in the kitchen, acoustically dead rooms, dead pianos, and hundreds of live guests all requesting different tunes simultaneously, can still rise to the occasion and see weddings as opportunities to have fun. The best way to make sure you're not hiring deadbeats is to get references from the people who've hired them before.

For an average quality wedding band, you can expect to pay $100 to $200 a person, for four hours of music, either in three long sets or four short ones. Musicians union standards vary, but an hour set, for many, is actually 45 minutes of music and a 15-minute break. They should have their own tuxedos, and not bill you if they have to rent them. You aren't expected to feed them either, but you may offer them a meal if there's enough to go around. They'll be happier and play better if you feed them, and require only a table in the kitchen, unless you want them mingling with the guests and corrupting America's youth. You might arrange with the bartender to give the band a limited number of drinks, but they are, after all, working for you, so it's okay to expect them to behave as if they're at work and not at a party.

The band bears the expense for any equipment they have to rent and for travel costs, unless it's excessive, in which case they may ask for more money. They should own their own PA system and supply tapes to play between sets. If the room you rent has a piano, you can ask the manager to have it tuned before your wedding. All of this should be worked out in advance and put in writing. The band will need time to set up before the wedding and tear down afterward, and are not customarily tipped, although you're free to do so if you wish. You should also go over set lists in advance, and you should make it clear how much participation you want from them. Some wedding bandleaders will think they're in charge of the entire affair unless you tell them otherwise. If you don't want to sing "The Bride Cuts the Cake . . . ," then you should say so in advance. If you have a theme song, or if there are songs you want the band to play that they don't already know, you must give them a list and/or provide charts at least four months in advance.

If you can't afford to hire a band, but really want music at your wedding, you can always hire a DJ. Before you do, you should call a number of DJs (they advertise in the Yellow Pages, or in the music/entertainment section of most newspaper want ads) and compare their prices. Ask what equipment they own (including backup equipment in case of failure), what records they have access to, and how many years they've been doing it. Ask him if he has a tuxedo to wear. Some DJs own their own colored lights, mirror balls, and fog machines, if you want a disco effect, whereas others may rent them and bill you for it. Some might be able to supply a microphone and a menu of popular songs from which the vocal tracks have been removed, with lyric sheets so that you or your guests can sing along. A DJ with a daytime job at a radio station might have access to a larger record collection than one who strictly free-lances, but a radio DJ might also feel obliged to fill the space between songs with snappy patter, which can be more irritating than enjoyable, and should be discussed before paying any deposit. Some DJ agencies have large record or CD libraries, from which, after a consultation with you, they premix tapes for your wedding containing the songs you request in the order you want them, a souvenir that might be fun to listen to, thirty years down the line. A DJ might cost $200 to $300—more if travel is required—for four hours entertainment, and a smaller fee, perhaps $25, for every hour beyond that.

Who's going to pay for all of this?

The band's fee is put on the reception tab, which traditionally is picked up by the bride's family.

Average cost: $882.

FORMAL WEAR

We would be gift wrapped as packages! And come on to one another stylish and spiff, pristine and groomed as the close-order drilled, as hand-in-glove, bespoke and customized, finally, as Goldilocks's just-right bowl and cereal, her chair and her bed, compartmentalized and discreet as wallets, smitten by proportion, scale, and all the tongue-in-groove congruities, by the dress-parade possibilities of a perfect human geometry.

And maybe that's the real meaning of the tuxedo. It corrects nature; it covers up flaw. It's designed, that is, to hide you. Like a sartorial Wite-Out, like a sort of male muumuu; its pleated shirt never looks wrinkled, its studs nail you together, its grosgrain stripes hold you upright, and its cummerbund turns on a dime, tucks hospital corners into your discordant, discrepant fabrics, the gap between your pants and your shirt. It papers you over, it bastes your body, it blind-hems your flesh and turns you seamless . . .

Not just to hide, not just to play the gigs of class or money, or watch the ladies or practice the trends, but, from time to time, to show the flag—of the civil, of the civilized, the secular glad rags and wraps of honor.
—FROM "MY TUXEDO: A MEDITATION," BY STANLEY ELKIN,
CHICAGO MAGAZINE, MAY 1986

You know how you feel in a tux. If someone asks you your name, you're as likely to say, "Bond . . . James Bond," as give your real one. When you wore a tuxedo for high-school prom, not only were you certain you were the swankest cat to ever swill lime vodka, but you were convinced you could pass for royalty, slip into the receiving line at Charles and Diana's charity ball, and not get thrown out. In fact, none of the high-school hangs that ever threw you out before could throw you out when you were wearing a tux. You'd look like you owned the place. Wouldn't dare.

Or if you were ever a groomsman or an usher at someone else's wedding—after the wedding was over, didn't you want to go out, go somewhere, and take advantage of your snappy tux before you had to return it? Drop into some nightclub at the top of a tall building, one of those places that rotate (the restaurant, not the building), lean suavely at the bar and order something only incredibly cool people drink, like a martini and a beer chaser, while all around you, miniskirted women so hip they wouldn't date Lou Reed if he begged them whisper, "Who's the Esquire in the tux? Bond? James Bond?"

A wedding is a show, and you are the star of it, pristine and spiff, groomed and customized. Actually, you're the costar, with second billing, but you'll still be expected to dress like a star. The tuxedo is the great equalizer, able to convert bums into contenders and make an auto mechanic indistinguishable from Henry Ford, a style of dress that is common the world over and hasn't changed much in 100 years. When you put one on, you feel exalted and aggrandized. It's fitting and suitable that you wear a tux to an event that exalts and aggrandizes your life.

The tuxedo was originally a scandalous prank cooked up by a nineteenth-century attention-seeking wise guy named Griswold Lorillard, a tobacco baron who, on October 10, 1886 (the year Liszt died and Ty Cobb was born), showed up at a white-tie ball being held at a country club in Tuxedo Park, NY, wearing a bright red vest and a tailcoat with the tails lopped off. Though Lorillard was considered a show-off and a swell, the fashion caught on because there were so many show-offs and swells back then who didn't know what to wear. Soon the tail-less dinner jacket found itself competing with traditional morning coats or cutaways at formal occasions, advertised in books by Fitzgerald and Thurber, worn on the movie screens by the likes of William Powell and Humphrey Bogart, in cartoons by Tennessee Tuxedo and Chilly Willy. During the gloomy malaise years of the Carter administration, tuxedos fell out of favor in this country, together with smiling or looking forward to anything. Washington parties served punch and were dull, and everyone was supposed to wear cardigan sweaters. In the go-lucky if not happy Reagan era, the tux came back with a vengeance, figures for both sales and rentals rising 50 percent from 1981 to 1985.

Those of us who remember prom in the sixties and early seventies (if we weren't too stoned to remember anything) had no more than a handful of styles to choose from, in a limited palate of black, white, gray, dork blue, goon maroon, or nerd beige. Flower children could rent tuxedos with lacy lapels, velvet piping, and flared bell-bottom pants, outfits now available in secondhand clothing stores and costume shops at bargain-basement prices. If secondhand stores give you polyester shock syndrome, you might want to rent a more contemporary tux from a formal-wear outlet, where you can choose from lines by Pierre Cardin, Bill Blass, Raffinati, Christian Dior, Oscar de la Renta, Lord West, After Six, in more styles than you could wear in a lifetime if you married all the women in Korea one by one.

Taste will inform your choice of what you, your father, your father-in-law, your groomsmen, your ushers, and your ring bearer will wear. Whoever is choosing the color scheme of your wedding will also want to have a say in the matter, but your vote should count the most. Custom may also inform your choice. The Wedding Mafia has designated certain kinds of tuxes to be worn at certain kinds of occasions. Any tuxedo rental store will probably have a chart for you to consult. It will look something like this:

Formal Day: Cutaway coat, striped trousers, waistcoat (vest), stiff white shirt with a collar that chokes you, and gray-and-black-striped four-in-hand or wing collar with ascot, gray gloves, black socks (as if anybody would wear white), and black shoes.

Formal Evening: Black tailcoat and trousers, white vest, wing collar with white bow tie, white gloves, black socks and shoes. You can wear a top hat, but if you do you will be expected to perform magic tricks or ride an elephant.

Semiformal Day: Black or gray stroller coat, striped pants, gray vest, turned-down-collar shirt, gray-and-black-striped tie, gray gloves, and black shoes.

Semiformal Evening: Black or white dinner jacket, tuxedo shirt, black cummerbund, black bow tie, no gloves, and black patent leather shoes.

Informal Daytime: A dark business suit in winter and a light one in summer, or a white linen jacket with white trousers, or a navy blazer with gray trousers. A conservative tie and a clean shirt.

Informal Evening: Tuxedo if the bride wears a dinner dress, or a suit if she's more casual.

California Beach: Shorts, T-shirt, sunglasses, no shoes, white or off-white zinc oxide cream on your nose, Frisbee, grin.

Greenwich Village: Black leather coat, black leather pants, black leather shirt, black leather tie, black leather underwear, black leather gloves, and black leather hat. Red tennis shoes. Hair optional.

You can rent your formal wear for $50 to $90 a person, including accessories, or you may want to consider buying your tux, if you think you'll ever have occasion to wear one again at Academy Award ceremonies or if you expect to become a mortician. A new off-the-rack tuxedo costs between $300 and $600. You can purchase used tuxedos from tuxedo rental stores for half or less what you'd pay for a new one. Obviously, used trendier styles sell for less, once they're out of style. You can also have a tuxedo tailor-made and hand-sewn. Custom-made tuxedos at Brooks Brothers stores start at $645, require two or three fittings, and six to eight weeks. A top-of-the-line men's clothing designer like William Fioravanti, also in New York, will make you a worsted cashmere tux for $3,750, or the cost of a stripped-down Yugo. The tux, of course, will outlast the Yugo. (Do they still make Yugos?)

One argument against formal weddings is that if your wedding is going to be informal, you'll at least get to buy a new suit to be married in. Suits cost about the same as tuxedos, but are a little more practical. If it's a quality suit, it should last you long enough to be buried in as well. It will be your special suit. You will never throw it or give it away. Maybe you'll hang it in a garment bag in the attic and take it out and look at it once in a while, but it will contain memories even when it doesn't contain you. You'll remember the man who sold it to you, a guy who seemed like some powerful captain of industry, a salesman who managed to intimidate you, even though he was only a poor schmo who worked in a clothing store and got to wear any power suit in the store for free. You'll remember why you spent more than you could afford, taking a chance that you'd be able to pay it off later, because it was only right to take a chance on a suit you'd wear to take a bigger chance in. You wanted to look dignified, stand with authority before the world when you spoke your vows. You'll remember putting the ring in your new suit-coat pocket and checking it a hundred times before the ceremony. Stuffing directions to the chapel in your inside coat pocket, even though you knew the way by heart. You'll remember how many people told you how great you looked. You'll remember how great it felt to finally take your coat off at the end of the evening and throw it over the back of a chair at the reception. You'll remember throwing it on the bed in your honeymoon suite, emptying your pockets on the dresser, reading a little tag from your shirt pocket, "Inspected by #19." It will become your lucky suit. Whenever you wear it, your wife will remember when she first saw you in it. If you're lucky, when you wear it as an old man, you'll tell people, "This is the suit I got married in," and hold the fabric out for them to touch, adding, "Doesn't even look worn. They don't make them like they used to."

Who's going to pay for all this?

You pay for your own tuxedo and accessories. You also pay for any gloves, ties, or ascots worn by the groom's party, and if you're going to rent ascots, you might as well rent monocles and top hats too. Your father, your father-in-law, and your groomsmen all pay their own apparel expenses. It will average out to about $75 a man.

CATERERS

At American weddings, the quality of the food is inversely proportional to the social position of the bride and groom.
                                                            —CALVIN TRILLIN

Caterers are among the most powerful members of the Wedding Mafia, and will probably account for your largest single wedding expense. Caterers are powerful because food is a powerful part of any celebration. Food and drink are what your guests are going to be looking forward to, what they get in exchange for the gifts they bring. Wedding ceremonies make people hungry and thirsty. Food is the reward for patience, the way you make a dog sit before you give him a treat. Wedding guests will begin to salivate as the ceremony draws to a close, from sheer Pavlovian conditioning. Food will be the cement that holds your reception together, because food is what people who don't know each other share in order to get to know each other, how strangers communicate in a common language, hamburgers for visitors from China, a western barbecue for anybody visiting Texas. It's why we feed Russian diplomats turkey at state dinners and they feed us caviar, the first tool of both diplomacy and hospitality. It's the first thing people who don't know each other talk about when they have nothing in common, and the second thing wedding guests talk about, "This *fejoada* is delicious, isn't it?" right after "Are you a friend of the bride or the groom?"

To put it another way, food is the most important part of a wedding reception, because if the food blows, the whole thing blows. If it tastes bad, or if you run out, that's what people are going to remember and talk about, and that's what's going to make both you and your bride furious enough to cause a scene, storm into the kitchen and tell the caterer she'll never work at another one of your weddings again.

The wedding feast is, again, a transcultural and historical tradition. The ancient Jews feasted for seven days. The Moors of Fez had three separate feasts, one on the night the bride was brought home, one the next day for the women only, and a third on the seventh day when the bride was said to have become a woman, a transition marked by the groom throwing fish at his wife's feet. The ancient Poles threw wheat, rye, oats, barley, rice, and beans at the doors, then sat down to a banquet at which it was forbidden to eat the flesh of any animal that had been gelded; that night, in the bedchamber, the bride would present the groom with a midnight snack, the testicles of a bear, which he had to eat, while wondering—disconcertedly no doubt—exactly how she acquired them. It's difficult to find any reference to any culture's wedding ceremony that does not involve feasting. Caterers know this, that you need them more than they need you. They know they have the most critical role at your reception, and they know you know they know.

The most important thing in choosing a caterer is to make sure it's someone you feel comfortable with. When you interview her, is she calm or nervous? Are you? Is she too aggressive, or not aggressive enough? Will she let you use the phone without asking if it's a local call? Does she listen to you, or does she do all the talking? You will be delegating more responsibility to her than to anybody else at your wedding, so you'd better feel certain you can communicate clearly.

It may be hard to know who to interview in the first place. Some restaurants or delicatessens cater out, and you can go there and taste the food for yourself, but many caterers don't own or work for restaurants, in which case you usually can't sample the food before ordering 100 or more servings of it. Such caterers depend on word of mouth for their livelihood, each job generating new jobs from guests who like the food. The best way to begin finding a good caterer is to ask anyone you know who attends or hosts a lot of catered affairs. Doctors or lawyers and their wives or husbands are a good place to start. Usually one or two parties will stand out in their memories.

Some caterers will charge a small fee for the first consultation. It might be a good idea to meet where the caterer does her cooking, to eyeball the premises, check the walls

for framed licenses, the windowsills for dead flies, and if one
or more cockroaches start crawling up your leg, terminate
the interview. Bring along a thick pad of legal paper and
take copious notes. You should know your budget before you
walk in the door, exactly how many guests you expect and
exactly what you can spend on them. This exact figure, of
course, is only a starting point, because both your guest list
and your budget are due to expand. The caterer should make
every effort to work within your budget. If she immediately
begins to try to goose it up, you could be in for a ride. Any
good businessperson will try to sell the customer more than
he needs, but a person getting married can be particularly
vulnerable, made to feel a piker for not choosing Norwegian
smoked salmon over the domestic brand, or Budweiser over
Corona, even though Corona is the most overrated beer ever
brewed.

The next thing to talk about is the menu. A wedding
is a bit like a second-grade birthday party, the one day of
the year when your mother let you have anything you wanted
to eat—Hostess Twinkies with chocolate syrup for an appe-
tizer, a bacon and peanut butter pizza for the main course,
and bowls of Marshmallow Fluff for dessert. It's your special
day, and you are entitled to your favorite foods. However,
your wedding is the only time in your life when you're going
to have everybody you know over to dinner simultaneously,
and you'll want to please as many of them as you can. If
your favorite food is liver or pigs' feet, maybe a side dish
will suffice. You should also ask if your caterer has any
specialties.

She should ask you what kinds of guests you expect,
what ages, how formal the wedding is going to be, how big
the room is and what facilities it offers. She should know
what dishes typically fail. If you expect a lot of elderly guests
with dentures, corn on the cob is out. You can't do barbe-
cued ribs at a formal evening wedding because people will
splash barbecue sauce all over their best clothes. You can't

do prime rib in a small room because at a crowded table, guests need elbow room to operate their steak knives. Hot food on a hot summer afternoon gets left at the buffet, as may gaspacho on a rainy day in November. Put fix-'em-yourself tacos on the buffet and the line will move about as fast as a dyslexic down an eye chart. Some dishes are just too exotic for Joe and Jane Wedding Guest, so you might want to pass on trying a traditional Bedouin wedding feast entrée: roasted camel, in which cooked eggs are stuffed into fish, which are stuffed into cooked chickens, which are stuffed into a roasted sheep, which is stuffed into the camel—it's just a little extreme. A compromise must be forged between the food you want, the food you can afford, the food that's possible, and the food the caterer does best.

When you've got a roughed-out menu, with three or four salads, a heated dish, a cold one, breads and relishes and condiments, appetizers and oyster bars and so on, ask what it will cost per person. If the food comes to $20 a person, and you have a $2,000 budget and expect 100 guests, you're golden, right? Wrong. Then you have to ask what extra costs there will be. How many waiters, servers, and cleanup help will the caterer need? What will they cost, per hour, and what will they cost if the party runs into overtime? When will overtime begin? Will the caterer bill you for any extra equipment she needs to rent? If your reception is outdoors, how much of what you need, in place settings, glassware, linens, and so on, can your caterer supply, and how much will she have to rent? Tables, chairs, lights, tent? If you pay the rental fees, will you be charged extra for the time your caterer spends picking up and returning the rented items? If the caterer has a wedding package to offer (buying ingredients in bulk to reduce cost), can you make substitutions? Who will you have to tip? Does the caterer have candelabras or centerpieces you can use? Breakage insurance?

What about liquor? You'll want to estimate for her how

many of your guests drink wine and how many drink beer, figuring a bottle each for every wine drinker and four beers for each beer drinker. What wines does she recommend? Will she supply the hooch? An open bar? A bartender? Brand-name labels or generic whiskey? Champagne, with glasses?

The next thing you'll want to look at are photographs of other banquets the caterer has done. Display is what separates a wedding feast from the buffet table at a Ponderosa Steak House. A knockout spread of cold cuts and salads and meats and vegetables, offset with flowers and attractive serving baskets and bowls, something truly stunning to behold, can make a guest think mediocre food tastes delicious. It doesn't matter whether it really is delicious, or whether your guests only *think* it's delicious, does it?

When you have an idea of what her meals look like, what they cost, and whether or not she's a person you can work with, then ask for references. The most experienced a caterer is, the better, because something new is going to come up at every wedding, even when the caterer works out of a function room or catering hall. The whole interview might take an hour. When you get home, call the references. In total, you should probably interview at least three caterers, and give the second two the same menu you worked out with the first caterer, in order to compare prices. Kosher caterers are listed separately in most phone books. You can pay anywhere from $15 a person for a cheeseboard and wine buffet, on up to $50 or more for a complete sit-down dinner. When you get the final estimate, don't say, "Hey, I could make the same meal for half that," because of course you could. You're paying her to make the meal so you don't have to. You're also paying her for her culinary/organizational/ managerial skills.

When you've decided who to hire, you have to go back and run through everything you ran through the first time. The second time, you must get an *itemized written contract* spelling out exactly what you're getting and what you'll have to pay. You should probably make several photocopies of everything you have in writing, for when you start losing and misplacing things. Make sure the list you have is the same as the list she has, that it says "Deliver 4-tiered 200 serving chocolate hazelnut cake at 4:30 to reception site on June 10th" on both your copies. She can't be responsible for bringing food you didn't ask for, only for the things on her work order.

Who's going to pay for all this?

Traditionally, the bride's parents pay for all reception costs, but because it's the largest single expense, it's probably the cost most often divvied up somehow. You can offer, for example, to pay for the booze, the rental, or for the help.

Average cost: $5,900 (200 guests).

BAKERS

If the wedding esthetic is that of the *Magic Fairyland of Eternal Wedded Happiness,* then the wedding cake is a scale model of the castle where the king and queen of the magic fairyland are going to live. Some cakes still have little plastic figurines of the two of you, standing atop the first tier, rulers of all you survey, ankle deep in it.

The use of cakes in wedding ceremonies goes back at least as far as the Romans, in which the eating of the cake was the most important part of the *confarreato* ceremony. The cake was broken over the bride's head (possibly another reason for veils) and the crumbs eaten by the guests. Both the Iroquois Indians and the Fiji Islanders used cakes in their ceremonies; cake is a symbol of the earth's harvest, made from grain that symbolizes fecundity, and sugar, standing for the sweetness of life. Eighteenth-century English weddings required the cake to be passed through a ring a specified lucky number of times. It's been said that if a young girl puts a piece of wedding cake under her pillow, she'll dream of her future spouse, though more likely, she'll dream of getting her hair stuck in a wad of goo. The Scandinavians make an 18-tiered wedding cake called a *kransekake*, a wreath cake that the bride lifts by grasping it by the top tier. Where it breaks off is said to predict the number of children she'll have.

Today most wedding cakes are three- or four-tiered. The record for the world's tallest cake, wedding or otherwise, was an 83-tiered, 70 foot 4.5-inch cake made by twenty chefs at the Collins Hotel in Melbourne, Australia, in 1987. Yours will be shorter, but no less ostentatious. Old-fashioned concoctions feature a white or yellow cake decorated with white and/or colored frostings sweet enough to give a piano cavities, and are almost as inedible as they are pretty. Modern cakes can be white, chocolate, carrot, angel food, pound, bundt, or anything you want. They may still resort to frosting for sculptural or pictorial effect, but may also decorate, in this health-conscious age, with edible flowers or fresh fruit, eaten in the belief a piece of sugary cake with fruit on it is better for you than a piece of sugary cake without fruit on it, which is something like saying a cigarette is better for you if you eat an apple with it.

Wedding cakes often have to be ordered from someone other than the caterer, though the caterer will probably be happy to recommend somebody or order it for you. The baker you choose will have a photo album containing pictures of cakes he or she has made in the past, to help you select the kind of fairyland castle you want. Wedding cake bakers consider themselves designers rather than bakers—artists—and charge about what Picasso charged for his doodles. Most bakers charge by the slice, about $2.50 per from a commercial baker, which, if you have 300 guests, works out to $750, or about what you paid for your first car. You will also pay extra, in some cases, for the cake top, some sort of plastic or crystal heart-shaped arch or other, which can be wrapped with ribbons and flowers and sells for $20 to $150. The fanciest bakers, who bake for Rockefellers or Du Ponts, and whose cakes truly are works of edible sculpture, adorned with lace and filigree and sugar flowers, cakes shaped like eggs or boats or tennis courts, often codesigned and customized by the bride and groom, can charge $10 or more a slice. A wedding cake with a butter- or shortening-based icing will melt on a hot summer day. Hostess cupcakes are 25 cents each, and they last forever. At any rate, you're not really paying for the raw materials, as much as for the "Ooohh-Aaahh factor," which is where wedding cakes have it all over Hostess cupcakes. The beauty and the grandeur of a well-built wedding cake will symbolize the beauty and grandeur of your marriage, something to think about, as you watch your guests tear your cake apart with their bare hands.

Who's going to pay for all this?

Whoever pays for the reception.

WEDDING CONSULTANTS

Wedding consultants are the *consiglieri* of the Wedding Mafia, underbosses who settle disputes between the various factions and families, subcontract out the work, and make sure the operations of the syndicate run smoothly. They are often people who previously involved themselves in only one aspect of the marital process, baking or floral arrangements, and decided to broaden their services, now basically a one-stop shopping center for all your wedding needs. The wedding consultant will arrange for tuxedos, gowns, caterers, flowers, have demo tapes of bands for you to listen to, book your rooms, possibly serve as a travel agent for your honeymoon needs, and do everything except write thank-you notes for you. You write a single check to the wedding consultant, who reimburses everyone else. Some wedding consultants will supply you with references, or have letters of thanks from previous newlyweds on file for you to read.

The drawback to using a wedding consultant is that it really is important to work with people you like, bands and florists and caterers, not just because things will go more smoothly when you have a personal rapport with someone, but because, after all, who wants disagreeable or weird people at your wedding? Let them have their own weddings. You might get along swell with the wedding consultant, but you might not like the same people your wedding consultant likes, or have an opportunity to meet and screen them beforehand.

Who's going to pay for all this?

The beauty of it is, for a change, the Wedding Mafia pays for it. That is to say, a wedding consultant is paid a percentage off the top from the subcontractors, like a travel agent. A band that tells you over the phone that they charge $800 will still cost you $800, but $100 of that might stay in the consultant's pocket.

TRANSPORTATION

Some newlyweds like the idea of being chauffeured around on their wedding day, and arrange for a limousine, or have one arranged for them as a surprise by their parents. Most limousine services have wedding packages, where, for around $40 an hour, you get a limo, a driver, and a bottle of champagne, usually for four hours. For approximately the same money, you might want to find an exotic car rental agency and rent a Corvette or a Porsche, which you can have for 24 hours and drive yourself.

Who's going to pay for all this?

Bridal party transportation costs are customarily picked up by the bride's family.

Average cost: $201.

BRIDAL REGISTRIES

The Wedding Mafia rakes in $17,982 per first-time bride, a figure comprising the total amount of money spent by first-marriage couples or their families for rings, honeymoon travel and apparel, wedding expenses, home furnishings, and household equipment. That figure does not reflect the full impact of weddings on the economy because it doesn't include money spent on newlyweds for wedding gifts. The cost of an average wedding gift varies from social class to social class, but if you're from an average middle-class family, and your friends are mostly middle class, you might use $50 per gift as a working figure. One hundred guests might bring fifty gifts (no, not each), which means that when you register in stores for gifts, you ostensibly have $2,500 to play with.

The bridal registry is a service stores provide, whereby the marrying couple lists the things they need to begin a household. Either by mention in a printed engagement announcement in the paper, or by word of mouth, the guests are told where the couple is registered. Guests then shop from the list on file at the store, and the items are crossed off as they are purchased, to insure you don't get five bagel toasters. If everything goes according to plan, you'll only end up with three bagel toasters. Registering for gifts is important, because if you don't, and people ask you what you need, and you mutter, "Gee, I don't know . . . a bagel toaster, maybe," then word will spread and you'll end up with ten bagel toasters, not counting the two your bride got at her shower, and you may not be able to return any of them without the receipts. If you say nothing at all, you'll still end up with five bagel toasters, or five espresso machines, or five lemonade pitchers, because there are only so many things you can buy for fifty bucks that are of the standard size and shape of a wedding present, roughly a cubic foot, wrapped in silver paper. In the fifties it was eight-slot bread toasters, fondue pots in the sixties, food processors in the seventies, and coffee machines in the eighties. Fine cutlery transcends the ages.

It used to be that you could only register at a few stores, mainly department stores, for items like china or place settings, but now almost any store that's gone to computers will take your list of gift preferences. You might be able to register through various catalogs, Crate and Barrel, Williams and Sonoma, maybe Victoria's Secret. Wherever you register, you should be both optimistic and conservative, and register for gifts in a wide range of prices to accommodate all your guests. Optimistic but not greedy, because if everything you register for costs $300, people are going to think you're jerks.

The wedding gifts you receive are considered communal property. However, the gifts your bride receives as shower presents are hers, separate assets received before the marriage, even though you're both going to use them. Showers are like stag parties in this regard, both orgies, one carnal and one materialistic. Shower presents comprise the dowry, stuff a bride brings with her to be used in the marriage, as well as the stuff she is entitled to take out of the marriage, should the marriage dissolve. If you register for a microwave, but she gets one for a shower present, remember to cross it off your bridal registry.

Who's going to pay for all this?
Everybody but you.

LEGALITIES

For all the hoopla about romance, a marriage is still a legal arrangement, a contract between two people entering into a lifelong partnership. The laws governing marriage differ from state to state, so you should check with a lawyer in your

area, but in general, there are a number of things for you
to consider, as well as requirements you'll have to meet.

1. *Blood tests.* In some states, you will have to be tested
to make sure you have blood. This is done to prevent clones,
replicants, and aliens from outer space from intermarrying
with humans and taking over the planet. Bloodless marriages
between humans are legal, and develop over time, but the
state tries to insure there's at least a little blood to begin
with.

The presence of blood is also a good indication that
both partners are alive. The ancient Persians believed that
married people were happier in the hereafter than unmarried
persons, and used to hire people to marry any dead relatives
who might have died celibate. In parts of China where ances-
tor worship is practiced, children must marry in order of
birth; it can therefore be necessary to posthumously marry a
dead eldest son, if he died single, to someone else's dead
eldest daughter, if she also died single, as a way of preserving
the order of things, the bride's casket often exhumed and
reinterred beside her new groom. Warring Mongol and Tar-
tar tribes used to marry their dead children to each other to
settle hostilities and create symbolic matrimonial alliances.
Marriage among the dead never really caught on in this
country, although it might not be a bad idea, in that divorce
among the dead is virtually unheard of.

Not only will you be tested for blood, but the blood
itself is tested for venereal diseases, primarily syphilis; in
Illinois, however, blood is also tested for the AIDS virus,
which is why a lot of newlyweds from Illinois drive across
the state line to get their marriage licenses. In North Carolina and Texas, you'll need a physical exam. A normal blood
test elsewhere should cost about $20. You take the test by
giving blood, then visiting your doctor when the results are
in to obtain them. You can still get married if you have
syphilis or AIDS, but if you do, your fiancée has to be
informed. You must take the blood test within a month or

two of the actual wedding. Your doctor knows the prescribed period in your area.

Who's going to pay for all this?

Your bride pays for her blood test, and you pay for yours.

2. *The wedding license.* When you have the results of your blood test, signed by your doctor, bring them in to your local town clerk who verifies that you've been tested and issues you a license. You can't just get a license on your own and walk up to someone in a bar to say, "Marry me, I'm legal"—you usually have to have two names on it, yours and your bride's. Your bride must be over 18 (or have her parents' permission to marry you), not your sister or cousin, and not my wife, or anybody else's wife, nor can you be married to anybody else. People getting married must also be mentally competent, to the extent that you are minimally aware of the fact that you're getting married. For example, the marriage of 87-year-old opera impresario Rudolf Bing to 50-year-old Carroll Douglas was recently annulled by a Manhattan judge, who ruled that Sir Rudolf was suffering from Alzheimer's disease and didn't know he was married. A likely story.

Your bride doesn't have to be a U.S. citizen, but marrying her does not automatically make her one, the way it used to, or confer permanent resident status. Since the Immigration Marriage Fraud Amendment of 1986, a two-year waiting period is required before such status is granted. If one of you is a dual-national already, you'll have to give up one nationality to gain American citizenship. Marrying an alien may grant or entitle you to citizenship in her country, or it may not. Calling the State Department will tell you for certain.

Who's going to pay for all this?

You pay for the marriage license. It will cost about the same as a dog license.

3. *The legal contract.* Marriage is a binding legal contract. Upon entering into it, you will be required to fulfill certain obligations. If you don't, you won't necessarily go to

jail, but your wife will have grounds to void the contract and file for divorce. You have to support her financially. You have to be faithful—in those states where adultery is still against the law. You cannot deny your wife sex without good cause. In some states it might still be on the books that you can be divorced for impotence. You can't be cruel or abusive in any way that causes her physical, mental, or emotional harm. She can divorce you if you desert her, or if you go to jail. In a no-fault divorce, she need only state that the marriage has irretrievably broken down without hope of reconciliation. Furthermore, you are legally obliged to pay her debts if she can't in those cases where you've used joint property to secure a loan, added your name to the title of property she was making payments on before she married you, or where you've established credit cards in both your names. Your wife, of course, has to do all of the above for you, because it's an equal partnership.

Who's going to pay for this?

Everybody pays when the contract is broken.

4. *Financial planning.* Maybe you've been asking yourself, "All I ever thought about before I met my wife was girls—now that I'm marrying, what else is there to think about?" Financial planning. If you're someone who always considered money to be something like a burning house—the faster you run through it, the better—you probably did so knowing that you weren't going to get anybody in trouble but yourself. Miss a payment on your student loan, bounce a check, wreck your credit rating, knock over an armored car, you lived dangerously because you could. When you were single. You can't when you're married. Now if you mess up financially, you're going to get someone else in trouble. Now you have to be responsible with money, save for the future, build equity, invest, divest, reinvest, re-divest, re-reinvest, think about life insurance, IRAs, the gross national product, junk bonds, municipal bonds, tax brackets, and death.

Financial consultants think about these things all day long. They *like* it. They can help you straighten out what you and your wife are going to own together and separately, as well as what you will owe together or separately. Combining lives with someone means combining both assets and liabilities, which may merge completely or partially. You must decide who owns what, or what can be disposed of without mutual consent, and what cannot. A financial consultant can advise you of what the most efficient way to do this is, how to save on your taxes, balance your checkbooks, put money aside, and so on.

Who's going to pay for all this?

Financial consultants work for the same fees as any other investment broker.

5. *Prenuptial agreements.* Marriage is an equal partnership, but the two people entering into it may not always be arriving with equal assets and liabilities. If you and your wife both own businesses, but your crook partner cleaned you out and headed south, leaving your business deep in debt and saddled with liens, you may want a legal prenuptial document to help separate your business from your wife's. If you are a free-lance writer, and you're worried that your wife is only marrying you for your money, you should get in your car, head for the nearest loony bin and turn yourself in, because free-lance writers don't earn big money. On the other hand, if your last name is Rockefeller, and you stand to inherit, say, Vermont, which has always been in your family, and which you want to stay in your family, you may wish to put that in writing, in case your wife divorces you, or you die, and she decides to sell Vermont to Canada. You don't have to be a Rockefeller, and it doesn't have to be Vermont—it can be as small as a 100-acre family farm, or a ring your great-grandmother brought over from Russia.

Most of the time, prenuptial agreements cover only the dispensation of assets upon divorce or death, who gets custody of the children, what their inheritance rights are, or what the rights are if you or your wife have children from a previous marriage. If neither of you has a lot of money, nor stands to inherit any, you probably don't have to worry about such agreements. You can also draw up prenuptial agreements that expire after a certain period, or agreements with terms that change if your situation changes, if you have kids, if your income goes way up or way down, or if hers does. Some prenuptial agreements may stipulate what constitutes grounds for divorce, as well as what any settlement will be.

If you find that unromantic, you might try thinking of it as a kind of living will, anticipating the death of the marriage but not preordaining it. It is, however, probably the worst time to be thinking about such things, when you're both prenuptial and have already been arguing over things as trivial as the wording on your invitations. If you can't agree on *"honour* of your presence," or *"honor* of your presence," how can you expect to agree on division of assets, houses, estates, businesses, or future children?

Who's going to pay for all this?

You and your bride. Each of you hires a lawyer (because it would be unethical for one lawyer to represent you both) and makes a full financial disclosure to that lawyer. You tell them what you have and what you want, and then the lawyers hash it out. Most lawyers will be happy to work for an arm and a leg, per hour, anywhere from $50 to $400. From the time you begin negotiating your prenuptial agreement to the drafting of the final document, it might take 5 to 8 hours, during which time your lawyer will scratch his or her head, scribble illegible notations on yellow legal pads, and say, "Shit—I wish I'd paid attention when this stuff came up in law school." It goes without saying that lawyers who've done a lot of prenuptial agreements will be better at it than those who haven't.

DETAILS

Life is easy, except for the details. As you prepare to combine yourselves, there will be a number of details to attend to.

1. *Will your wife be taking your name?* A woman is under no legal obligation to do so. She may not want to, arguing that the practice of taking the man's name is sexist, implies he owns her, or at least that it signifies and validates marriage as something that changes a woman's status more than it does a man's, the old "honest woman" tag. If she wants to take your name, because her maiden name is difficult to spell, like "Mary Xiphisura," or because her maiden name is sesquipedalian, as in "Sara Sesquipedalianstein," or awkward, as in "Edda Deadfrog," or just because she loves you and doesn't mind, then you will feel honored. If she keeps her maiden name, you should still feel honored that she's marrying you.

You also have the option of hyphenating your names, and subsequently fighting to see who gets to go first. The hyphenation of names has a long tradition in England, where a bride from a hoity-toity family, marrying a man from a hoity-toity family, would splice her name onto his, in order to make the most of their mutual hoity-toititude. If you choose to hyphenate, don't forget that your children will have to spend their whole lives explaining it. Nor should you forget that it's possible your child will fall in love with someone else with a hyphenated name, so that when Marie St. Jacques-Inne marries Klaus deBachs-Hamburger, their names will be Marie and Klaus St. Jacques-Inne-deBachs-Hamburger. You can also fabricate an entirely new portmanteau name, if that seems fairer to you. Mary Bigelow and Jim Butterfield can become Mary and Jim Bigbutt.

You need to know what your names are going to be because you're going to have to fill out a lot of forms.

2. *Where are you going to live?* You'll need to put your new address on your forms as well. If you both own homes,

which one do you sell? If you both rent, who's going to break their lease? Does she move into your groovy bachelor pad, forcing you either to wash or get rid of half your stuff, or do you move into her bachelorette pad, forcing you to wash or get rid of half your stuff? Or do you find a new place altogether? If you're marrying in August, but you live in a college town where all the best apartments become available June 1, do you move in together on June 1, and then try to conceal the fact you've been "living in sin" for two months from your parents or in-laws? And if you move, where are the RSVPs going to go to? Or the wedding gifts that people send early? You'll need boxes—who's going to start collecting all the boxes?

Who's going to pay for all this?

Moving expenses can be paid from your general wedding fund, or you and your bride can each pay them separately.

3. *Joint checking.* The general wedding fund can be created after you know your new names and address, and can then open a joint checking account. This is one of those cute couple things you'll do together, like shopping for rings. You will probably both be keeping your previous checking accounts, so you'll want to choose a check or design you don't already have, on different colored paper. When you fill out the forms, this may be the first time you or your bride sign your new name. It will feel strange, after signing the name you know yourself by all your life. Deposit in the account whatever moneys your parents give you to pay for the festivities. You should each get an ATM card, so that you can both make emergency cash withdrawals, forget to tell each other about them, and completely annihilate your balance in no time at all—which will prompt you to call a financial consultant (see legality #4).

The cost of opening your new account comes out of the money deposited into it.

4. *Insurance.* You'll want to put her name on your insurance policy, and if each of you has a car, she'll want to

put your name on hers, unless one of you has a terrible driving record with consequently high rates to pay, in which case it may be cheaper to sell the bad driver's car to the good driver for a buck, while you're both still single, and insure it as a second vehicle on the less expensive policy. Only your insurance agent can tell you exactly. Though not officially a member of the Wedding Mafia, your insurance agent will still want all the money out of you he can get, and then some. Life insurance. Home equity insurance. If you and your fiancée find yourselves arguing excessively over money, you might inquire about alimony insurance.

You both bear the costs of new insurance, according to your ability to pay.

5. *New IDs.* Once you combine your car insurance, whoever is changing his or her name will want to get a new driver's license. You will have to show your marriage license in order to do so, which means that if you combined your car insurance policies before the wedding, you'll have to go back and change the name on the policy after the wedding.

You each pay separately for whatever new licensing fees you incur.

6. *Health benefits.* You may find it less expensive to combine your health coverage or benefits, especially if one of you is covered by an employer-paid insurance policy that includes spouses, but the other is not. This can mean having all your medical and dental records transferred. It can also mean changing the name on file at the pharmacy for her birth-control prescription. If you feel a major illness coming on, you might want to move up the date of your nuptials, to take advantage of your new coverage.

You each pay for yourselves.

7. *Credit.* You may want to put your wife's name on your credit cards, or yours on hers. However, it's possible that a husband can die and leave his wife without any credit rating at all if she's been using his. When that happens, she may have to reapply for loans or credit cards, and possibly

not get them. She should ask a financial consultant, and think
about establishing or keeping credit accounts of her own.

You should each pay for whatever you charge.

8. *Taxes.* Will you save money filing jointly or separately? If separately, and you're planning a December wedding, would it be wiser to wait until after the first of the
year? Whoever changes their name has to change it with the
Social Security Administration as well.

9. *Miscellaneous.* Are there any other legal complications
to consider? For example, in some states, a married couple
is not allowed to own, together, more than one liquor
license, which can prevent two single bar-owners from
marrying.

10. *Luggage.* If you're going to surprise your bride with
a set of luggage for the honeymoon, you have to know what
name she intends to use before you can monogram it. That
goes for anything else you intend to have monogrammed—
linens, towels, tablecloths, and so on. Monogramming used
to be a big part of combining households, but it's not done
so much anymore.

You buy the luggage.

11. *Tattoos.* As a sign of their undying love, former
New York Jets defensive lineman Mark Gastineau and former
actress/barbarian Brigitte Nielsen supposedly had each other's
name tattooed on their butts. I'll believe it when I see it,
and believe me, I don't want to see it. If you and your bride
intend to engrave your monikers into each other's buttocks,
allow time for the wounds to heal, because you'll want to
sit down at your reception. And under no circumstances
should you show anyone at the reception, no matter how
insistent they get. Unless they're a member of the Wedding
Mafia, in which case, feel free.

Traditionally, the man pays for all tattoos.

The "Wedding Mafia," of course, is just an expression.
A great many men and women in the wedding industry—

possibly the majority of the men and women in the wedding industry—are decent and honest and competent and reliable and give you exactly what you pay for and don't take advantage of you in the least. The image of a mafia, a criminal conspiracy out to grab your precious wedding dollar, is useful only insofar as it makes you cautious, and aware that you are going to see your expenses rise and rise if you're not careful, and rise even if you are careful. It can distress you, make you fight with a woman you love enough to marry, or with her family, or with your own. As anyone in the Wedding Mafia will take you, again and again, the most important thing to remember is to have fun.

Have all the fun you can have. When you sense yourself going sour, make a joke of it, allow yourself to feel you're fighting the Wedding Mafia, a syndicate of evil, seeking to undo you at every turn. It's only a metaphor for all the other pressures and forces, accommodations and compromises, vagaries and vicissitudes, goods and evils you'll face as a married man.

COSTS

Here are the estimated costs you can expect:

Invitation and printing costs	$ 286
Flowers	$ 478
Music for ceremony and for reception	$ 882
Officiant and chapel fees	$ 166
Limousines	$ 201
Attendants' gifts	$ 238
Engagement ring	$ 2,285
Wedding rings	$ 1,004
Rehearsal dinner	$ 501
Bride's wedding dress and veil	$ 963
Apparel for five attendants	$ 745
Bride's mother's apparel	$ 236
Groom's tux (rented)	$ 82
Groom's tux (purchased)	$ 340
Best man's, ushers' suits	$ 333
Reception for 200 guests	$ 5,900
Honeymoon apparel	$ 936
Total	$15,576

In all, first-time marrying couples in this country spend $3.3 billion on rings, $4.5 on honeymoons, $16.4 on the weddings themselves, and $7.8 billion on home furnishings—$32 billion dollars total. The average amount spent on a honeymoon is $3,200; 13.7 percent spend under a thousand, 36 percent spend $1,000 to $2,500, 39.6 percent spend $2,500 to $5,000, and 10.7 percent spend more than $5,000.

All figures in this chapter are from a poll of *Bride's Magazine* readers.

6

ARE WE NOT MEN?

Barker took his beer and the plastic bowl of pretzels, half of them broken, to a table where he sat down to think about marriage. Those who were in the cage wanted out, those outside wanted in. Sometimes Barker saw marriage as an asylum for losers. The best of unions eventually soured. Hadn't even Bennie—all unknowingly—looked regretful at having to go home? And Bennie liked his wife. Think of the man whose ardor has grown cold as a frozen hamburger patty. At other times Barker feared marriage as not sharing—the way you were supposed to feel—but as relinquishing: the right to privacy; the right to leave things on the floor and in the sink, to make lousy decisions, and to go to bed whenever you felt like it—fully clothed, if that's what turned you on; the right to misspend money and sit for hours in a brown study. The minute you were married you gave up your right to act like a rat. On the other hand, that ineffable warmth beneath a woman's skin, the smiles of gratitude it was possible to arouse. Someone to cut the pain of being alone at night, and worse still,

*at Dusk. Dusk was the terrible hour. Once in a while Barker wept
before turning on the lights. He would sit in his livingroom, feeling
it grow darker by the second, testing himself to see how long he
could stand it, the fumes of loneliness invading his room like carbon
monoxide from a faulty stove.*

—FROM *PROFESSOR ROMEO*, BY ANNE BERNAYS

What are your beer and pretzels saying to you? Something similar?

You're alone in a bar. Thinking about everything. The
day is approaching. You thought you gave yourself time, a
long engagement. Time flies when you're juggling time
bombs, riding shotgun on a million small details, monitor-
ing your feelings for signs of weakness, trying to keep your
spirit from flagging while the goons from the Wedding Mafia
do their best to wear you down. The day is approaching,
like a train, on tracks you've tied yourself to. All you can
do is grit your teeth and let it hit you. Everyone says it feels
good to let the train hit you. Every day a response card or
two trickles in, and everyone offers congratulations. They're
happy for you. What do they know?

The news is out. Even the grocery boy knows. Bartenders, gas station attendants, waitresses, traffic cops, people
walking their dogs, passengers in airplanes flying high overhead—they all know, and they all congratulate you. They're
all trying to push you into it. "I'm going, I'm going," you
want to say, "don't push me."

The day is approaching. The day is Mike Tyson, glaring
at you from across the ring. The day is a funnel cloud on
the horizon, headed toward you, civil defense sirens howling
like wolves in the green air, and everyone's down in the
storm cellar but you. The day is the smoke you smell in the
middle of the night, the noise the dog barks at, a prowler's
screwdriver scraping against the front door hinge.

While you count the bubbles in your beer, grab a napkin and write down the names of your heroes. What were

they doing when they were your age? Ten years older? Twenty? Thirty? But you can't plot your life like a novel or plan it like a trip. Too much can change. For better or for worse. Those are the terms you've agreed to.

Take another napkin and draw a picture of your dream house. Add everything you'd add if you had all the money in the world. Helicopter pads, a bowling alley, glass elevators from your cliff-top mansion to the beach below, a sauna, fireplaces in every room, porches all around, a gazebo overlooking a trout stream, a dining hall for all your friends, a master bedroom with a walk-in fireplace on one wall and floor-to-ceiling picture windows opposite. A two-acre garden of home-grown tomatoes. Just draw. When you're done, ask yourself if you remembered to leave any room in your dream house for your wife. You didn't, did you? What would her dream house look like? Do you know her well enough to guess?

REALITY

Order another beer, take out another napkin, and draw the real house you and your bride will occupy after the wedding. Make a list of what you'll have to do. Get a million boxes and start packing. Paint walls. Sand floors. New toilet seat, if you can figure out how to get the old one off. Rent a Bob Vila tape. Pot rack in kitchen. Move refrigerator. Install porch swing. Paper towel rack over sink. New clothes bars in closets. Bookshelves. Call cable TV company. Phone, gas, electric. New water heater. You find yourself getting into it, don't you? You feel tribal about it, a brave hunter building a new mud hut for his woman, a woodsman hand hewing a log home for his missus, a sodbuster building a sod hut for his wife. Nestmaker, carpenter, shelter giver—you like the sound of that.

When you're done with that list, take another napkin

and write down all the things you should do to make not just a *house*, but a *home*. Buy matching towels, plant a garden in the back, make a kitchen breakfast area just like the one she slurped down cereal at when she was a kid, buy a couch big enough for both of you to curl up on, get the nice wooden dish rack she likes, a new rug so her feet won't get cold in the morning. What else? New window shades, her favorite kind. What else? It's hard to think. New bedspread and sheets. A new bath mat. Everything color coordinated and pastel.

When you're done with that list, take another napkin and start list number three—all the things you'll have to do to make not a house, and not a home, but a *life.* If you look at your first two lists, you'll realize all you've thought about are objects. Things you can buy and ways to arrange them. Ways to improve the things you already have. Ways to nail one thing to another thing, or store those things inside that thing, or cover an old thing with a new thing. But no woman ever divorced her husband on the grounds that they didn't have enough things, that the objects weren't arranged properly in the house. You can figure out nest-building, but can you figure out life-making? Meaning what? Giving your wife the intimacy she wants? Learning how to talk to her? How to be generous, and how to let her be generous? How to show your gratitude? How to remember all the things that are important to her, and make them important to you? How not to let your work, your pursuit of money to buy things with, overwhelm your pursuit of *happiness,* which has nothing to do with working for money, unless it's work you'd do for free, and has everything to do with companionship, the warmth beneath a woman's skin, a hand to hold at dusk when the lonelies start creeping up through the floorboards to blow cold on your ankles. It's too confusing. Why not just fix the floorboards?

WHAT YOU NEED

The waitress asks you if you need another beer. You don't need another beer. What you need is a friend, someone to talk to, bullshit with until the fog clears and you can think again. What you need, in fact, is a best man.

If you haven't realized it by now, men need other men to help them make emotional decisions. We pretend it's only women who act in groups and all go to the bathroom together in restaurants, but we're no different, except in the way we deny we need each other, and conceal our need for each other in time-honored codified language and usages.

For example, a boy going through puberty, who wants the answer to some simple question like, "Do girls like sex as much as boys?" would never actually ask a friend if girls like sex, because that would be admitting he doesn't know. Instead, the boy, little Eddie Fournier, now over his heart-breaking love affair with Kathy Barron (see Chapter 3), will say to his friend Jim, "I heard Gail Whetherhill really likes sex," and Jim will say, "Gail Whetherhill makes me sick," and then Eddie will know girls like sex because if they didn't, why would Jim have gotten embarrassed?

In college, Jim and Eddie might join the same fraternity, for more of the same sort of support. Jim will sleep with a lot of girls and get the reputation as a ladies' man, and Eddie will look up to him, even though most of the women Jim slept with and promised to call back think he's scum. They'll both graduate, and then at their five-year high-school reunion, Ed will see Gail Whetherhill again and hardly recognize her, she looks so terrific. They'll date, fall in love, and get engaged, and Ed will ask Jim to be his best man. In the stress of planning the wedding, Ed will worry that the passion is going out of their romance, so he'll go out one night to have a long talk over beers with Jim, who'll tell him not to worry—Gail has liked sex ever since the eighth grade. "Don't you remember," Jim says, "we used to talk about it."

Who says men don't talk to each other? It doesn't matter what you say, as long as you both speak the same code. Sometimes when we're either jogging or drunk, we'll drop the code and speak plain English. Either way, we get what we need out of it. A marrying man needs a best man.

WHO TO CHOOSE

Some people think the tradition of a best man goes back to the days when marriage by capture was practiced. The best man, then, would be whoever you'd most want at your side in a war or conflict. Today he should be the person who knows you the best, knows what mistakes you've made in the past and can point them out to you when you're making them again. Someone, perhaps, who knows most of your ex-girlfriends, and can tell you how and why your fiancée is better than any of them. Someone you trust and can turn to for counsel.

There are other criteria for choosing him.

First, proximity. Maybe your best friend lives too far away to be of any help to you. The best man is going to be someone who should be there at your side, kind of a designated gofer. If he's not available, you're going to have to do everything yourself. It might be wise as well to choose someone who has the time to help you, someone with a nine-to-five job and no kids, rather than a doctor on call to both hospital and family. He should be a reliable person too, somebody who is punctual and doesn't forget things or constantly lock his keys in the car.

He should be tactful and articulate. Tactful because he's the person at the reception who's going to have to deal with any complaints or crises involving the help or the guests. If a guest drinks too much at the reception, the bartender tells the caterer, who tells the best man, who tells the guest, takes his keys, and finds him a ride home. He should be articulate because, at many receptions, the best man gives the first toast.

Finally, you have to ask yourself whether you want someone to help smooth the transition into husbandry, a best man who is himself married, or someone to help you celebrate your last days of bachelorly freedom, a friend who's still single.

THE BEST MAN'S RESPONSIBILITIES

1. To collect money from the other groomsmen and ushers, consult with them, then order and deliver a gift, from them to you. It can be any sort of gift, but in general, it's for you, and not necessarily for your household or your bride, a gift a man would get at a shower if men had showers. Cigars, ammunition, that sort of thing.

2. To coordinate the clothing worn by the groom's party. He should call the men in your party—fathers, groomsmen, ushers, and ring bearer—get all their sizes and make sure the rental store receives that information in time to set aside the proper outfits. If you intend to take off on your honeymoon right from the reception, the best man is supposed to make sure your tux gets returned. He should also return anybody else's tux, if they can't do so themselves.

3. To help you pack for your honeymoon. Normally, of course, your butler does this, while the best man leans against your armoire, smokes a pipe, and says, "I say old chum—Majorca is frightfully cold this time of year—do take an extra ascot." It's silly to have anybody help you pack, but remember—you'll be under pressure. You forget to pack things even when you're not under pressure, don't you? Pack alone for your honeymoon, and you could easily find yourself heading out to sea for a two-week cruise with only your

bride's lingerie to wear. (If you're into cruising in women's underwear, maybe you shouldn't be getting married.)

4. To provide transportation to the ceremony and from the ceremony to the reception. After he helps you get dressed, usually by standing around watching television while you get dressed yourself, it's his responsibility, perhaps his most important responsibility, to make sure you get to the church on time. If you're renting a limo, he rides in the limo with you, saying, "I've got two hundred dollars in my pocket—we could still drive to Florida and become shark fishermen." If you rent a car to take off in with your bride, after the wedding, he's in charge of that. Don't forget that if you're both wearing tuxedos, you can drive as fast as you want, because when you get pulled over for speeding, if you tell the cop you're late for a wedding, he'll let you off with a warning. Maybe. *Almost nothing is as crucial as getting to the church on time,* because if you're late, apart from the emotional strain you will have placed on everyone (including your bride, who'll be wondering if you've left her at the altar), you're going to back up everything else, until the food at the reception is cold, the champagne's warm, and all the help finishes the night on overtime.

5. To stand at your side during the ceremony. He can proceed down the aisle with you, or enter from the side. He's there to prompt you if you go up on your lines, and catch you if you faint. He also has the ring in his pocket. He's at your side, waiting in the anteroom before the ceremony, or riding in the car, because it would simply be too strange for you to be alone. If you were left alone, you'd start talking to yourself: "I'm getting married, I'm getting married." You'll mutter even if he's there, but at least you'll know you're muttering, because he'll tell you.

6. To act as bursar at the reception. When it's time for the Wedding Mafia to collect their cut, you don't want them pestering you for the vigorish, while you're busy being buttonholed by everyone else. Instead, you write out the

proper checks and give the checks to the best man. He pays the clergyman, the band, the caterer, the waiters, and anybody else who needs paying. And again, he intermediates between you and the mafia. If the bartender runs out of club soda, the best man sends someone to get it. If the ring bearer can't find the bathroom, the best man shows him. He's also supposed to be the one who keeps your friends from writing JUST MARRIED all over your car, or from putting BABY ON BOARD signs in the rear window. Half the time, however, he's the one who instigates it.

7. And he's in charge of the stag party.

THE STAG PARTY

Think of it as a descent into hell. Descending into hell is a part of a great many purification rituals, which, when all is said and done, is what a stag party is supposed to be, a journey through the profane toward the sacred. All sorts of characters from story and mythology have descended into hell, from Christ to Orpheus to Hercules. Sometimes it's figurative hell, the soldier who emerges from fierce battle a new man, as in *The Red Badge of Courage*, or the slave girl who endures a life of cruelty to emerge strong and free, like Celie in *The Color Purple*. High-school and college football teams often have intense practice periods called "Hell Week," or "Hell Days," three-a-day workouts in searing August heat, in which an athlete learns where to dig down to find that something extra by being drained of whatever it is he finds more of when he locates the extra amount he didn't know he had. Courage, strength, stupidity, or maybe steroids.

A stag party is a chance for you to touch bottom, to resist the *Seven Stag Temptations*, to publicly debase and humiliate yourself and your entire family, flirt with low-level alcohol poisoning, risk incarceration, and emerge purified and ready for marriage. It's a chance for you to get your yah-yahs out, once and for all. As if yah-yahs come out, once and for all. Yah-yahs actually return faster than rain behind a windshield wiper. You only get your yah-yahs out once and for all symbolically. But, then, it's the thought that counts.

If you don't care about your health or potential chromosome damage, you may agree to let your best man surprise you with a stag party. If you do care, you should sit down with him and give him an idea of the kind of party you want, on a scale of 1 to 10, one being a Mormon Tabernacle Choir potluck, ten being a saturnalia debauched enough to turn Caligula's stomach. A lot will depend on how old you are, just because it's a simple fact an older body cannot do what a younger body can, usually because it did, when it was younger, and it damaged itself doing it. If you were smart when you were young, you would have paced yourself, but you didn't, which is what makes you smart when you're old, knowing your limits and having a vague notion of mortality.

But suppose you're twenty-five years old. You're still young, and you want to have a stag party to remember. You've told your best man that, on a scale of 1 to 10, you want a 7, and you've given him a list of the names and addresses of all the guys you want him to invite. What can you expect?

THE SEVEN STAG TEMPTATIONS

Your best man comes to pick you up at your place. It may be the day before your wedding. If you have your druthers, *it should not be the day before your wedding*, because no bachelor who ever survived his own stag party the day before his wedding has ever said he enjoyed getting married hung over. You want to feel good on your wedding day, not sick. Unfortunately, when the people you want at your stag party are arriving from out of town, and will only be available to get together to act like morons the day before your wedding, you have no choice. Two days before is preferable.

You may be picked up early or late. If early, then you might be headed for a traditional bachelor's dinner, an old-fashioned smoker in which all the men of the merging families—fathers, grandfathers, uncles, and cousins—gather for a sit-down meal, usually hosted by the groom's father, with cigars and toasts and speeches and mildly risqué jokes, rating a 3 or 4 on the Stag Scale. You will be expected to make a formal toast at your bachelor dinner, something like, "To my bride, the luckiest woman on earth . . . because she's marrying the luckiest man" (remember, her father is listening), and in general comport yourself with dignity. If your best man picks you up late, it will probably be a stag party with friends and people your own age there, in which case dignity becomes less important. On your way to the party, your best man will say, "I hope everything goes okay—the guy said the donkey hasn't eaten in days," or, "You're not allergic to penicillin, are you?" He is trying to scare you, which is the *First Stag Temptation*: the temptation to call it off and go see a movie, disappoint your friends, and betray the entire spirit of the occasion. Staying true to the spirit of the evening indicates you can be true to the spirit of a rite of passage, and will therefore be true to the spirit of your wedding.

When you get to the party, either at someone's house or in the hotel room of an out-of-town guest (no cleanup), you will be greeted with the Stag Welcome, whereby the guests at the party say your name loudly and curse, as in, "Eddie, you asshole," or "Fournier, you stupid sonofabitch." You may be hailed as well by the Stag Salute, whereby someone lifts a beer in your direction and belches. By cursing and acting macho from the get-go, everyone has proven they're not . . . you know . . . vegetarians . . . and then you can get on with the festivities.

The festivities, for the main part, involve imbibing oceans of alcoholic beverages, accompanied by boozing and occasionally heavy drinking. The descendants of the ancient Babylonians drank something called "raki" at prenuptial celebrations, then stuck coins to the groom's forehead. The ancient Norwegians drank ale, probably on Thursday night, "Thor's Day" being a pagan day on which no Christian ceremonies were performed. Drinking is a stag party tradition. Drinking to excess should not be, but sometimes a groom's friends don't think they've done their duty unless they've forced at least a quart of whiskey down his throat and left him in a pool of vomit, listening for trains on the bathroom floor.

The *Second Stag Temptation*, as you descend into hell, is to drink too much. You want to have fun, and let go a little. All the same, the occasion is a coming-of-age rite, during which you are expected to show maturity, and it's a clear sign of immaturity to think it's macho to drink a lot. You never saw John Wayne wrestling with porcelain. Needless to say, but worth saying anyway, you can't let anyone drive home drunk, and should arrange with your best man beforehand for designated drivers, cabs, or a bus. If you or anyone in your party is arrested for drunk driving, that's all anybody will remember about the wedding, and you could do a *lot* worse, driving drunk, than just getting arrested.

Lubrication is required, because you're all going to feel the need to be prepared to say honest, emotional, intimate things to one another, in which case you have to be loaded so you can say later you didn't mean it. The floor for the discussion of feelings and intimate emotions opens when your friends start insulting your bride, their way of telling you how much they like her. "I think I saw your fiancée yesterday on the back of a Harley with her arms around a guy who looked like David Crosby." Or, "I remember when I dated

Gail in college—all she wanted to do was go back to my place and do the dishes. She kept telling me how much she wanted to get into my pans." Or, "How tall is she when she stands up on her hind legs?"

This is the *Third Stag Temptation*: to betray your bride to your friends. Your loyalty is being tested, your friends trying to get you to choose between her and them. They are also trying to see if you're still man enough to show your independence from women, not that anybody present really wants to be independent from women, just that, you know, you could be if you had to be. You must show tact in how you reply, careful not to betray your bride, while still showing affection for your friends. The proper replies to the preceding questions are: (1) "That wasn't Gail on that Harley, it was your mother—but it was David Crosby"; (2) "That's funny—she doesn't remember dating you"; and (3) "Go fuck yourself."

The *Fourth Stag Temptation*, which usually occurs further on into the drinking, comes when you are asked to represent yourself as a chauvinist pig. It's just us guys, right? In a sense, the stag party is a modern version of the victory party a groom and his mates had after successfully capturing a bride. It's a man's world, isn't it? Men have always captured brides, held dominance over them, haven't they? Sometimes the capture was or is simulated. In other cases, there was nothing symbolic about it. Among the ancient Assyrians, young women were gathered together in the marketplace and auctioned off like slaves by the public crier, the large sums brought by the prettiest girls divvied up and given, in part, to the ugly ones, to make them more marriageable. In czarist Russia, after the ceremony, the bride was conducted to the bedchamber by old women, who urged her to be gentle and obedient, followed by the groom and his groomsmen. The groom would order his new wife to pull off his boots. In one boot would be a trinket, and in the other, a whip. The bride got to enjoy whichever she discovered. In some cases, brides would present their new husbands with whips they'd made themselves, as a token of submission.

You don't have to be overly sensitive to see what's wrong with this picture. Yet it's true that to a degree, a part of male bonding still involves slamming women, us versus them, one groups's strength coming unavoidably at the expense of the other. Male self-interest now pays lip service to the women's movement, as indicated by the polls taken of modern men who are asked what they're looking for in a wife, where greed has replaced the desire to dominate, men wanting, "Someone with a healthy income," a modern superwoman, over the traditional compliant female to raise our children and cook our dinner. We blame women for our troubles, as much or more than we blame our bosses or our fathers (they can't very well expect us to blame our*selves*), and find companionship in commiseration, as much as women ever find company in pissing and moaning about us. That's fine.

Even so, you should avoid the temptation to surpass commiseration and cross into sexist blather, if only because it's not appropriate to the occasion. Or rather, the occasion of a stag party is exactly when you're supposed to be thinking about how you feel about women—usually you miss them and wish there were some at your party—and since you're getting married to one, the fourth temptation challenges you to defend them. You shouldn't say anything you couldn't repeat to your bride. You'll feel as though she's looking over your shoulder anyway.

The *Fifth Stag Temptation* involves money, some form of gambling in which both your luck and your fiscal responsibility are put on trial. Craps is sometimes played, although poker is the game of choice. In poker, you will be forced to think under pressure, read the subtle nuances in your opponents' expressions, complete exacting mathematical equations under the influence of alcohol, and show yourself willing to risk everything on a flop of a card, a sign that you are ready to risk everything in the wedding ceremony. Under no circumstances, however, should you risk the money you need to pay for the wedding or the honeymoon. You'll probably feel that, because it's your bachelor party, you're going to be lucky, that the cards owe you and you're supposed to win, but remember—the cards are part of the universe, and the universe doesn't care. Trying to find a lesson in whether you win or lose, as if a successful night were a sign that your marriage will be successful too, is not going to help you, either at cards or love, even though you'll be looking for signs. If you really want to enjoy the poker game, you might bring in a deck of pornographic playing cards, not because it's fun to play with dirty cards, but because in many cases you can tell who has the aces, just from reading the expressions on their faces.

The *Sixth Stag Temptation* involves the flesh, the traditional part of the bachelor party where risqué or bawdy entertainment is provided. Titillating entertainment is furnished, in theory: (1) to get the groom aroused so that he'll be ready for his wedding night; (2) to demonstrate to him what he's supposed to do on his wedding night, if he's a virgin and doesn't know; (3) to provide him with cheap casual meaningless sex, if he's not a virgin, on this, his last night to avail himself of cheap meaningless sex and get away with it; or in general (4) to demonstrate his virility in front of his peers, by his reaction to the entertainment, and thus demonstrate to them that he's ready for marriage. In theory.

There are, of course, varying levels of bawdiness, and various forms of entertainment to choose from. This is something you should discuss in specific detail with your best man. Every man has a notion of what's arousing to him, and of what's disgusting to him, and a gray area in between where the taboos are not so absolute. Some people might find taped highlights of past Miss America Pageant evening-gown competitions exciting. Others would not. Some best men think it's their duty to find what's disgusting to you and then show it to you, as a way of embarrassing you. It's probably safe to say that every level and act of human or subhuman depravity has been put on videotape by now, and can be bought or rented if you look hard enough. It's the nature of taboo and human curiosity to peek one step past what you can stomach, test yourself by saying, okay, I'll watch two minutes of the Swimsuit Competition. At a stag party, if it gets carried away, you can end up with guests more nauseated than invigorated.

Triple X-rated videotapes are the easiest form of entertainment to obtain, sometimes as close as the nearest 24-hour Stop & Rob. It's hard to know what to expect when you're shopping for them, because you usually can't tell from the cover. Some purport to have a legitimate story line requiring actual acting skills from the people on film, who invariably possess none, nor would it help the story line if they did. Some show men and women who enjoy having sex engaged in pleasurable acts by mutual consent, whereas others contain violence and cruelty, which can be sickening. In the video age, where cameras are inexpensive and rental outlets are everywhere, Triple X movies have proliferated, sometimes made by anyone with a camcorder and a few friends who somehow don't seem to mind airing it out in public or on tape, presumably people with deceased parents. A movie made on the more expensive 35mm film might have better production values than a cheaper movie made on video, if you're into production values. At any rate, you can't tell from the package, because every skin flick on the shelf will have a seal on the box claiming to have earned HUSTLER MAGAZINE'S HIGHEST XXX RATING!!! Guidebooks to Triple X-rated films are available with, believe it or not, plot summaries ("A guy walks into a room and has a lot of sex") and content indexes. A Triple-X video in the VCR and a bunch of guys sitting around watching television and drinking beer make for a lovely evening, but then it's almost obligatory, and helps drive home one of the hidden lessons of stag parties—that parties, like life, are more fun when there are women present. Now that XXX-rated videos have become so widely available, there's nothing particularly novel about watching them anymore. Videos can also ruin a good poker game, when at the sound of somebody moaning from the TV, players put down their cards and run into the next room to see what the noise is all about, instead of paying attention to the deal.

The alternative is live entertainment, anything from ballet dancers to belly dancers to ecdysiasts. Under the best circumstances, you get entertainers who share a genuine pride in the human body and a love of the expressive possibilities of motion. In the worst circumstances, you get fat babes hopping around buck naked.

If you want ballet dancers at your stag party, you're probably going to have to go to the ballet, whereas belly dancers will come to your house. Depending on how far they have to travel or how experienced they are, a belly dancer will cost from $100 on up for a single performance, which can last 10 to 45 minutes. The dance form is more than 5,000 years old, and so are some of the dancers. In the Middle East, most of the best dancers are over forty, because it takes years of practice to learn the muscle control required of a true professional, who will perform "isolations," where a single muscle pulses while those around it remain still. Belly dancers will perform "The Dance of the Seven Veils," but none will perform "The Dance of the Whole Shootin' Match." For that, you need strippers.

The stag party at the strip joint is a classic American image, the kind of thing Norman Rockwell would have painted if he'd lived in the real world. You sit up front, right on the ramp, drink and holler and tuck dollar bills in the dancers' garter belts until the bouncer throws you out for asking the dancer if she can change a twenty. You can enjoy the show and defy authority at the same time. Stag party members in a strip joint can be easily identified, because they're usually the only members of the audience who smile. The businessman with his tie loosened, the old Chinese guy still in his chef's uniform, the slick at the bar in the polyester shirt, the table where the last three guys in America still wearing Elvis sideburns nurse bottles of Miller—everyone else sits stone-faced and silent, eyes open but draining the battery, like a parked car with the headlights left on.

In addition to traditional ecdysiasts, you can also choose from mud wrestlers, oil or Jell-O wrestlers, nude female boxers, midget tossing, or midget bowling (the midget is placed on a skateboard and rolled toward a set of pins).

You can also hire strippers to come to your house for a private show. Exotic dancers usually work out of booking agencies. A feature act might put on a one-hour show involving twenty minutes of dancing and forty minutes of mingling and teasing the groom, for about $300. Dancers arrive accompanied by their managers. Hiring a stripper for a private show is not the same thing as hiring a prostitute, but many men confuse the two.

It still happens that stag parties sometimes engage the services of prostitutes. You might think, since three-fourths of the female characters you see on TV are hookers, that prostitution is more common than it is, or that, inferring from rumor and hearsay, the majority of stag parties involve prostitutes. As an average college-educated middle-class American male, I've never personally heard of a stag party involving prostitutes, and don't know anybody who's had one or been to one. It probably happens, but it would be wicked stupid to take the chance, given the diseases you'd put yourself at risk of contracting. It could be more than a little awkward, should someone think it funny to surprise you with such a party, when you don't want them to. It could be dangerous to your health, and to your marriage, should your bride find out, and she will. It's also illegal.

A few years ago, a state legislator in Iowa was busted at a stag party thrown by lobbyists on behalf of a fellow politician, in a strip joint hired for the evening, for receiving oral sex from a prostitute on a tabletop, evidently unaware that among those in attendance were two newspaper reporters. I'm not sure, but I think he was busted for failing to report a campaign donation worth more than fifty dollars.

Whatever the form of sexually stimulating diversion, and whatever the theoretical reason behind it—to get you ready, to teach you, to demonstrate your virility—in practice, it serves a somewhat more noble ritualistic purpose. Despite what you've heard about hookers at stag parties, for the most part, at least in an ostensibly monogamous society such as ours, when the groom is offered sex at a stag party, temptation in its purest and perhaps oldest form, *he is supposed to refuse it.* Smile and say thanks but no thanks, publicly swearing off such behavior, in front of his friends, and thereby demonstrating himself ready for marriage. For all the stories about grooms at stag parties getting laid, when you stop to think about it, how many of those stories can you believe? What kind of person would do that? How many guys would really sleep with prostitutes, the day before their weddings?

Don't miss the symbolism. The temptation to become impure is offered. You refuse it. Instant purification. Which may not be as hip as instant gratification, but in this case, it's a lot more apropos.

THE LAST TEMPTATION

As the evening draws to a close, after you've done the Stag Dance and all taken the Stag Oath (neither of which I can go into here, because there may be women reading this), and after everyone has told all the embarrassing stories about you they know, smoked their cigars, rewound the videotapes, and ground the last cheese curl into the carpeting, it's time to gather a second wind and go get something to eat. Males, after all, haven't really bonded until they've gone on some sort of public rampage in which mob rule subsumes individuality and the identity of the group is affirmed. Any all-night diner or pancake house will do. Whoever won the most at poker should buy food for whoever lost the most. Somebody has to put a french fry up his nose. Somebody has to try to put a french fry up somebody else's nose. Somebody has to tell the waitress if she ever needs a place to sleep he'll be happy to make her a pallet on his face, and somebody else has to apologize to her and tell her it's a bachelor party. Someone should unscrew the cap on the salt shaker so that somebody else dumps a half a cup of pure sodium on his burger. Wrappers should be blown off straws whenever possible. Someone should take a straw and make his Coke bubble, while someone else engages a nearby table in loud and preferably obnoxious conversation.

You know the scene. In fact, you know it too well, almost have a sense of déjà vu about it all. When you realize what's so familiar, you will confront the *Seventh Stag Temptation*, the desire to go back in time and be eight years old again, because as it draws to a close, after the posturing and the videotapes and the adult games are over, you'll realize a stag party is just a third-grade birthday party with beer. It will feel, for a moment, like a gathering from a far simpler time, when the only relationship you had to think about was with your dog, and the only games to play were baseball and football. You might look around the restaurant and try to remember the last time you had a party with all your friends, and all your friends were guys. Birthday parties. Food fights. Bowling.

You wouldn't really go back in time, and couldn't if you wanted to, but you might be able to pretend for a while, at the end of a stag party, remembering prolonged sunsets during daylight saving time, endless summer afternoons when everything buzzed, from the insects to the electric wires, and a can of soda was only a quarter. Shopping for new school clothes every September. Almost getting caught shoplifting at the mall. Sneaking into the movies. Talking in the cafeteria about some cool new TV show you saw. Arguing with your friends about whether or not a lion could beat a tiger in a fight. The days when you ran in a pack, knew all the secret places in the neighborhood, and could kill an hour just throwing stones at a stop sign.

When you've waxed nostalgic all over everybody's hamburgers, and can't keep your eyes open any longer, it's time to pay up and leave. You'll say good-bye to everyone in the parking lot, and tell them you'll see them at the show. They will take their leave by giving you the Stag Handshake, which is just like any ordinary handshake, except it lasts a split second longer, and there may be an extra foot-pound of pressure to it, or an additional squeeze at the end, some way of telling you this time, they mean it when they say congratulations. You'll drive home, waxing nostalgic, off and on, and if your friends have kept you up late, you might even get a good night's sleep, something that can be harder and harder to come by as the wedding day nears.

Who's going to pay for all this?

They do. You may contribute to defraying expenses if you choose to, but it's supposed to be a party thrown for you, by your friends.

7

LAST DETAILS

W*hen I came to myself I was bewildered and exhausted. The white light of the corridor shone in the polished floor. I was not among the immortals, not yet. I was still, as ever, on this side of the riddle of suffering, of wolf-men and torturing complexities. I had found no happy spot, no endurable resting place. There must be an end of it.*

—FROM *STEPPENWOLF*, BY HERMANN HESSE

Having a best man to help you do things like pick up the tickets from the travel agency or shop for ascots will take some of the load off your shoulders, but there's still a lot you can't delegate. There may be several meet-the-new-in-laws' parties you'll have to attend, and you can't very well send your best man in your place, because the new in-laws are going to be at the wedding too, and they'll know you've pulled a switch. You must, in the month before the wedding, attend to the following final arrangements.

RECEPTION SITE

Check again with the reception site to make sure they didn't hire somebody new who mistakenly double-booked the hall for the day of your wedding. Check to make sure the place hasn't blown up, burned down, or gone out of business. Check for road construction, chemical leaks, and termite infestation.

CEREMONY SITE

Check with the ceremony site for all of the above. You should also double-check the reservations you made for the rehearsal, which usually takes place the night before the wedding.

REHEARSAL RESERVATIONS

Finalize whatever plans you have for a rehearsal dinner. Make the reservations and make sure everyone invited knows where it is.

CATERER

Give the caterer your final guest list. When you send out your invitations, you should have requested that all RSVPs be returned to you at least a month before the wedding, but some people will forget, so you may have to call them. With a finalized list, you'll be able to get exact costs from the caterer. When you do, now that you have a better idea what the budget is going to be, you might be able to make substitutions on the menu—salmon, when you thought you could only afford whitefish, a better wine perhaps. When you know exactly how many guests you'll be having, you should probably visit the reception site, with the caterer, eyeball the room, figure out where the tables are going to be, and make a list of what you'll have to rent. If you're using a catering hall, you may only have to choose napkin colors and order from the menu.

LIQUOR

If you are ordering the beer, wine, or liquors yourself, you'll have to place your order with a liquor store. Your choice of wine will depend on the food. The caterer will offer her own suggestions, as will the wine expert at the liquor store. Some liquor stores order large quantities of wedding wines, and can give a discount for bulk orders. Some will deliver for free, or charge extra if the delivery is not in the area. You might want to order wines with a particular theme in mind. If your bride is French and you're from California, you could both order wines from your home regions. Some marrying couples choose wines with the same vintage as the year of their births; 1958, 1961, 1962, 1964, and 1966 were good years for Bordeaux, 1958–1961, 1964, and 1966 for California wines. Kosher wines once consisted basically of fermented cough syrups and Welch's grape drink that had turned, but now offer almost as wide a selection as nonkosher wines. The guy to watch out for is the beverage manager at a Wedding Mafia–owned function room, a man who has a basement full of bad Chianti he'll try to foist on you at a 300 percent markup, but because you're nice people, he'll knock off 50 cents a bottle. Be cautious around any wine merchant or potables vendor who tries to talk you up by making you feel cheap, but still order at least a case or two of your favorite wine or beer.

FLORIST

Check with the florist to finalize the decorations. Ask if any new flowers are available. Get the prices, itemized and totaled, in writing, and ask if they'll deliver. If not, you'll have to find someone to pick them up. They'll have to know when to pick them up, where to take them, and exactly what to do with them. Check too to make sure all the boutonnieres and bouquets have been ordered and properly recorded.

RINGS

Pick up the rings. Make sure the engraving is correctly spelled, with enough time to spare that it can be corrected if it isn't. If you're getting married in a suit, put the rings in your suit-coat pocket and hang the suit in the closet. Check the pocket every day to make sure the rings haven't disintegrated or vanished.

CLOTHING

If you are wearing a suit you've purchased new, make sure the final fitting leaves enough time to retailor any mistakes, or in time to let it out, if you've gained 100 pounds since the first fitting. (You'll probably gain weight before the ceremony.) Everything you're going to wear should be clean and pressed and hanging in the closet beside your suit.

GIFTS

You need to buy a gift for your best man, as well as smaller gifts for the groomsmen and ushers. The gift for the best man can be personal, a new fishing reel or a picture frame with a photograph of the two of you in it, taken on some trip you took together. The groomsmen's gifts are more general, something everybody can use, and something that will last a lifetime, to serve as a souvenir—wool scarves, tiepins, pen sets, that sort of thing. Such gifts are usually presented at the rehearsal dinner.

GIFTS FOR THE BRIDE

You should buy your bride a gift as well, maybe something she can use on the honeymoon, and something she's not going to get at any of her showers or as a wedding present.

GIFTS YOU RECEIVE

You are entitled to open wedding presents as soon as you receive them. They'll start to trickle in a month or more before the show. Many will be brought to the reception, even though guests aren't supposed to do so. You must keep scrupulous lists of who gives what, and you'd be smart to write thank-you notes for gifts as you receive them. The gifts that arrive early are the ones you'll be most likely to lose track of. Even if you write it down, you'll forget where you put what you wrote it down on. There's nothing you can do about it, other than slow down and try to effect a degree of redundancy in your planning, you and your bride checking each other's work as often as possible. Carefully tape all cards to the boxes they arrive in.

TIME OUT

As you check each other's work, you'll become testy and snappish. Set aside an hour each day during which the wedding cannot be discussed. If necessary, take an entire weekend off to drive in the country and talk about anything other than the wedding.

PHOTOGRAPHER

Give the photographer a finalized itinerary of the wedding day and add to or subtract from the list of special pictures you'll want him to take, depending on what guests you know are or aren't coming.

ACCOMMODATIONS

Make a list of the nearby hotels and motels, together with their phone numbers and prices. You should, in fact, have sent a copy of this list to anyone coming in from out of town, along with the invitations, because some will want to book rooms well in advance. You'll still need extra lists, for when guests phone and ask you to recommend lodging.

TRANSPORTATION

Make a list as well of rental-car agencies. Know the names and phone numbers of five different ways to arrange transportation from the airport to your town or to where your guests are staying. You aren't expected to pick up anybody at the airport, but you might want to offer.

WEDDING ANNOUNCEMENTS

If you're sending out wedding announcements, have them stamped and addressed and ready to mail on your wedding day.

SEATING ARRANGEMENTS

If you plan to have a head table at the reception, you'll want to go over seating arrangements with your bride. In some cases, you'll need assigned seating for all your guests. Remember that all the people you've ever wanted to meet each other actually can. The guy you knew in Tucson can meet the woman you worked with in Portland, two people you always thought would hit it off if only they could meet. Assigned seating can make it happen. You and your bride will probably have an argument or two, working out the seating arrangements, particularly when one or more parent is divorced and/or hates the other. Your father's present and former wives should not have to stare at or talk to one another if they don't want to. Better to have any ugly disputes settled in the planning stage than at the reception itself.

Generally the parents, the clergyman who performed the ceremony, and his or her spouse, and any grandparents or close relatives who will fit, should sit at the parents' table. The bride and groom, best man, maid of honor, their spouses or dates, and all attendants male or female, sit at the bride and groom's table. You can have separate tables for her parents and your parents, but this might look like they don't get along. When the plan is agreed upon, you should write the names on placecards (or have a calligrapher do so), label and number the cards, and give the cards and the seating plan to the caterer, who will screw everything up by seating your new wife next to your old girlfriend, putting teenagers at the same table as old people, and having your partially deaf grandmother by the kitchen door where she won't hear anything.

BABY-SITTING

If, from your finalized guest list, you can tell there's going to be a lot of small children or infants present, you should consider having a playroom handy, a cloakroom or empty storage room off the banquet hall, with toys and a baby-sitter or two on hand, as well as beds or soft places to put kids down if they get sleepy. Friends with children will be able to stay longer and be grateful to be relieved of parenting duties. To find a baby-sitter who brings along her own play-room full of toys, call local day-care centers. You should be able to make some arrangement for under $100 for the whole evening.

THIEVES

You'll need a place at the reception for guests to leave presents. You may also want to arrange for a groomsman or brother of the bride to guard the presents from thieves who actually show up at weddings dressed like guests and cart the booty away. The same person may be in charge of loading the presents in a car at the end of the evening and bringing them back to your house. That person should have a roll of Scotch tape with which to tape all cards to the packages they belong to, to avoid having to wonder later who gave what, when the cards get loose or mixed up.

MORE THIEVES

You should arrange for somebody to watch your house during the ceremony and reception. Thieves also check the paper, read the wedding announcements to see exactly who is going to be absent when, and clean out the house while you're partying. If you're going away on a honeymoon, you'll also have to arrange for a house-sitter to water plants, feed the dog, and watch the loot.

GUEST BOOK

You should designate someone to sit by the guest book and make sure everybody signs it, or have several people to alternate, since it's a pretty boring job.

PAPERWORK

You should double-check to make sure the blood tests and your marriage license are in order. The marriage license goes in your suitcoat pocket, along with the ring. If you're wearing a tuxedo, put everything you can't get married without—license, rings, honeymoon papers, along with the pickup slip from the tuxedo rental store—in a steel box, and put the box in your top dresser drawer. Put the dresser on top of your bed, so you don't forget where it is, and then the night before your wedding, sleep on the couch.

THE BAND

You should check in with the band to make sure they haven't broken up or been arrested. If you hired a six-piece band at $100 a man, and the sax player quit, make sure you know in advance not to write your best man a check for $60. Make sure the band has learned any special songs you've requested, and that they know where to set up. The place where the band sets up is determined after the caterer knows where the tables go.

YOUR HOUSE

If people are going to be coming over to your house, be sure to clean the place as thoroughly as possible. This won't be hard, because in the week before the wedding, unless you have the serenity of a Zen monk, you will wake up several times during the night, and not be able to get back to sleep, leaving you plenty of time to clean. Since people are coming over, you should stock your refrigerator with whatever you give people when they visit. Keep hi-fat milk on hand, to put in a pan on the stove and drink warm, if you need help in getting back to sleep. On the other hand, if you're moving into a new house after the wedding, you will want to be completely packed.

YOUR TEETH

Have your teeth cleaned.

YOUR CAR

Change the oil, spark plugs, and windshield wipers on your car. Tune the engine and have the brakes checked, as well as the tires and anything else that could fail. If you're driving your own car, you'll want it to be able to take you to the church, and if you're taking it on the honeymoon, it has to be ready to go farther than that. After the reception, you will be exhausted, and driving even a short distance on a straight road may be taxing. You don't want either mechanical failure or pilot error to cause an accident. You should do the same for your bride's car, so you can loan it in case someone from out of town needs to borrow an emergency vehicle.

YOUR MIND

You should do relaxation exercises daily, breathing deeply, learning to calm yourself down. If you exercise, you should strive to maintain your normal regimen. Both you and your wife will want to look fit and trim for your nuptials. There is, in fact, a great likelihood that neither of you will ever weigh as little again.

YOUR WORK

You might even be so bold as to try to get some of your own work done. It's next to impossible, but you can still try. If you work for yourself, you can give yourself time off. If you have an understanding boss, you're in luck. If you have a boss who's not understanding, you're out of luck. It's frustrating to find yourself unable to work, at the same time as you find your bank accounts inexorably dwindling while you write check after check to hundreds of Wedding Mafia collectors with their hands out every day. Don't schedule major projects for the months preceding or following your wedding. You won't be up to it.

YOUR HONEYMOON

If you're going to leave on a honeymoon directly following the reception, have all your reservations in place and con-

STRESS

You've been told by someone already married that planning a wedding can be stressful, but exactly how stressful is it? Look at the first 10 (of 43) listings on the Holmes-Rahe *Social Readjustment Rating Scale*, designed to measure the adverse effects of stressful life-events on human health.

1. Death of a spouse
2. Divorce
3. Marital separation
4. Jail term
5. Death of a close family member
6. Personal injury/illness
7. Marriage
8. Getting fired at work
9. Marital reconciliation
10. Retirement

Marriage, generally considered a fortunate event, is the seventh most stressful thing that can happen to you. Five out of the top ten are marriage related.

No doubt part of the stress comes from telling yourself you're getting married and you're supposed to be happy—therefore you aren't entitled to feel stressed. Vehemently denying stress only creates more stress. By marrying, you are putting yourself in a position to be affected by the top three stressors—separation, divorce, or death of a spouse. At the same time, you are planning an enormously complex event, a wedding, full of details you are expected to assimilate and retain, which would saddle you with enough work to stress you out, even if you weren't denying everything you're afraid of.

Fear is a physical state, your body perceiving danger and preparing to do one of the only two things it can do in the face of danger—run away, or stand and fight. Your muscles tense, your heart beats faster, your blood pressure rises, and your breathing becomes short and shallow. It's a physical state of red alert.

The solution is to relax yourself, physically. In a relaxed state, you reduce your oxygen consumption, lower your heart rate and blood pressure, reduce serum lactic acid levels, increase skin resistance, cause alterations in blood flow and, in general, suppress the arousal of the sympathetic nervous system. Relaxation brings on a synchronicity of brain-wave activity, more alpha and theta waves. It activates the right hemisphere of the brain, which is thought to be responsible for nonverbal, intuitive, nonsequential, and spatial-holistic thinking. As a result, you are more likely to engage in what is called primary process thinking, which is creative and illogical, flexible and multidimensional, nonlinear. You free-associate, daydream, break down barriers, and see the whole picture.

The way to relax yourself is to start with the body and let the brain follow. Here are a number of ways to begin.

1. *You can modify your behavior.* If you are a Type A individual, driven, impatient, a perfectionist, in need of a lot of stimulus, afraid of failure, then you can make yourself do things opposite the way you ordinarily do them. Take off your watch and put it in a drawer. Walk to work. Force yourself to sit in a chair without anything to do for an hour a day. Slow down everything you do. Eat slower. Talk slower. Stare off into space intentionally.

2. *You can modify your activity.* You can exercise

vigorously, until all your muscles are tired and all the tension has gone out of them. You can take up yoga, t'ai chi, or karate. You can take saunas or sit in hot tubs. It might be a good idea to get a professional massage the day before the wedding. Sensory deprivation tanks, available at some spas, are extremely efficient at breaking down muscle tension. Tapes are available in most New Age bookstores, which are designed to help you relax using soothing sounds: ocean waves breaking on the shore, thunderstorms, or birds chirping in a meadow.

3. *You can do relaxation exercises.* These exercises are designed to make you aware of your body and what it's doing. Hypnosis, self-hypnosis, and biofeedback are similar ways of teaching you to feel and negate the physical presence of tension. In progressive muscular relaxation, you are taught to focus on one muscle or group of muscles at a time and work at relaxing that muscle. Tapes are also available to help you do this.

4. *Meditation and prayer.* Both are, in effect, ancient forms of relaxation exercises, performed through concentration, usually in dark or quiet places. Both can lead to insight.

It's sometimes thought that alcohol or drugs can help you relax. They can have that effect, but it's only temporary. The negative effects of both are well documented.

The important thing is to take whatever path to relaxation you favor and commit yourself to it. Find an exercise and make a habit of it, repeating it until it becomes natural to you. Then, when you find yourself tensing up, you can catch yourself, stop the process before it goes too far, and realign yourself.

firmed, and all tickets in your possession. Make sure the place you're spending your wedding night knows you're coming. The tickets and itineraries go in the same suit-coat pocket or metal box in the dresser drawer on your bed as the rings and the wedding license. Your passports have to be updated if you're leaving the country, and both you and your bride should get the necessary visas and inoculations. You may be hassled by a confused customs inspector somewhere if your bride's new driver's license shows her new married name, but her passport bears her maiden name. You may need to bring along a copy of your marriage license. Traveler's checks should be withdrawn, signed at the bank, and placed in the suit-coat pocket or steel box. You should know the balance on your credit cards as well, in case you find yourself needing emergency cash abroad. Pack your suitcase at least a week before you're due to leave, and check it several times a day to add what you forgot to pack.

THE REHEARSAL DINNER

Your last responsibility, before the wedding, is to attend the rehearsal and rehearsal dinner. The rehearsal is just that, a dry run. It gives you a chance to walk through the ceremony, to get your timing down. In some cases, it's no more than a matter of trying to make sure people don't bump into one another and put an eye out. In other cases, the rituals and routines of the marriage ceremony may be quite complicated and involved, requiring actual learning. In most cases, the rehearsal is more fun than the real ceremony. Nobody's watching you, and you and your family or friends can joke around, ask questions, and throw paper airplanes from the balcony. It gives you an opportunity to visualize, which, according to sports psychologists, is the key to successful performance, envisioning what you'll do and where you'll be under controlled, calm conditions. You might want to stand at the altar, turn around and visualize, thinking, the minister is there, I'm here, my bride beside me, parents in the front pew, best man on my right, beyond him the side door about twenty feet away, down the hall forty feet and outside to the parking lot, where a car could be waiting with the engine running.

The rehearsal dinner is where your entire families meet, sometimes for the first time. It's a chance for them to break the ice and get together informally before they officially merge through matrimony. It gives you a chance to visualize again, and reflect that what you're doing affects other people. You thought it was just you and the woman you love, making a deal for life, but it's more than that. When you see your parents and her parents, sitting together at the head table, you're looking at your children's grandparents. To you, they're separate people from separate places, with separate histories and experiences, but to your kids, it will all be one thing, two limbs converging in a single family tree. Your children will claim the heritage and the blood of both families. You'll feel like a mixing bowl, the creator of a whole new blend of humanity. You can look at your bride's aunts and uncles and cousins and grandparents and wonder what genetic traits you'll be combining yours with. Maybe all her nieces and nephews behave like little angels. That may give you hope. Perhaps all the women in her family over fifty have thick dark mustaches. That may not give you hope. You'll wonder as well what she's thinking of your family. Or what your families think of each other, as you notice your great-uncle Rudolf at a corner table, showing her great-aunt Rosemary where they put the metal plate in his head.

The rehearsal dinner is also the time for toasts and speeches, a feudal banquet where rival warlords make peace by praising each other over raised cups and speak in glowing terms about the forthcoming union. The toasting usually begins with the heads of the families, often the fathers. Your father toasts your bride's family.

"We've only known the Whetherhills for a few weeks now, while we've all worked on organizing the wedding, and we've had such a good time that I think we both envy our children, knowing they'll get to enjoy this merging of families more often than we will. We're proud to welcome your daughter Gail to our family and we're grateful that you're welcoming our son Edward to yours. If we can agree to take the grandchildren every other weekend, I'm sure we'll all get along fine. To the bride and groom."

Her father responds.

"We've known Ed for about two years now, and in all that time, he's never asked me for money, so I guess he's all right too. But seriously, if I may be serious a moment . . ." He goes on for a while, telling those gathered what a prince you are, maybe embarrassing his daughter by telling a little about some of the chumps she used to date, and concluding on a warm note. "When Gail was six years old, she told me she wanted to marry a man just like me, but I think she's done that one better. We're glad to have Ed in the family, and look forward to getting to know the Fourniers. Grandkids every other weekend? It's a deal, but we alternate Christmases. To the bride and groom."

Then maybe your grandfather speaks.

"Ed's grandmother and I have been married for fifty-nine years," he might say, pausing for applause. "Fifty-nine years. People often ask me what the secret is. Well, I'll tell you what the secret is. For a happy and successful marriage, the man should make all the big decisions, and the woman should make all the little decisions." He pauses for effect, while the bridesmaids roll their eyes. "I've been married fifty-nine years, and so far," he says, smiling at his wife beside him, "there haven't been any big decisions."

Gail's uncle Jake goes next.

"Ruth and I have been married a good while too," he says. "Seems like a hundred years or so. Anyway, our secret is, never go to bed angry. So Ed, Gail, remember—stay up and fight."

The maid of honor might tell of a night in college when Gail had just been stood up for a date and swore off men forever, only to realize she really liked men, and needed them, but needed to feel independent too, and how you are the kind of man who will both support your wife and allow her her independence, which should make for a successful marriage. Eeeeeeyuck. Then Jim, your best man, may respond by repeating something stupid you said on a camping trip when you were eighteen, about how as far as you were concerned, you were going to marry the richest girl you could find, because then if it worked it would be great, but if it didn't, you'd still get half of all the stuff you bought together, with enough money left over to buy a Corvette, and then with so much really nice stuff and a Corvette, you could get somebody incredibly beautiful and intelligent and nice to be your second wife. "But Ed never could count very well," your best man says, "because it looks like he's marrying the second one first."

When everyone is done toasting you, it will be your turn. The words you speak during the ceremony will be from a book, but the words you speak at your rehearsal dinner will be from your heart. You can talk about how you met, what your first impression was. Describe what your feelings were when you first saw all the Fourniers and the Whetherhills gathered together, what the idea of family means to you. How you're going to need all the advice you can get. Describe a petty spat you and Gail had, wording the invitations, how you were both afraid because it seemed like the rest of your life was at stake, and how you resolved the argument. And how the rest of your life is still at stake, but you're looking forward to it. Thank everyone for coming, propose a toast to your new relations, and say you'll see everybody tomorrow.

Tomorrow.

8

THE BIG DAY

*T*o *measure up to all that is*
demanded of him a man must overestimate his capacities.

—GOETHE

Your life, so far—can you sum up?

Your life is contained in two kinds of boxes. Your past is all around you, in plain old cardboard boxes, and your future is on its way, arriving in silver- and white-wrapped boxes with bows and frills. The past is a dark cave. Then again, the future is a dark cave too, the entrance disguised as Magic Fairyland. Not a convincing fairyland either, more like those luridly painted semitrailer trucks that pass as Haunted Houses in traveling carnivals. Two caves, future and past. The space between the caves is limbo, littered with fake-looking rocks, like the planets where the old Star Trek landing parties used to beam down to. You have to carry the boxes from the cave of your past into the cave of your

future, except that the things you need to make the move
are packed away, boxes unlabeled so you can't find anything.
Like, your clothes. You realize, slowly, you're standing there
naked as the day you were born, while all around you a
crowd gathers, made up of all your friends and family, as
well as Captain Kirk and Spock and Dr. McCoy. Dr. McCoy
is going over you with his medical devices.

"He's in shock, Jim," McCoy reports. "Something must
have happened to him."

"Or is going to happen, Captain," Spock says.

"Spock, explain," Kirk says.

"Most interesting, Captain," Spock says. "An apparently healthy earth male, approximately 24.8 years old, at
the peak of his physical and emotional life, and yet he is
frozen by fear, incapacitated by the proximity of what he
wants most in life."

"And what would that be, Mr. Spock?"

"Unless I miss my guess, this creature has chosen a
mate for life and is about to marry. My tri-corder reports
his nervous state is high, his imagination aflame, yet his
instincts are working at cross-purposes, not knowing whether
to stand or flee."

"Forget your damn tri-corder readings, you pointy-eared
freak," McCoy spouts. "Can't you see the man has no clothes
on?"

Never mind the tuxedo, you want to say—what about
the boxes? Who's going to move all the boxes? You can't
move anything until you unlock the fairyland door to the
cave of the future, and in order to do that, you need the
key, but the key is in a small box, and the small box is in
a big box. Everybody starts looking through the big boxes
for the small box. Meanwhile, Kirk and Spock are blasting
the fairyland door to the cave of the future with their phasers.
It glows bright red, but won't budge. Your fiancée reaches
into a box and pulls out a Smurf. She holds it up to you by
the ears.

"What the hell is this doing here?" she asks.

You're humiliated. Suddenly, everybody is pulling Smurfs from boxes. "These are not my Smurfs," you want to say.

"I found it!" somebody shouts. It's the small box with the key in it. The box is two inches square and covered with gray velvet. You crack it open like a clamshell. Inside is a wedding ring.

You're about to hand it to her, but suddenly, for no reason, the ring melts in your hand, turns to liquid, made out of mercury instead of gold.

You wake up.

Your heart is racing. What? What is it? Where are you? Somewhere strange. You're lying on the couch. You fell asleep on the couch, and you were having a bad dream. Your head starts to clear. The last thing you remember, before you fell asleep on the couch, was watching a Star Trek rerun, and now you're awake. It's Saturday morning. What a weird dream. The television is still on across the room from you. Smurf cartoons. That explains the Smurfs and Captain Kirk. Why did you dream you were naked? Because you *are* naked. You're surrounded by boxes because it's June 10, your wedding day. You've packed all your belongings. What a mess. You slept on the couch because you put the ring and the marriage license and all your tickets and everything you can't afford to misplace in a metal box in the top drawer of your dresser, and you put your dresser on the bed so you wouldn't forget where the dresser was. Can't be too careful.

The ring! The dream was trying to warn you about the ring. You go into your bedroom and open the dresser drawer.

It's empty.

You panic, and sit up on the couch.

You wake up.

You're still on the couch. You went back to sleep, while lying on the couch, trying to interpret your first dream, and had a second dream. No point trying for a third. You look at the clock. It's 5:47 A.M. Might as well get up and do something useful.

There's nothing useful to do at 5:47 A.M. except deliver newspapers. You decide to take a bath. Any other day, you'd take a shower, but this is not any other day, and at 5:47 in the morning, you have time to kill. Brides were once given ceremonial prenuptial baths. Now they give them showers. The ancient Jews bathed. Athenians bathed before their weddings in water from the fountain Callirrhoe, at the foot of the Acropolis. Forget about it. Slip down into the hot water, a Paleozoic preamphibian, submerged in the primordial ooze of life, contemplating his own evolution. That's what you're doing, isn't it? Evolving, crawling up out of the water to breathe air on dry land. The caves in the dream, and the weird zone in between—that's what getting married is, isn't it? A passage from one place to another, during which one must endure a confusing transition. Why caves? What, in a dream, does a cave mean? Darkness. Maybe the womb, birth, another confusing transition from one stage of life to the next. Don't the aborigines of Australia use caves in their rebirth rituals, into the cave as one thing and out as another? Isn't a church just a man-made cave, a stone room with windows? Into it as one thing, out as another. Ontogeny recapitulates phylogeny, which recapitulates evolution, which makes incarnate the ineffable modality of the visible, unless you're a solipsist, in which case taking a bath leaves you somewhere between Berkeley and Hume. The only way to get clean is to resort to Hegelianism, applying the antithesis, the soap, to the thesis, which is you, in need of a bath, and through synthesis, washing and rinsing, arriving at a higher state of being.

You wake up.

How can you wake up when you weren't asleep? Daydreaming, waxing philosophical in the tub.

It's going to be a strange day.

You prepare to shave, staring at yourself in the mirror. The person you see in the mirror is getting married. Not you, him. He looks older than he used to look. He still looks single. What will he look like married? Like your dad? You take a new razor blade from the plastic rack of razor blades, then change your mind and put the old one back on. You always cut yourself with new blades. You don't want to show up for your wedding with your face lacerated and little pieces of toilet paper stuck everywhere.

There is a pair of patent leather shoes on your dresser. For a while, you can wear jeans and sneakers. Continuity. You can't find your sneakers though. You wander around

YOU WANT VIDEO WEDDINGS?

If you want to see weddings on video, why not just run down to the video store and rent one, of somebody else's wedding? There are plenty of movies with wedding scenes available.

The Godfather. Sonny's upstairs playing Bridesmaid Revisited, while Dad's in the den putting out murder contracts—what *really* goes on behind the scenes at a wedding.

The Graduate. Ben Braddock in the backseat of the bus with Mrs. Robinson's daughter. Now everything's okay . . . right?

Father of the Bride. Spencer Tracy marries off Elizabeth Taylor. Wedding as emotional ordeal. Tracy as a portrait of equanimity.

A Wedding. Robert Altman's version of the same idea, wedding as chaos. Not nearly as chaotic as other Altman films.

Cousin-Cousine. Mooning as a toast: "To the bride and groom!"

Mystic Pizza. Jojo overcomes her fear of turning into a fat Portuguese lady. Julia Roberts as a bridesmaid.

The Philadelphia Story. Hepburn, Grant, and Stewart answer the question, "Do you invite your ex?"

How to Marry a Millionaire. Marilyn Monroe, Betty Grable, and Lauren Bacall are golddiggers on the loose. If you had to choose one . . .

It Happened One Night. Heiress Claudette Colbert wants to marry a playboy, but her father won't let her, so she runs away, chased by Clark Gable. Moral: Don't let your bride meet Clark Gable.

Our Wife. Laurel accidentally marries Hardy.

Other Movies—Drama or Comedy: *Camelot, Royal Wedding, The Scarlet Empress, Ivan the Terrible (part 1), Quiet Wedding, The Member of the Wedding, The Catered Affair, June Bride, A Kind of Loving, Lovers and Other Strangers, Brigadoon, The Bride Wasn't Willing, I Married a Witch, The Runaround, You Gotta Stay Happy, The Bride Went Wild, The Lion in Winter, I Love You, Alice B. Toklas, The Man in Gray, The In-Laws, A New Leaf, The Wicked Lady, Wedding Night, The Family Way, My Little Chickadee, True Love, Betsy's Wedding;* Horror: *The Night Walker, Bride of Frankenstein, The Bride and the Beast, Chamber of Horror;* Movies Not to See: *Betrayal, Fatal Attraction;* Great Movies About Love: *Unbearable Lightness of Being, Modern Romance, Annie Hall, What Now My Love.*

As listed in *Halliwell's Filmgoer's Companion,* 8th ed. (New York: Scribner, 1985).

your apartment looking for them. In the kitchen, you wonder
what you might have in the refrigerator for breakfast, so you
open the refrigerator door and stand there, staring blankly.
Looking. What were you looking for? Oh yeah, your sneakers. You know you put them somewhere. You just had them
yesterday.

Wait a minute.

Sneakers in the refrigerator?

Maybe it would be safer to go out to eat. Your sneakers
are on top of a box, near the couch where you fell asleep.
You get dressed. You go out for breakfast, buy a newspaper,
and plop down in a booth at a steak and eggs joint, surrounded by truck drivers and serial killers. You look in the
paper for omens, good or bad, your last breakfast as a free
man. No apparent increase in the threat of nuclear war. No
mention of a plague. No tidal waves, swarms of locusts,
ministers' strikes, tornadoes, hurricanes, blizzards, Amway
conventions, or serious leaks from nearby biological weapons
plants. The wedding looks like a go.

In the People section, you read where Bill Wyman, of
the Rolling Stones, at fifty-two, is marrying a nineteen-year-
old, Mandy Smith, who he's been dating since she was thir-
teen. How do you date a thirteen-year-old? What's there
to talk about—gum? Wyman's twenty-eight-year-old son is
dating Mandy's thirty-eight-year-old mother. On your wedding day, it makes you feel better to know somebody's life
is more bizarre than your own. You decide to drive home
and do some more packing, but in the parking lot, you can't
get the key in your car door. Of all the days to be locked
out of your own car. Then you realize you're trying to get
into someone else's car.

Maybe a nap, you think, when you get home. You'll
do better when you've had more sleep. You lie back on the
couch at 9:23, and fall into a dreamless, Smurfless sleep.
You wake up. It's 9:29. The phone rings. It's your fiancée.

"Hi," you say. "How are you?"

"Nervous," she says. "I was wide awake at five in the morning. How about you?"

"I just got up, actually."

"Is it supposed to rain?"

"The paper didn't say anything about rain."

"Paper? I thought you said you just got up."

"I did. Then I got a paper and went and ate breakfast. I had an affair, robbed a bank, and came straight home."

"Mom called and said the florist is going to be a half hour late because the orangutans want more bananas and the airlines can't fly to Russia."

"What did you say?" you ask. You told her two nights ago that you couldn't hear another detail about the wedding.

"I said the florist will be late but it's okay because she's bringing an assistant to help her set up."

"That's what I thought you said."

"Remember now—I told the caterer you'd pick up the ice and bring it to the hall by three o'clock. You also have to pick up the balloons. The caterer has the helium already, so just get the balloons and ribbons to tie to them. The order's all ready to go and paid for, so all you have to do is get it."

"No problem."

"Say it back to me."

"Ice by three o'clock, and get the balloons and the ribbons."

"You won't forget?"

"No, I won't forget."

You go over to your parents' house for lunch. If entropy describes the disintegration of the universe as order gives way to chaos, then your parents' house is contributing more than its fair share of chaos to the process. Everyone's back in town, your brother from LA, your older sister from Montana, your baby sister from Santa Fe, and everybody's got their kids and their husbands and wives with them. There hasn't been this much family in the house for years. Your older sister's room looks ransacked with diapers and car seats and baby clothes everywhere. Your nephews are sprawled out on the living-room floor, playing with the same toys you used to play with, the ones your mother saved in the attic. Not particularly high-tech toys—they don't transform into anything—but they seem to be satisfying your nephews. You say as much to your mother.

"That reminds me," she says. "There are some boxes in the attic I want you to go through before I start throwing out what people don't want. There's also furniture, if you think you're going to need anything."

More boxes.

It's hot and dry in the attic. Dust motes float in a ray of sunlight, the beam of light like a buttress holding up the wall. Maybe the exact same dust particles you stirred up twenty years ago. One box contains souvenirs from high school and junior high school, old athletic awards, team letters you never managed to sew onto your jackets, photographs from prom or Sadie Hawkins Day, when you were amazed that Kathy Barron asked you out, after jilting you so heartlessly in junior high school. Off you went, with twenty whole dollars burning a hole in your pocket. Remember cheap dates? What's your date tonight going to cost? Ten grand?

It hurts to see these things again. It's always been the bride who laments leaving home, her mother, sisters, aunts, and friends, sobbing for three days and nights at her loss of innocence, her childhood days drawing conclusively to an end. In China a girl had to take the bedding from her childhood bed with her when she got married, and never return to that room again. Grooms are less frequently permitted such feelings. The Roman bridegroom threw walnuts around at his wedding celebration, for the boys in attendance to scramble after, an acknowledgment that he was giving up his childish things. Imagine never being able to play with your nuts again.

A second box contains souvenirs from grade school. A cracked superball. More than 100 baseball cards you'd forgotten about, which, you realize with glee, could be worth real money. A chain of paper clips 20 feet long. A stupid clip-on bow tie your grandmother gave you. Which you'd put on if she were still around and go show her, but she's not. A scout knife with half the plastic handle missing. A peace sign medallion you swiped from your older sister. The heads off your sisters' Barbie dolls. An old cigarette lighter needing only a new flint, wick, spring, cap, screw, wheel, and a little lighter fluid to be perfectly operational. A thing architects use, although you're still not sure what it does. A real bullet. The magnifying glass you used to fry ants with. Six plastic wallets, given as Christmas gifts over six consecutive years, by your great-aunt Trudy. A cherry bomb and a roll of caps. And a single 3″ × 5″ notecard with a phone number scrawled on it in your immature fist.

"See anything you want to keep?" your mother says.

"Yeah," you say. You want to show all this to your bride someday. It seems important. "I can't deal with this right now. I don't know where I'd put it."

"Okay, but I'm not going to hang on to it forever," she says, even though she's already kept it for twenty years.

In your old bedroom, you stare at the phone number on the notecard. You bring the phone into your old room and dial the number.

"Hello?" a woman's voice says. "Yankowskis."

Donna Yankowski! The first girl you ever noticed, because she was the first girl in school to get breasts. Not breasts, exactly, but she was a little overweight, and when she started wearing a bra, it gave her prepubescent pudginess a pseudo-womanly form. Less pseudo with each passing summer.

"Sorry," you say. "Wrong number."

In the den, your brothers-in-law are sitting on the couch, watching a baseball game on television. You lie down on the floor to catch a little of the game. You decide to rest your eyes, just for a moment, when the phone rings. It's your fiancée, telling you she just found out the reception hall was double-booked after all, and you're going to have to move your party. Her mother wants to kill the reception hall manager, but your fiancée thinks killing the manager for double-booking is traditionally the groom's responsibility. Okay okay, you tell her, you'll kill the manager, but just then, your baby sister is shaking you.

"Wake up," she says. "Someone wants you on the phone."

You wake up.

It's your fiancée, and there is a crisis. The bartender the caterer hired is sick, and the caterer said she's going to try to find a replacement, but the other two bartenders she uses are already working somewhere else—is there anyone you can think of who could fill in?

"I can't think of anybody. Maybe we could just let people serve themselves."

"I'm not going to worry about it. Everything's going to be okay. Tell me everything's going to be okay."

"Everything's going to be okay."

"My sisters are driving me nuts. Do you remember what to bring?"

"Absolutely. Ice by three o'clock. Piece of cake."

"Balloons and ribbons! I knew you'd forget."

"I'm teasing you. Ice, balloons, and ribbons. No sweat."

Meanwhile, you can't get ahold of your best man, who you were supposed to get together with at 2:30. Did you tell him to meet you at your apartment or at your parents' house? At 2:35, you're about to go back to your place to wait for him, when he pulls up in his car with the right front fender smashed in. He had a little accident at an intersection. This is the guy who's supposed to get you to the church on time. By the time the whole family is done saying hello to him, it's 2:50. You've got to get the ice. Your family says good-bye, see you at your wedding.

Your wedding.

You throw your best man's tuxedo in the back of your car and rush to the liquor store, where your order of six 40-pound bags of ice hasn't been made up yet. It should only take a moment. It takes more than that, but you finally load it all into the trunk of your car and go in to pay for it. You don't have any money. You put it all in the pocket of your tux, so you wouldn't forget it. Your best man only has a twenty, and the bill comes to twenty-five with tax.

"Hey, listen," the liquor store owner says in the end, "forget about it, okay? Let the extra bag of ice be our little wedding gift to you."

You thank him and drive like a maniac to the hall. It's a hot day, and the ice melts and gets the carpeting in the trunk soaking wet, but you deliver the ice and make it back to your house by 3:45. Zero hour is an hour and fifteen minutes away. It's going to happen.

The church is fifteen minutes away, so you have roughly an hour to change. Your best man asks if he can take a quick shower. You want to call your fiancée and ask her if she's all right. You wonder what she's doing. Getting dolled up, putting on makeup, shaving her legs, getting teased by her sisters. At this very minute, she's getting helped into her wedding dress, pinned and tugged and patted. A big full traditional wedding dress with a veil and a train? She wouldn't tell you even that much. You wonder what's keeping your best man, so you pound on the door and shout, "Three minutes!"

He opens the door with shaving cream on his face.

"Relax, would you?" he says. "This is a very important day for me, and I want to look my best."

When you finally get a chance to shower, you discover he's used all the hot water, so you take a cold shower instead, which is probably good for you.

You dress, girding yourself for battle. The socks feel thin and useless. The pants feel slick and strong against your legs. The shirt is stiff as a bulletproof vest, the cufflinks and studs like military insignia. The shoes are light as a feather— you could dance like Fred Astaire. The suspenders make you feel not just suave but important, capable of making quick decisions with the fates of nations hanging in the balance. You put the jacket on. You can hear the minister.

"Do you, Bond, James Bond, take this woman . . . ."

Look at yourself in the mirror. Shaving cuts? Massive facial blemishes? Then look yourself in the eyes. You will look just like this, when it's all over. No one will be able to tell you're different, but you will be different. You want to be different, should be different—that's one reason why you're doing this—but remember this moment. You can't believe you're doing this. Then you can easily believe it, piece of cake. You knew when you proposed that it was the right thing. You're dressed for it, prepared and rehearsed— might as well do it, as long as you've got the suit on. Got everything? You look around. You stuff your sneakers and your blue jeans, remembering to take your wallet out of the back pocket of your jeans first—and they say you forget things on your wedding day—into your suitcase and tell your best man he can start loading the car. You empty the steel box from your dresser. Tickets. License. Money. Ring. Keys, wallet in pocket, everything you need.

"What the hell is the dresser doing on the bed?" your best man asks.

"I put it there so I wouldn't forget it," you say. "Just load the car."

"Anything you say," he tells you. "You clearly have a grip on things."

You notice that the plants need watering. Where's the note you wrote to the house-sitter (thinking ahead) on how to feed the fish? In the kitchen you smell gas. How could that be? You have an electric stove.

Your best man clears his throat from the doorway.

"We should probably be going. It's 4:55."

"It's what? Oh shit, we're late."

"Just kidding," he says.

"I know I'm forgetting something."

As you drive, your best man behind the wheel, the light of the sun seems particularly intense, coating the world in gold, shadows impenetrably dark, white spots blindingly bright. The colors on advertising signs are extra vivid, everything heightened, buzzing, throbbing. The grass burns green, trees reach into the sky, where the clouds are alive. You can smell the food in every restaurant you pass, and hear the softest things, flies, distant lawn-mower engines, the jingle of a woman's keys as she opens the door of her parked car. You're not thinking about anything, exactly. Random images, of the past, the future, the moment you met your fiancée, the moment you proposed, other weddings, the baseball game you saw two seconds of this afternoon, Donna Yankowski, the dream you had this morning.

"Last chance," your best man says. "I can take you to the airport . . ."

"Drive."

It's 4:55. The actual service starts at 5:30. You recognize half the cars in the church parking lot. You should have eloped. Your best man turns off the ignition. You could just sit in the car. Duck down, lock the doors, pretend to be asleep.

"You gonna make it?" your best man asks.

"I'm fine," you say.

"Here," he says, pulling a flask from his inside coat pocket. "I thought you might appreciate this."

You take a swig. The whiskey scorches your throat.

"Keep it," he says. "A little present."

"Well, then," you say, slipping the flask in your pocket, "let's go. I've got a woman to marry."

"If she's here," he says. "A lot of people are betting she doesn't show."

"Like who?"

"Me. Your dad. The minister."

The soles of your shoes click against the linoleum of the church hallway. In the anteroom of the chapel, you see your father, your mother, your soon-to-be mother-in-law, the officiant, the florist, the ushers. The florist buttonholes you, literally, pinning a boutonniere on you. Her breath smells like Lavoris. She's wearing a corsage too—people are going to think she's your mother. Your mother gives you a hug and tells you you look great. Your father shakes your hand and tells you he's proud of you. He says he was nervous on his wedding day, but his father, your grandfather, said something wise to him.

"And what was that?"

" 'Don't screw up.' "

"Thanks, Dad."

Why didn't you elope? All you want is to be alone with your bride, at a time when nothing is less likely to happen. You ask where she is.

"She's here," her mother says. "She's with her father. You don't get to see her until the ceremony."

"We should probably go take our seats," your mother says. "See you after the service." She kisses your cheek and hugs you. Your father hugs you. Your mother-in-law-almost hugs you. The minister tells you it will be about ten more minutes. Your best man asks if you want to talk. You say you think you'd just like to sit and think.

You review.

Love. Marriage. The old photographs on your grandparents' walls you stared at as a kid, wedding pictures of their grandparents. The one formal portrait anybody ever took of them. Standing straight. Women in neck braces of lace. No one smiles in old wedding photographs. They knew the difficulties ahead. More difficult then than now? They had

oceans to cross, new languages to learn, dirt full of rocks to
till and plant, sixteen-hour days in factories. Loaded 16 tons
of number nine coal and owed their souls to the company
store. Simpler lives? Harder lives? Was a drought, to them,
less a thing to worry about than nuclear war to you? They
lived in solid houses, alone with each other, no phones, no
radio or television, nothing but each other and the wind
outside the window. Marriages lasted hundreds of years back
then. Whether they should have or not. Husbands and wives
protected each other. Eskimo wives chewed their husbands'
shoes so they'd be soft in the morning, and in return, husbands brought home the blubber. Fair enough. What's fair
today? Dual incomes. Dueling incomes. The more money
you have, the more you worry, except when you don't have
any. Money. Possessions that possess you. A man is richest
according to those things which he can do without, Thoreau
said. Your boxes of stuff. Her boxes of stuff. New silver-
wrapped boxes full of entirely new stuff arriving as wedding
presents. Boxes of your old stuff in your mother's attic. Boxes
of her old stuff in her mother's attic. Too much stuff.
Remember when you could fit everything you owned in the
back of a station wagon? When you'd just graduated from
college, and spent time staring at maps, wondering where
you were going to end up? What you would do there? And
who you might do it with? Life was rich with promise
then, no less rich now but different somehow. Then you
could fly solo, leave without asking permission, come and
go as you pleased. Now you have a traveling companion,
or you will soon. A consultant. An aide-de-camp. A boss.
Coconspirator. Confederate. Ally. Consort. Sidekick. Nurse.
Flunky. Stooge. Backer. Accomplice. Advocate. Exponent.
Associate. Antagonist. Opposite number. Competitor. Abet-
tor. Helpmate. Copilot. Backup singer. Straight man. Bos-
well. Miss Kitty. Significant other. Crucial other. Everlasting
other. Absolute other. Eternal fierce and benevolent other.
Squaw, better half, spouse, yokemate, helpmeet, bone of

your bones and flesh of your flesh, match, bride, esposa, frau, gwraig, kvân, cwèn, genoot, zmona, supsuga, malzonka, patni, tàitai, wify, kone, maka, uxor, moglie, femme, nevasta, supruga, cèile—wife.

"Five minutes," someone says.

It's not the stuff that matters. She matters. She is good. She is great. She makes you feel right. She takes you as is. She likes the things about you that used to drive other people crazy. She sleeps like a baby, curled up on the couch, mumbles with her eyes closed when you try to wake her. She talks to herself when she irons clothes. She has a soap opera. She loves shoes. She will eat chocolate anytime, anywhere, any amount, at the drop of a hat. She can drive all night. She's short. She's sexy when she flashes her eyes at you, and she's sexy when she doesn't. Gives good backrubs. Knows how to hit a softball. Likes Sambuca. Can't type, bake, or waltz. Never worked as a waitress, a secretary, or in a nursing home. Hates snakes, beef stew, and social injustice. Has a laugh you need to hear every day. A smile you need to see more often than that. Kisses like a banshee. What do you know about her? What are you going to learn about her? You'll be learning for the rest of your life. Growing old. What will she look like at forty? Fifty? Sixty? Ninety? Always beautiful. Ever more lovely. Like looking at your own hand, your feet, a part of you. If you can't imagine life without her now, what will it be like then? You've seen them in restaurants, old married people. Sometimes they don't even talk to each other, or look at each other, order their food, drink their coffee, smoke cigarettes, and leave without ever saying a word, cemented together, stuck without imagination or ambition. Other times you see old people in a tacky truck-stop dive by the side of some highway in the middle of Nebraska, a retired couple out to see America in their new RV, "Never been to Nebraska, wanted to check it out," who plop their weary bones down on the Naugahyde and smile at each other, just glad to be together, eating another meal in a new place, so close to each other they don't need words. God how they love each other, indivisibly. Not necessarily happy every single day, but together. And that's what you want. You want that togetherness, and you're willing to risk anything to find it, risk heartache, divorce, death, any calamity a married couple might expect to encounter, on the chance you'll be lucky. That's the bet you're placing. All or nothing. On your wedding day, you feel lucky.

"It's time," your best man says. "You ready?"

You wait in the hallway at the side door to the chapel. You can hear organ music. The music stops. The minister nods, and you follow your best man into the huge stone room. You take your place at the mark where you stood at rehearsal, and turn. The room is full, your family smiles at you from the front pews, but you barely notice anybody, because all your attention is focused on the light at the back of the room, the doorway at the end of the aisle. She's going to walk toward you, through the parted sea of friends and families, the dearly beloved and newly begathered. She'll come through the door any second. Your heart pounds. The door opens. You see her father first, then your bride.

And she takes your breath away.

You try to draw air. You feel woozy. You clench your teeth. This is the moment, and she looks unbelievably absolutely astonishingly beautiful. Not the dress, or the hair, or the veil, or the train, or the room, or the candles, or the music, or the windows, or the flowers—the impossible look on her face. A smile as big and broad and real and true as any smile you've ever seen, and it's all for you. The tears behind her glistening eyes. You lock eyes with her from across the sanctuary and reel her in, or she reels you in. You've gotten your wish. You're alone with her. You told yourselves you were doing this for your parents, would have eloped if you'd had your way, but now you barely notice your parents are there. You feel no eyes upon you except hers. Everything else is blurred and out of focus, miles away, beyond the envelope you and your bride feel enclosed by, some sort of invisible barrier. You feel isolated with her. Somebody sings a song. Somebody gives a sermon. Somebody reads a poem. You try to listen, pay attention, but you've heard it all before. You can hear individual words and lines, but they rush past you without connecting. It's like trying to count the cars on a moving freight train—you get lost. "Put aside my childish ways." Sure sure. "Love is the one thing . . ." It's a million things. You feel protected in the armor of your tuxedo. Safe with a companion by your side. You're moved beyond words with gratitude, to her for doing this with you, to the universe for sending her to you.

You're told to turn and face her, take her hands in yours. Your faces are a foot apart, eyes locked. Her eyes are wet. Yours are salty too. She squeezes your hands, and you squeeze hers, hanging on to each other for dear life, rescuing each other from something less than a dear life. You're glad you didn't try to memorize anything, because it's all you can do right now to repeat after the minister, the rabbi, the justice of the peace.

Do you take this woman to be your lawfully wedded wife?

No—you just wanted to know what it felt like to go through the wedding process, up to this point.

To have and to hold . . .

What does he mean, *have*? You mean, like, sex?

For richer or for poorer . . .

That cuts both ways, in the age of dual incomes, right? So even if your business goes bankrupt or you go totally broke, you'll still be together, right?

In sickness and in health . . .

When you get sick, you want to be nursed, mothered, and mollycoddled. Ginger ale, Beaman's gum, cold wash-cloths on your forehead, sponge baths, and no jabbing you under your tongue with the thermometer. When she gets sick, she wants you to leave her alone so she can crawl under a rock. It's a deal. No matter how bad it gets, it's a deal. If she's lying in a hospital bed with cancer at eighty, wracked with pain, begging you to help her—you will. In the day to day, she will tell you to eat more oat bran. You will suggest no ice cream after midnight. You will take care of each other's health. It's a deal.

For better or for worse . . .

Through everything. Any fights. Misunderstandings. Fuckups. Mistakes. Poor choices. Forgotten appointments. Missed buses. Unmet airplanes. Cold insults spoken in anger. Hurting misstatements spoken in distraction or innocence. Bad meals. Warm beers. Reruns of "Love Boat." Promotions and demotions. Relocations and re-relocations. Heat waves and blizzards. Bad roads and blown head gaskets. Anxiety attacks and nervous breakdowns. Strained backs and strained bank accounts. Feuds with in-laws and disownments. Windfalls and pratfalls. Rainbows and rain-outs. Conquest, Slaughter, Famine, and Death. Pride, Covetousness, Lust, Anger, Gluttony, Envy, and Sloth. Indigestion and indecision. Drunkenness and crankiness. Bombs bursting in air and the rockets' red glare. Boring winter afternoons. Mosquito-infested camping trips. Seasick cruises. Hard nights. Tax time. Super Bowls and World Series. Winning the lottery or losing your shirt. All of it. All of the above, because all of it sounds more interesting for two people than for one.

Till death do you part?

Until then. No sooner. Maybe not even then. How could death part you, the way you feel right now?

They're waiting for you.

So what do you say?

Was Queen Victoria ugly?

"I do."

You wait your turn for her to say it. Squeeze her hands. Count the cadences, scan the prosody, the spondees and pyrrhic feet of names and questions, "Do you, Gail, take this man, Edward," flowing into a rivulet of iambic tetrameter, "to be your lawful wedded husband" with an extra accent for stress, into anapests, trochees, and dactyls, "for better or for worse, for richer or for poorer, in sickness and in health," onto the final five accented words, "till death do you part?"

She does.

You're stunned. The past and future meet.

The best man whispers, "The ring."

He hands it to you. You take her hand gently in yours. It's not the right hand, or rather, it is the right hand, and she offers you her left one instead. Snickers from the peanut gallery. She wiggles the correct finger at you. You slide the ring on. It fits. She takes your left hand and slides the ring she bought you down your fourth finger, up over the knuckle and snug into place.

"According to the laws of this state, and by the powers vested in me, I now pronounce you husband and wife."

It's done.

"You may kiss the bride."

You will never forget this kiss. It's not a show-off kiss, a hammed-up Hollywood kiss, or a bent-over kiss, or an aroused kiss. It is a soul kiss. The visible physical uniting, a kiss of life. You know how to kiss, don't you? Put the softest parts of your bodies, your lips, next to the most dangerous part, your teeth, and surrender.

They let you out of the cave shortly after the kiss. You stand in the sunlight, in a line with your families (note the plural) and friends, and shake hands with everyone as they leave the church. The people you don't know tell you their names, sometimes where they're from and who they're related to or acquainted with. You can't begin to remember any of this information, but you'll be expected to when you meet these people again at the reception. Your fiancée—make that your wife (get used to it)—is at your side, and you feel like you haven't seen her or had a chance to say anything other than "I do" to her in days, but already other people are tearing her away from you. Uncle Bob from Des Moines.

WEDDING DON'TS

Don't tongue anybody when you kiss them. Including your bride, at least not in a showy way.

Don't pretend to screw the ring onto her finger.

Don't write anything on the soles of your shoes, so that when you kneel before the congregation, they can read, HELP ME. And don't let anybody else write on the soles of your shoes.

Don't pretend to be making up your mind, by stroking your chin in contemplation, when the minister asks you if you take your bride to be your wife.

Don't look over your shoulder, when the minister asks if there's anybody present who wants to speak now or forever hold his peace.

Don't make any jokes about your bride being pregnant, even if you know they're funny, because half the people at the reception don't know you and won't be sure if you're joking.

Don't talk about money, or what the wedding cost anybody.

No risqué toasts. If someone else makes one, ignore it.

Don't smash the cake in your bride's face when it's time for you to feed it to her for the photographer. It's stupid.

Don't dance with any ex-girlfriends until the last set.

Agnes Schrumpf, a former neighbor before your in-laws moved. Mr. Dennis. Who? The organist's husband. Thank you for coming. You neither wrote nor performed the music, but people compliment you on it anyway. A piece of rice—birdseed among the environmentally correct—hits you in the eye.

You're finally alone with your bride in the car on the way to the reception, except for the best man, who is driving.

"Hello, wife."

"Hello, husband."

"Oh, God—get a grip," the best man says.

It sounds, feels, and in fact is utterly absurd. You can hardly help but laugh. You're married. It's great.

At the reception, you can barely make it in the door before you're accosted by somebody who wants to shake your hand again. You wish you'd brought a joy buzzer. You want to tell people with bad breath, "Hey—there are mints inside." Your bride is hugged from all directions, set upon by wedding wolves. You intended to stay by her side, but inch by inch, she drifts away from you. You keep seeing her out of the corner of your eye, getting hugged, three feet away, then five, ten, but people keep coming up to you, wanting to pat you on the back. Finally, when you've lost sight of her, you feel a tug on your elbow. You turn, and it's her. You smile.

"Hello, wife," you say. "Think we'll ever make it into the dining hall?"

"Where are the balloons?" she says.

"What?"

"The balloons. I don't see any balloons."

"I was supposed to get the balloons?"

"Yes. I told you three times today to get the balloons."

"You never told me to get any balloons. You said I had to pick up the ice, and I did."

Both of you are being completely sincere. She believes

with all her heart she said it three times, when she only said it twice. Twice should have been enough, but her clear and concise instructions went into your head and formed tiny little engrams of memory that were immediately and irretrievably lost in the whirlwind of your brain.

She goes into the bathroom. She's upset. What are you going to do about it? Someone pulls you into the main hall. The room looks festive enough, flowers and candles and white tablecloths. Balloons aren't exactly conspicuous by their absence.

"You did it—how does it feel?"

"Feels great."

The band is still setting up. Everyone but the bass player is wearing a tux. Five out of six ain't bad. Aunt Pam hugs you.

"We're so happy for you. How does it feel?"

"Feels great."

Your wife's mother's sister's oldest friend, Mr. Lupescu, easily the most boring man you've ever met in your life, has already got your baby sister cornered by the gift table, which, you notice, is stacked halfway to the ceiling, and not everybody's here yet. You ought to go rescue her, being your baby sister and all, but before you do the caterer has you.

"Hi congratulations excuse me but we need another case of club soda which one's the best man I don't want to be bothering you is he the person I should be talking to he is good then congratulations how does it feel?"

"Feels great."

You see a group of friends and head for them, shaking three hands on the way. Everybody has equal claim to you, so it's difficult to excuse yourself from anyone to get to where you'd rather be or need to be.

"Welcome to the club," a married friend says. "How does it feel?" He wants to know because married people come to weddings as a way of reliving their own weddings.

"Great."

"Where's your better half?"

"Of what—my mind? I wish I knew. She's in the bathroom. I forgot to get the balloons."

"No, she's not—she's over there."

You see her chatting with people by the door. You head toward her. On your way, your friend Karen stops you to tell you how beautiful your bride is. You say you know. There was a point, a few years ago, when you considered dating Karen, which means that in some way you entertained the possibility, however remote, that it could have been her wearing the big white dress today, had events not conspired otherwise. Odd.

"That's a gorgeous dress she's wearing," Karen says.

"It is," you say. "I like the one you're wearing too. Excuse me for a moment. I'll be right back."

Try not to say you'll "be right back" too often, you realize, because the odds are, you won't be. You fight your way through six more people, shake eight more hands, tell seven more people how you feel, and finally reach your bride's side.

"You all right?"

"Yes," she says. "I just had to scream. I wanted to scream into a pillow, but I couldn't find one, so I screamed into a roll of toilet paper instead."

"I'm sorry," you say. "I forgot to get the balloons. My mind is a sieve."

"It's all right," she says. "It's a stupid thing to get upset about."

"It looks pretty good in here without them."

"It would look better with them," she says. "But don't worry about it. I'll think of a way to get even."

The best man hands you a beer. The guests have arrived. Waiters and waitresses in black pants and white shirts are handing out plastic champagne glasses and filling them with bubbly from thick green bottles with huge punts in the bottom. The best man raises his glass in the air and calls out, "To the bride and groom!" You set your beer down, raise your glass, and drink champagne while everyone shouts out, "To the bride and groom." When you turn around, your beer is gone.

Then it's time to eat. You and your new wife lead the guests through the buffet line. Everything certainly looks attractive, candelabra, flowers, knives and forks laid out like rows in a marching band, moraines of bread and rolls and buns, crystal bowls of fluorescent punch, fauvist fruit salads, jumbles of exotically spiced filler like taboule and groats and couscous and bulgur, piles of vegetables, steaming bloody slabs of fresh-killed meat glowing on the carving board beneath the heat lamps, college student servers in snappy outfits with puffy white doughboy hats.

"Is this what we ordered?" you ask your bride.

"I guess so," she says. "I'm not really hungry."

"Neither am I," you say.

You eat. Your parents eat beside you, telling your bride's parents all the foods you hated as a kid. "Hear that?" your mother-in-law says to her daughter, as if it's going to be your wife's responsibility to feed you for the rest of her life. Her father tells the story of how sick your bride got, the first time she ate lobster. "Daddy, please," she says. Your new father-in-law asks you a question.

"What do you think you'll be doing in ten years?"

"I don't know," you say. "Probably writing thank-you notes."

"What about kids?" your mother asks you.

The band finally starts playing the dinner set. "Tangerine," "Moonlight Serenade," "Tenderly." Over the music, you hear a tinkling, growing louder. The guests are tapping their water glasses with their forks and knives, trying to get you and your bride to stand up and kiss each other. Customs. Sometimes the dearly begathered think it's funny to interrupt your meal, force you and your bride to kiss each other and heckle you if you don't. Indulge them once and they'll be on you all night. All you can really do is get up and leave. Your bride needs another glass of wine, and you could use another beer, so you go to the bar. The bartender, as he fills your order, looks oddly familiar.

"Aren't you the guy who owns the tuxedo store?"

"Yeah," he says. The caterer called him up at the last minute. They've been doing each other favors for years. He used to bartend for her on a regular basis, before he became a made member of the mob with his own business. "This way I get to keep an eye on my merchandise. You look terrific, by the way. I told you that cummerbund would fit."

"Thanks. Excuse me."

After dinner, you and your bride are called upon to cut the cake. As a joke, somebody hauls out a Carvel "Fudgie the Whale" ice cream cake with "Good Luck, Ed and Gail" written on it in edible red wax. You laugh. The genuine wedding cake is wheeled out, a real Magic Fairyland production with three tiers, plastic arches and bridges and pillars, flowers, white icing that looks solid as dental plaster, and a little plastic Ed and Gail on the top. The photographer positions himself, tells you both to hold the knife, a little higher, up, to the left, okay now back, big smiles, look like you're in love. You briefly wonder if a jury of your peers would convict you for stabbing him, and if so, since you're both holding the knife, would you both suffer the same penalty?

The dancing begins. You take a tour around the floor with your bride, another with your mother, another with your mother-in-law, your sisters, your grandmother, the flower girl. Your mother asks the band if she can sing, "Our Love Is Here to Stay." Someone else asks the band to play the honeymoon song, you know, "What Is This Thing Called, Love?" Or the Canadian version of "Take the A Train"—"Take the Train, Eh." Nyuk nyuk nyuk—wise guys. You circulate. You introduce everybody you know to everybody you know. You boldly tell two of your single friends, who've just met, that they should ask each other out on a date. You stand and listen while somebody you don't know tells you something you don't want to hear. When anybody gives you advice, you say, "That sounds like good advice." You sit down with the people who've traveled a long way, say, "Geez, I haven't had a chance to say hello to you all night," and chat for about two minutes, until somebody grabs your elbow and says there's somebody you should talk to. At least 10 times, you'll tell the story of how you and your bride met. Comment on how lucky it was that you had good weather 20 times. "I'm glad you could come," 100 times, "Excuse me," 200 times. You'll take an extra minute or two to be by yourself in the men's room, alone at last, quiet at last, until somebody bursts in the door and says, "What are you doing here—you're supposed to be out there dancing."

"No," you say, "I'm supposed to be in here, peeing."

Around ten o'clock or ten-thirty, older people or people with kids or baby-sitters start to leave. They find you to say good-bye, sometimes people you haven't even had a chance to say hello to yet. If you walk somebody to their car, you see a waiter doing dishes in the parking lot with a garden hose and loading things into the caterer's van. The party is slowly drawing to a close. Back inside, you find your bride sitting alone in a chair, and plop down beside her.

"I'm exhausted," you say.

"So am I," she says.

"Time for a second wind."

"Absolutely," she says.

This really is your evening, and you don't want it to end. You start finding people on the edges, leaning on the railings or balconies or sitting in dark corners. The band starts playing blues numbers now that the demographics of the crowd are changing. You take off your jacket, loosen your tie, and ask the bartender for a glass of ice water.

"Peel onions," he says. "That'll make your eyes water."

"That's really funny."

"You didn't hang the jacket over the back of a chair, did you? They get spilled on that way. Put it on a hanger and nobody will spill on it."

"I'll tell my valet."

Your parents say they think they'll be leaving soon. People are planning after-hours parties back in their hotel rooms. You want one last dance with your mother. She hugs you when it's over and says she loves you, that they love your wife, and are happy for you both. You make similar farewells with your in-laws. You thank them for their help, both financial and otherwise. When they're gone, only the hard-core partiers are left, but it's still a good crowd, and the band is paid for until midnight. Your bride says she's going to go change out of her wedding dress and get ready to leave. You say you think maybe you'll change too. You give the best man the checks to pay off the help, then get your luggage from the trunk of your car. The blue jeans and sneakers you've been waiting to put on all night were in a separate bag from your honeymoon luggage, a nylon athletic bag. You take the athletic bag into the men's room, open it, reach in, and find a bottle of champagne, with a note from your buddies—"Good luck." You also find that your clothes are wet, because the bottom of your car trunk got soaked when the ice melted earlier in the day. You dry your clothes over the hot-air hand drier in the men's room and put them on. Comfortable at last. You arrange with the best man to return the rented clothes. He says sure thing, takes them and hands them to the bartender. Your bride, in a simple sundress, is also comfortable at last, smaller now without the petticoats and padding. You kiss her. Waiters and waitresses are pulling the tablecloths off the tables. The bartender is stacking empties. The trumpet player is blowing into his hat while the band plays nothing but slow dances, "Goodbye Porkpie Hat" or "Days of Wine and Roses." Your bride looks at you.

"You wanna go?"

"Yeah."

"Where we going?"

"It's a surprise."

You booked a room for the night at an inn, a forty-five-minute drive away. It should have been closer. You can't remember ever being this tired. It is, as they say, a good kind of tired, but still, it's dangerous. You've been dancing, eating, merrying, and marrying for hours, up since five in the morning—the white line in the middle of the road is a blur, a wiggling snake. You can't see to read anything, road signs or maps. You speed because you can't help it, lurch around the corners.

It's 1:00 A.M. by the time you find the inn. A sleepy desk clerk gives you your keys. You find the room. You asked for the honeymoon suite, but it has two double beds in it anyway.

"Which one do you want?" you say to your bride.

"Either one," she says. "I don't care."

You drop your bags without even trying to set them down gently. You both take showers. You unwrap the sanitized plastic drinking cups from the bathroom and open the champagne your friends snuck into your luggage. It got warm in the car. The cap hits the ceiling and the champagne foams all over one of the beds. You still have a dry bed left. You brush your teeth. Your bride comes out of the bathroom wearing something special she bought for this occasion, a lace teddy or a silk camisole. She looks adorable. You get into bed. After brushing your teeth, the champagne tastes awful. You kiss her. She kisses you.

You try to keep your eyes open.

She tries to stay awake.

You both fall asleep with the lights on.

ANIMAL SEX

Many people hope, after they marry, that they will have wild animal sex. Wild animals, however, long to have human sex, the luxury of a nice dinner, soft music, romance, and then smoke cigarettes in bed afterward without having to worry whether or not your mate is going to have you for dinner. The birds and the bees do not have it as easy as you might think.

A male bee's goal in life is, like any English schoolboy, to have sex with the Queen. Female worker bees are sterile, frigid, ugly, and mean. As soon as the male drone has his way with the Queen, he's driven from the nest by the workers, doomed to hang out in drone bars for the rest of his life, bragging about how he had sex with the Queen.

The Emperor Penguin has sex once a year for three minutes. Both male and female penguins are frigid, but they prefer it that way.

Turtle foreplay involves a long head-bobbing dance, after which the male sucks on the female's toes.

Male cobras have two penises.

Lobsters mate face-to-face. The female conceals herself in a kind of hut she has built, and the male comes knocking. If she likes his looks, and he's not too kinky-looking (rubber bands on his claws), she lets him in.

Sea lions and beavers make love while floating side by side. That is, with other sea lions and beavers. Sea lions have harems, with only the dominant males copulating with the best females, something like our high school.

Rhinoceros foreplay involves males and females smashing into each other at high speeds. The male has a 2 foot penis, copulates with his lovely bride for about an hour and a half, and ejaculates every ten minutes.

Elephants go into musth every 3 to 6 months, secreting a strong-smelling substance from a gland below the eye that makes them look like they've been crying. Foreplay involves the male squirting the female with water, chasing her around or bringing her snacks, while she ignores him. He chases her, dragging his 4 foot 100 lb 'S'-shaped penis on the ground. Finally, he mounts her from behind, standing on his hind legs. Copulation lasts a minute.

Tiger sex is, well, tiger sex, perhaps the loudest and most raucous mating this side of Cher. The male tiger bites the female by the neck while he copulates with her. She swipes at him with a paw when it's done, and it's done perhaps as often as 50 times a day, when she's in heat.

Chimpanzees play with themselves, enjoying both masturbation and oral sex. Young chimps observe older members of the group copulating and imitate them by dry humping each other. Female chimps in estrus are extremely horny, and have sex many times a day, with any chimp who's interested. Yet while chimps are promiscuous, they sometimes form "consort relationships," in which two might pair off, for a time, out of what seems to be simple affection.

Sources: David Wallechinsky and Irving Wallace. *People's Almanac* (New York: Doubleday, 1975). Jamie Shreeve, author of *Nature: The Other Earthlings* (New York: Macmillan, 1987).

9

THE HONEYMOON

Married men ought never to attempt or hurry their initial enterprise if they do not find themselves ready for it. If a man discovers himself to be agitated and on edge, it is better to give up outright any attempt at marital commerce and await further occasion when he is less upset . . .

Till possession be taken, our husband should leisurely and by degrees make several little trials and light offers, without obstinately committing himself to an immediate conquest. Those who know their members to be naturally obedient need only guard themselves against an overwrought imagination.

We are right in remarking the untamed liberty of this member. He puffs himself up most importunately when we do not need him, and swoons away when our need is greatest. . . . Is there any member more rowdy and indiscreet?

—FROM *THE AUTOBIOGRAPHY*, BY MICHEL DE MONTAIGNE

One good thing to be said about the sexual revolution of the sixties and seventies is that it took a lot of pressure off the wedding night. According to the myth, this is the night you've been waiting for, when you finally get to enjoy each other fully, physically and passionately, with society's and the church's and your parents' and anybody else's blessing, suck face, slip slurp and slide and bounce each other off the walls and make the beast with two backs until you're plumb worn out, wasted, and ruined. It may even still happen that way, to virgins, oversexed eighteen-year-olds or people who for whatever reason really did wait until they were married to wet their whistles. If you ask around though, you find that most preconceived notions of what a wedding night is supposed to be like are inaccurate, because most couples are already worn out, wasted, and ruined by the time they reach the honeymoon suite. A lot of people don't even bother trying to make love, whereas others try and report mixed results, often the disappointment you can predict will ensue when expectations are unreasonably high. It's hard to think of a single night when a man's performance anxieties might be any greater. It once was true that a marriage could be voided if the couple proved unable to hang the bloodied sheet out the window the morning after the wedding. We still think of an unconsummated marriage as unfinished business, something you can annul, declare to be nothing, not worthy of divorce, because it was never something.

You may or may not feel like having sex on your wedding night. You may be exhausted, sleep-deprived, or drunk, or you may simply feel the burden of too much tradition and mythmaking upon you. You have the rest of your lives for that. You certainly have the rest of the honeymoon for making love. It will suffice, on your wedding night, that you're alone, at last, quiet, at last, lying by the woman you love, at last, with no further wedding details to think about, at last. You'll be tempted, recalling something you forgot to tell the photographer, or wanting to make sure the caterer remembered to return the candelabras your mother loaned her. Drop it. Somebody didn't get a check? The hell with 'em.

The honeymoon is the time to put everything on hold. You can put more on hold than you know. Psychiatrists going on vacation tell their patients to put all their pressing urgent neuroses on hold, and somehow, their patients manage. The wedding night is the first night of your honeymoon, a time to decompress and unwind. Bills. The work you're missing. Deadlines. Employers and employees—behind you. On hold. Out of sight and out of mind.

Some scholars believe the practice of allowing for a period of sequestered respite, following a wedding, derives again from cultures that practiced marriage by capture. The honeymoon was a time to go to the mattresses and lay low, so to speak, until the bride's brothers had given up their search for her. It may go as far back as prehistory, when human beings evolved the custom of copulating in private. They were primitive people, but they weren't so stupid that they couldn't count to nine, and know that if a newly mated pair disappears for a month and turns up ten months later with a baby, it's probably their baby. Primitive man was obsessed with knowing, and making sure the rest of the tribe knew, whose babies were his.

The word *honeymoon* comes from an alcoholic drink made from honey, called *mead*, favored by the Anglo-Saxons, who drank mead for thirty days after a wedding. Possibly thirty days before one too, considering that all you'd need would be twelve well-timed weddings a year for a 365-day mead binge. *Moon* refers to the thirty-day monthly cycle during which Anglo-Saxon newlyweds put their lives on hold and got away from it all, without thought to the Druids, Picts, Celts, and Viking hordes back home, burning their huts to the ground and stealing their chickens.

There's nothing, however, particularly Anglo-Saxon about the idea of giving a newly married couple a break.

Among the Jews, a newly married man was exempt from military service for a year. The Incas let their newlyweds go a year without paying any taxes, an idea whose time, I think, has returned. In this country, honeymooning probably didn't begin to catch on until after the Puritans stopped making the rules. The Puritan idea of a honeymoon would have been standing on the stoop, watching the sun set for a minute or two before heading back inside to go about the grim business of being Puritans. Napoleon's younger brother Jérôme (hard to imagine, Napoleon introducing himself, saying, "I am Napoleon, Victor of Borodino, Hero of the Italian Campaign and Emperor of France—and this is my kid brother Jérôme") took his new bride, a woman named Betsy Peterson, to Niagara Falls in the early part of the nineteenth century.

Jérôme was neither the first nor the last pilgrim to do so. Mark Twain visited the falls, noted the tourists and honeymooners there, having their pictures taken, and wrote, in 1869:

> *Any day, in the hands of these photographers, you may see stately pictures of papa and mamma, Johnny and Bub and Sis, or a couple of country cousins, all smiling vacantly, and all disposed in studied and uncomfortable attitudes in their carriages, and all looming up in their awe-inspiring imbecility before the snubbed and diminished presentment of that majestic presence whose ministering spirits are the rainbows, whose voice is the thunder, whose awful front is veiled in clouds, who was monarch here dead and forgotten ages before this hackful of small reptiles was deemed temporarily necessary to fill a crack in the world's unnoted myriads, and will still be monarch here ages and decades of ages after they shall have gathered themselves to their blood relations, the other worms, and been mingled with the unremembering dust.*

The Poconos, the Catskills, and the Lake George/Sara-

toga area in upstate New York picked up the slack when
people started getting tired of Niagara Falls. Today people
travel farther and spend more money on their honeymoons
than ever before. The most popular domestic honeymoon
destinations are, according to *Bride's Magazine*, Florida, the
South, the West, Pennsylvania, the Northeast, California,
and the north-central states. The most popular destinations
outside the continental United States are Hawaii, Mexico,
the Virgin Islands, Jamaica, the Bahamas, Canada, Bermuda,
and Europe, followed by other Caribbean places like Puerto
Rico, Aruba, or Barbados. According to *Bride's Magazine*,
the average honeymoon lasts 8.8 days, and costs $2,515.

This is *your* $2,515. The groom pays for the honey-
moon. In theory, now that you're married, whatever moneys
you earn will be shared, but the money for the honeymoon
is supposed to come out of what you managed to set aside
before the wedding. In practice, many couples both pitch in
what they can in order to get the most out of the trip. Many
couples also divide up wedding responsibilities such that the
bride does all the planning for the wedding and the groom
does all the planning for the trip afterward. Then, if both
are somehow disastrous, your bride will at least be able to
have the last word.

Sometimes a groom may try to surprise his bride, telling her only what kind of clothes to pack and what shots to
get, and to bring her passport. Your bride may like the idea
of being swept away somewhere, carried off like one of those
women with the bare shoulders and the severe neck injuries,
on the covers of bodice-ripping romance novels, with you
playing the part of the dark brooding laird. If she's been
making all the decisions regarding your dealings with the
Wedding Mafia, she might enjoy having all the travel plans
and arrangements made for her, so that she can just sit back
and enjoy.

Playing the dark brooding laird and surprising your
bride could also, obviously, backfire in a major way, if, for

instance, you plan a two-week tour of Antarctica, and she has a deathly fear of penguins. She may have somehow concealed from you the fact that she gets seasick just watching Alka-Seltzer commercials, in which case you'd be wrong to plan a cruise. Maybe she took a solemn vow before God to sleep with Don Ho if she ever came within 100 miles of him, married or not, in which case you might want to avoid Hawaii.

You can, of course, go anywhere you can afford to go and do anything you want. If you plan the honeymoon together, you can take breaks from your wedding planning to read travel books or pass brochures back and forth and fantasize. Every bridal magazine on the stand (often the fattest publications on the newstand, as true testimony to the power and prestige of the Wedding Mafia as any) includes several travel articles in the back of each issue on where to honeymoon. There are many other magazines dedicated strictly to travel. You can visit travel agents, who often get dollar signs in their eyes when they see newlyweds approaching, and would be more than willing to help you with your travel plans. Usually they can save you money as well. Without trying, in this limited space, to discuss all the places you might want to go on a honeymoon, there are still a few general things you might want to consider and talk over with your bride to be.

WHERE TO GO

Do you want an active or a passive honeymoon? Many people, after the ordeal of planning and carrying off a wedding, want to check themselves into the Mayo Clinic, be fed intravenously, and allowed to sleep for two weeks. The honeymoon is the one time a poor man can live like a king. It's the dream vacation of a lifetime, when you can sit, for as long as you can afford to, in the lap of luxury, call room service, be waited on and fawned after, fed peeled grapes all day long, and find chocolates on your pillows at night. Other people get bored lounging at poolside waiting for Ramón to bring the mango daiquiris. Do you want to go to one place and stay there, or travel through several places? Do you want your days filled with activities, two weeks at an archaeological dig, or idle, two weeks at the beach, reading John le Carré novels?

You also should talk about what kind of weather you prefer. It's always summer somewhere in the world. A January honeymoon in Australia might just shine away the winter blues. Even in the same hemisphere, some places appreciate summer more than others. You can go to Martha's Vineyard in July and find peace and quiet in a little harbor town like Menemsha, or go somewhere like Sweden. In the land of the midnight sun, the Swedes go nuts in the summer, and don't turn in at night until they've soaked up every last ray, recharging their batteries for the long winter ahead. If you marry in summer, but like where you live in the summertime, you might want to postpone your honeymoon and take a trip when you really need it, or, considering all the money you shelled out for the wedding, when you can better afford it.

What kind of landscape are you interested in? You can visit the north woods for very little money if you feel up to taking a canoe trip into the Boundary Waters, along the Minnesota–Canada border. For $500, two people can eat and live well, and once you get into the deep woods, there's very little else to spend your money on. For more money, you can drive up into the spectacular Canadian Rockies and spend some time in Banff, at the Banff Springs Hotel, or drive an hour north to Chateau Lake Louise, get in all the hiking and mountain climbing or horseback riding you want and come home to one of the most rustically luxurious hotels in the world.

Maybe there's a specific activity you wish to pursue.

Trout fishing on Montana's Smith River, floating north from White Sulphur Springs. Golfing at Pebble Beach. Pugil sticks at Camp Lejeune. Or maybe you want specifically not to pursue anything in particular, or set any destination, setting off, instead, in a rented RV, camper, or a pickup truck with a cap and sleeping bags in the back, down the blue highways for an undesignated period of time, for parts unknown.

Such a trip would more resemble the course of a marriage, and be good practice for married life. Wise travelers know the pleasure of travel comes not in the arriving but in the going, that you don't pass up a thousand things in a rush to see one thing, but rather, that you stop along the way, in Wall Drug, South Dakota, or Bartlett's Water Show in the Wisconsin Dalles, or at South of the Border off Highway 95 at the North Carolina/South Carolina line, stop anywhere you want, buy stupid trinkets, take chances, rent Jet-Skis off the Baja, take a balloon ride in France, indulge yourselves and try not to press. The only sure way to have a bad time is to tell yourself *you have to have a good time or else*, that this had goddamn better be the best goddamn vacation you ever had or that goddamn travel agent will be sorry.

The Wedding Mafia will tell you that money should be no object as a way of acquiring more of it from you. The wise traveler will tell you that money should be no object because the more you spend, the more you expect, and the more you expect, the more you might be disappointed, because you almost never get what you pay for in this life. You can have as much fun honeymooning in Salina, Kansas, as in Rio, if you're willing and able to relax and make your own fun. Though, of course, Carnival is better in Rio. Your attitude and spirit are more important than what you do.

Fortunately, people are usually in pretty high spirits following their weddings, so the honeymoon often is the best vacation they ever had. It is a blessed lull, a time without criticism or fault, duty or responsibility, harshness or somber reflection. You'll come home to find your hut burned down and your chickens gone. Your life will get hard again. Your marriage will get hard again. When they say the first year is the hardest, they're not kidding. You will have to learn how to live with another person, which, if you've never done it before, is no walk in the cake. You will have to learn that your job is not more important than her job even if it pays you twice what her job pays her—work is more than money. Work is a thing a person does to the best of his or her ability, in order to feel useful and valuable and fulfilled, in which case all jobs are equal, even if society thinks lawyers are more important than poets. You will have to learn to respect each other, to avoid overwhelming each other, to listen, to talk and to *guess* what to say when you don't *know* what to say, to give more than just your time. You'll have to learn how to write a whole new script for being in love and living in love together, since the prepared speeches you each had in your pockets, coming into the marriage, don't work as conversation, monologues becoming dialogue. Fears and emotional issues are likely to be buried deep in your psyche, things you told yourself you could postpone, in other relationships, things you said you'd deal with when the time came, when you settled into a serious relationship—well, the time has come, Jack. There are new things to learn that you're not prepared to learn, couldn't be expected to be prepared to learn, but now you're in a whole new school. If you thought it was hard enough trying to control your own life, get your single life headed in the proper direction at the correct speed, how hard is it going to be to coordinate that life with someone else's?

If marriage is a journey, then the wedding is the first leg of the journey, and the honeymoon is the end of the first leg, maybe the first rest area. There are plenty of stories of honeymoon disasters, lost luggage, accidents, and ship-wrecks. The first step can be a misstep, may well be a misstep or a full stumble. It's almost to be expected, that somewhere in the first month you take a misstep, because marriage is not an ordinary journey, more like a three-legged race. You have a partner. You've tied yourselves to each other. If you persevere, you find you're not hobbled but strengthened. At that point, you might find it's the only way to go. Many wise travelers say it's true.